JOURNEY OF HOPE
Towards a New Ecumenical Africa

JOURNEY OF HOPE
Towards a New Ecumenical Africa

Nicholas Otieno
with
Hugh McCullum

WCC Publications

Cover design: Chaz Maviyane-Davies

ISBN 2-8254-1466-2

© 2005 WCC Publications
World Council of Churches
150 route de Ferney, P.O.Box 2100
1211 Geneva 2, Switzerland
Website: http://www.wcc-coe.org

Printed in France

Table of Contents

This book is respectfully dedicated to
Dr Aaron Tolen (d. 1999, Yaoundé, Cameroon)
President of the World Council of Churches (1991-1998)

During his term as president, WCC called on Dr Tolen to represent the Council at numerous functions and occasions. In 1993 he was a member of a delegation of Eminent Persons to South Africa to monitor the situation in the run-up to the first democratic elections in that country at a time when many feared civil war might break out. In October 1994 he headed another delegation of Eminent Persons visiting the USA for hearings on Racism as a Violation of Human Rights. He also led ecumenical delegations to Burundi in 1995 and to the Democratic Republic of Congo (then Zaire) in pursuit of peace and reconciliation. On all those and many other occasions, Aaron Tolen provided valuable leadership and made the ecumenical voice heard and respected, especially in Africa and within the ecumenical movement.

His most recent involvement, before his untimely death, was at the WCC's eighth assembly in Harare, Zimbabwe, December 1998. He very ably moderated the Africa plenary which helped the assembly to understand the history and contemporary situation in Africa. He was a relentless champion of the African cause and African interests. For him, the search for a peaceful, just and democratic society in Africa was a life-long commitment. He struggled for the respect of human rights and human dignity for all. It was Aaron Tolen, back in 1991 at an executive committee meeting, who boldly challenged the WCC "to look at Africa with new eyes."

Aaron was God's precious gift to the ecumenical movement in general and to the World Council of Churches (WCC) in particular. His distinguished service and contribution to the life and well-being of the ecumenical movement spanned a whole generation. For thirty years he dedicated his life and abilities to promoting the unity of the church and of humankind. He generously put his professional skills and gifts at the disposal of the ecumenical movement.

Aaron's gifts as a leader and visionary were already evident between 1969-1974, when he served as World Student Christian Federation (WSCF) secretary for Africa and Madagascar. In that capacity he addressed the All Africa Conference of Churches (AACC) general assembly, Abidjan, 1969, where he articulated the integral nature of ecumenical work in Africa. His participation in WCC work started during the same period, when he served on the executive committee of the CCIA (Commission of the Churches on International Affairs).

Dr Tolen was a key participant at the WCC's first assembly held in Africa, at Nairobi, 1975. His insightful contribution led to his election as moderator of CCPD (Commission of Churches' Participation in Development). He served in that capacity from 1976-1983.

From 1983-1991 he served on the Central Committee as moderator of the then Unit on Renewal and Education. During the meetings of the Central Committee, he moderated the Public Issues Committee, where his skills as a professional political scientist were put to great use.

Preface

At the Harare assembly in 1998, the covenant by Africans both from the continent and the diaspora affirmed the cultural and social wealth of the churches in Africa and their wonderful gift of faith to the global ecumenical family. In response to the Africa plenary, the WCC committed itself to accompanying the churches in Africa in their struggle to actualize the fullness of life to the people of the continent. The motif of consensus-building during the Harare assembly was enriched by the language of ecumenicity, as the assembly experienced "padares" as the market place of ideas towards building new communities of hope in Africa.

The Ecumenical Focus on Africa (EFA) was mandated by the Central Committee following the Harare assembly. This was meant to be a process that would go on until the ninth assembly. The EFA has worked closely with the African churches and the All Africa Conference of Churches (AACC). It provided a framework for WCC's accompaniment of AACC during a very critical period when the latter went through a serious leadership crisis. The *"Journey of Hope for Africa"* as the EFA theme for the process of accompaniment, facilitated work on theological education, ecumenical formation, democratic change, peace and reconciliation, conflict resolution, as well as economic justice, development and addressing public issues. In partnership with AACC, National Councils of Churches (NCCs) and Regional Fellowships, significant work was done in addressing ethical, economic and missiological issues around the motif of "Behold, I create a new Africa". The Ecumenical HIV/AIDS Initiative in Africa (EHAIA), which is the most comprehensive ecumenical initiative on HIV and AIDS, was established within the framework of the EFA.

Special mention is needed of our accompaniment of the peace talks for Sudan. It was with joy and thanksgiving to God that we welcomed the signing in January 2004 of the Comprehensive Peace Agreement for Sudan. In our congratulatory message to the principals of the peace process we stressed that the peace dividends must be extended to Darfur which is today the worst human-made disaster in the world.

Since Harare there have been the historic transformation of the Organization of African Unity (OAU) into the African Union (AU) and the invigoration of the New Partnership for Africa's Development (NEPAD), the British-initiated Commission for Africa, the UN Millennium Goals, the re-invention of regional economic zones, and the emergence of an African Parliament. These are signs that Africa is on the brink of a new season of hope. At the same time, those developments are frustrated by continuing conflicts in several parts of the continent. The burden of debt continues to weigh heavily on the shoulders of African states and African people. Without doubt the biggest problem in Africa today is HIV and AIDS. The cumulative effects of this pandemic are frightening and bring about a tendency towards an attitude of social nihilism among African men, women and children.

Today Africa is the only continent which is regressing in economic terms. Some call Africa the lost continent! Yet there is an emerging trend in the way many parts of the world are relating to Africa. After a period of seeming neglect, the international community is beginning to "look at Africa with new eyes" – something the WCC started to do more than a decade ago.

During the run-up to the Porto Alegre assembly, we see the ecumenical accompaniment of Africa reaching a new level in the area of peace and conflict resolution. In partnership with AACC and Church World Service of the National Council of the Churches of Christ in the USA, an organized and sustainable framework of intervention, namely the Eminent Persons' Ecumenical Programme, has been established. Other initiatives in multifaith dialogue and cooperation are showing hopeful signs in a region where the politicization of religion is likely to be a source of conflict. Ecumenical formation, the search for new ways of being church to the younger generation, the disabled, poverty eradication and addressing climate change issues are other initiatives taken within the framework of the EFA.

Ecumenical engagement with Africa has been, and should continue to be, deepened. This is not a call for yet another special focus on Africa, but it is an indication that this region should remain one of the main WCC priorities in the foreseeable future.

"Being Together Under the Cross in Africa" was the title of the Assembly Message adopted by the delegates on the final day of the Harare assembly in December, 1998. Some delegates had suggested that a more dynamic phrase might have been, "moving together" or "building together." Both of these phrases appear in the official report, suggesting that there had been movement at the assembly and that there was an act of building. Being together, moving together, building together, these had special meaning for our African Plenary on the afternoon of 8 December called "Ubuntu and the African Kairos".

We heard from Rev. Barney Pityana that footprints found recently by paleontologists on the west coast of South Africa were about 117,000 year old and are considered to belong to an ancestor of modern humanity. Later evidence found by archeologists and historians shows that Africa is the cradle of humanity and the birthplace of modern people. Set against these dramatic discoveries, Pityana entitled his presentation "The Footprints of God".

The God of Africa is coterminous and coexistent with the people of Africa. God has no existence other than with the people. This God is weak and vulnerable because we have known no other God. This is the God who shares our human condition because God has no other existence but ours. We have only known God in the people of our everyday existence. As Pityana said: "To understand the people of Africa, therefore, requires a paradigm shift about God and religious life."

In this book, *Journey of Hope: Towards a New Ecumenical Africa*, we are reminded of the pledge made at Harare to accompany the African churches and peoples. Africa's pilgrimage through these many centuries and millennia has been, especially in recent years, long and hard. At Harare we said we must caution ourselves to avoid the negatives, the "basket case" scenarios, not through denial but because we know only too well that during our modern history, exploitation, corruption, war, poverty and disease have made our people suffer so deeply. But we also know how far we have come together. And together we will affirm that Africa, as the primordial home of humanity, is rising to the occasion and taking leadership in the struggle to create a new world in which all will live as good neighbours to each other.

We set out, this ecumenical movement of ours, after Harare, on a journey with full expectation that it would be difficult and challenging, but one filled with hope that we would be accompanied by, and be in solidarity with, one another and share the burdens too heavy to carry alone. We would eliminate on this journey the barriers and walls that divide us. We would reconcile broken relationships and heal wounds inflicted by conflict. And we would journey together in the spirit of

Pan-Africanism and manage our human and natural resources responsibly, ethically and in true partnership with one another and with Creation.

We know well that Africa is all too invisible, that it has been robbed of its soul by slavery and colonization and there have been forces at work wreaking negative power on a hapless continent. But we must avoid the subtle appeal of victimization.

One must always remember that during the independence and liberation struggles there were major investments in great and good ideas by leaders such as Kwame Nkrumah, Mwalimu Julius Nyerere, Amilcar Cabral, Leopold Sedar Senghor, Patrice Lumumba and Nelson Mandela which had strategic impacts for the future of Africa.

However, these initiatives were all too often overwhelmed by the intrigues and polarization of the global power struggles during the Cold War. Then, as we were emerging from this turmoil, Africa became hostage to a new global order in the 1980s and 1990s in which international financial institutions intruded into the internal economic and political arrangements within nation-states. In this regard the public commitment of the churches in Africa always included a comprehensive response to the dilemma of development and a search for economic justice.

The ecumenical movement has embarked on a path of accompaniment, self-renewal and commitment to the issues facing the continent. Peace-making initiatives among peoples in conflict continue to preoccupy the churches in Africa. We have always regarded the advancement of sustainable development to include a critical assessment of the conditions that have perpetuated poverty. This has required a deeper understanding of the global environment and the struggles of people in rural and urban Africa.

It is in this context that the contribution of the ecumenical movement ought to be understood and appreciated. The moral and ethical obligations of the churches acting together in all of life have always been a source of inspiration to the community of faith. This enables the people of God to comprehend the global social, political and economic trends and intervene on behalf of the poor in order to transform the conditions of poverty and injustice in our world today.

So much has happened since the Harare assembly and we have witnessed the urgent need for a redefined ecumenical engagement on the continent in the light of the challenges and opportunities facing Africa in the 21st century.

Journey of Hope is a moving account of Africans and churches around the world accompanying, supporting and helping them with the realization of the agenda launched in Harare. This book assesses some of the impact of ecumenical accompaniment to African churches on their journey of hope. We have just begun our pilgrimage and already so much has been accomplished towards ensuring that never again will Africa suffer humiliation such as had been experienced previously.

Samuel Kobia
General Secretary
World Council of Churches
Geneva, 2006

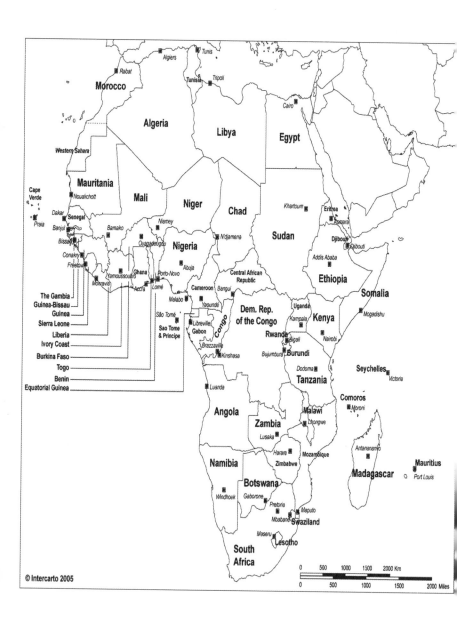

© Intercarto 2005

A Letter to My Ancestors

Dear Ancestors;

In 1998 the World Council of Churches is once again in Africa and we the children of this soil were trying to show them round our home, the heritage from God which you preserve for us. Once before this council was here in 1975 and we dramatized our history and our humanness in the play "Muntu", indeed some of you were there in the flesh. As I pour these words to you like a libation, my heart and soul are full of grief and hope, quite conflicting, but that is the truth. You see, I have just heard the hurt of your children. I am re-living in my bones and hearing in my ears the voices of the pain of the "family-ghosts of the Middle Passage".

No wonder that Ali Mazrui says that you are angry with us. True, often we find that we are angry at ourselves and continue to vow "Never Again". But even as we say "never again" and defeat apartheid, we find ourselves reaping the whirlwind of racism at every turn. We yearn to be authentic, we yearn to discover the strength with which you resisted total obliteration of what you had received from your forebears and indeed of the total annihilation of our kind from this soil. We yearn to rediscover your wisdom, for who knows but that we may glean insights and inspiration for our contemporary struggles and dilemmas for we too resist total absorption into a Euro-centered global culture we have not helped to shape. We know you have something to say to us.

I remember you, Anowa, you had taught us how to live in harmony with ourselves and with the rest of creation.

I remember you Creator, that moving away from the smoke and fire created by man, you charged woman to teach her sons to honour God and to apologize when they have wronged others. I remember you, God of Many Names, you taught us to seek reconciliation when we fall into strife, you gave us padare where we can have our palavers.

Honourable ancestors, our land knows a lot of strife and I have just seen and heard more. We grieve for you as we grieve for ourselves. But it seems in the very turmoil and decay that is Africa, is the seed of the New Africa determined to sprout so that Africa might make her own unique contribution to the global community.

Dear ancestors, you had a religion, you were led by the Creator. Some of you like Nehanda, held on to it even with your dying breath. Some of you enhanced it with tenets from Islam, others of you enriched it with Christianity and many of you struggled to abandon it totally and taught that we too should abandon that African religion outright. But you preserved the essentials of the religion ingrained in the culture, you passed those on to us. I am not complaining. We too are creative beings, so we have taken the challenge to craft a Christianity that does not obliterate our Africanness, but rather contributes to its enrichment globally.

We make bold to seek the new, for if we are afraid of positive change we shall be over taken by decay and simply perish from the face of the earth as a distinct people.

Did you not say that the one who is blazing a trail does not know that the path behind is crooked? We too have to take the responsibility for the choices we make. Nevertheless I have an urgent need to tell those of you who opted for Christ that, we who followed your footsteps continue to grieve the Holy Spirit. You remember how Jesus, our spiritual ancestor, prayed that we may have peace, and how he wished us fullness of life.

This was nearly 2,000 years ago. The world has known very little peace. For us in Africa, the only peace we have known in the past 500 years is that which comes from acquiescing in our own dehumanization. I am not unmindful that some of you resisted the imposition and paid with your earthly lives.

I can hear Anowa say, "enough is enough". I see Jesus weep to see our inability to identify and adhere to that which makes for our peace. Our refusal to stay under his motherly wings gives him grave sorrow for the hawkers hovering around us are ready to sell us any and all ideologies and world views as long as they line their pockets and feed their racism. It was not too long ago the Western media was telling us that Africa has been "abandoned". We did our own analysis and steeled ourselves, for we came to know the reality of the siphoning of Africa's resources by transnational corporations and the newly named fad "globalization". We know the economic exploitation, which promotes the misery of Africa, as Africans enrich the West and, increasingly, the East too. We seek a way out and a way forward and we count on you our ancestors to accompany us throughout. Today, we are reminded that:

"It is not the material poverty that constitutes the biggest problem of Africa in the bid for social transformation. It is the lack of a vital inner force, a moral will and a capacity for sustained initiatives in the struggle for positive change".

We have been through liberation struggles that you know so well. Today we continue where you left off..., retrieving our lost humanity. Today, it is our very humanity that is being belittled and overlooked by the powerful ones, both internal and external. Today we aspire to a cultural liberation by distilling and incorporating the valuable norms you tried to preserve.

This is why I make bold to pour these words to you, my ancestors. I am convinced that both our African and our Christian heritages as well as the Islamic, have something to say to us. "Tete wo bi ka, tete wo bi kyere?" ["the past has something to say: the past has something to teach"]. But the past has nothing to impose.

Do hear me out a little my ancestors in Jesus. What has the Christian past to teach us as we struggle with our contemporary realities? Can we find a healthy and health-giving Christianity in Africa? Well, say something. OK! You too have questions to ask. You ask: What are we doing in our community-based organizations? Are we carefully examining the concepts of structural adjustment, of liberalization, of privatization, or do we contain our efforts within "rescuing the perishing and caring for the dying"? I hear you urging us on, "God beyond changing, transforming, reconstructing so you might continuously nurture, enhance, build and sustain beautiful lives in beautiful environments. That is the way to claim our descent."

You call us to the need to face the impunity with which we violate the humanity of others. How right you are! We are promising ourselves a new day. We have begun with gender-sensitivity and gender equity. If only the churches will develop awareness of women's perspectives, involvements and contributions we would not lose so much potential. Whatever the context and agenda, you call us to pay particular attention to those whom the world considers "marginal". New voices will help shape the new Africa. We have vowed to help bring an end to social exclusions in our communities; so why not begin in the church?

Jesus, you specifically prayed that we be one; just see what we have made of unity on this continent. We have promised ourselves to develop ecumenically-minded leadership, to replace our confessional fundamentalism with the zeal for joint-work in mission. We shall not be partners only, but companions, a people walking the Emmaus road with you.

My esteemed forebears, in 1970 David Barrett made a statement that still today fills me with fear and trembling. He wrote under the title "AD 2000: 350 Million Christians in Africa". I can see you smile, because you told us that "if might were right, the elephant would be king of the forest." What does this numerical strength represent? I thought of the onion that once disappointed me to the core of my being; it held a theological message. This big perfectly shaped glossy-skinned fruit of the earth had a hollow centre. The life-sustaining growth point had dried up. So I ask, what is the theology and spirituality at the core of African Christianity, dried, rotten or alive? Our claim to relevance depends on the answer.

Today what fills me with fear and trembling is that Africa is perceived and treated as marginal in all spheres of world concerns except as a source of wealth for others and in matters of faith. Both Islam and Christianity run high on the crest of visibility as people grope for shalom. So the concerned observer is bound to ask: What faith? What practice? What theology? What church? Now, ancestor Blyden, I do not know if you remember, but you once prophesied concerning Africa that it will become the spring of spirituality for the whole world. I do not know whether we are entering into the heritage of this prophesy. What I do know is my own question on which you may perhaps enlighten me. "How can Christianity in spite of its nineteenth century legacy of Western impact become a frame of reference for the expression of African ideals of life?"

Living with our history we declare the twentieth century as African's Christian century. You will bear us out that even though the churches of the first Christian centuries were concentrated on the shores of this continent, this century that is closing has seen more dramatic presence of Christianity. The church has grown, yes, but it seems little has changed from 1951 when it was said that "the church has grown evangelically without corresponding theological, liturgical and economic maturity." This 'lamentable' situation needs to be addressed with all intentionality. There is an understandable concern that under the stress of political and social change, organized Christianity may start to disintegrate at the centre while it is still expanding at the circumference.

Well, honourable forebears, you know that we are expanding, there are many more churches, many more expatriate missionaries, many more charismatic movements and many more people who confess

Christ as their personal saviour. There are many who leave it to The Christ to deal with their enemy, the devil, and to dispel the fear of some of you whom they had demonized or are beginning to do so. We too want to leave behind a path of faith and on that we shall faithfully work.

We do not deceive ourselves. When we protest the dismal image of Africa projected in the Western media, we do so fully aware of our own complicity and domestic exploitation. Bessie Head has observed that "the root of cheating and stealing" is that of "despising the people". People at the helm of affairs in Africa or related to Africa say the people "know nothing simply because they do not read and write". We despise ourselves as others despise us, while we proclaim that wisdom does not come from reading and writing many books. We are aware of our "social defects". We experience or inflict "a form of cruelty, really spite, that seems to have its origins in witchcraft practices. It is a sustained pressure of mental torture that reduces its victims to a state of permanent terror. And once they start on you they don't know where to stop, until you become stark, raving mad. Then they grin."

In the second half of this century, as in the first, we have seen politicians, colonial, civilian and military do this to those who challenge them. In another context this is a picture of the economic strangulation of Africa by global monetary powers which makes Mazrui ask "Is there life after debt?"

Nananom, you are around us and so you are witness to the fact that political sagesse [wisdom] on the part of religious bodies is at a very low ebb in Africa. The dramatic discontinuation of the structures that served you has not served us well and where they continue, they are often in conflict with the imposed Westernization. We still have the churches and the mosques. They have the opportunity to touch the lives of people at the least on a weekly basis not to talk of the daily and the one-on-one encounters with these living roots of our nations. But one still asks "How is this availability of the people utilized?"

Political parties use their opportunities to cultivate people to rally around the interests of the party said also to be the best interest of the nation. But the results are ambiguous, for while mouthing the needs of the people, our political leaders are forced to implement "externally induced projects of democratization and population control", economic structural adjustments that pass on the responsibility to stay alive on the people themselves puzzled. "To what purposes are our taxes beyond the maintenance of armies and an ill-equipped police force?" The complex political and economic challenges overwhelmed us and have resulted in social decay that sends people scrambling for spiritual support. "What is the churches response?"

The consultation just mentioned, warns clearly that "It is deceptive and dangerous to preach a Gospel of Prosperity in the midst of massive poverty." It is deceptive because we do not bring the people to an analysis of the "socio-structural constraints that prevent many African communities from enjoying decent living by any standards". It is dangerous because we claim that religion is "an agent of welfare" but do not empower the people to seek this welfare. And above all it is deceptive to continue to teach that religion and politics do not mix, when both claim to cater for the welfare of the people. It is deceptive because while on this side of the grave, we dare not separate body and soul hence we have to see to it that religion serves our humanity.

Beloved ancestors, you gave up your people for labour, then you gave up the land to be colonized. You were the first to experience the globalization of our economy. You moved from maize to coffee to satisfy the trade terms. You were forced out of traditional statecraft and made your way into modern statehood and "the blackening" of the UNO in the 1960s. In the process, we, your children have been incorporated into a Euro-centered world culture. I am not saying all is unambiguously bad. By the imperial languages some of us your children can communicate beyond our mother tongue. But whether we speak these tongues or not we find ourselves bound by Euro-centric "international" laws we did not help to craft. I knew you would say, "But you can change some of these". We have to shed the carefully groomed inferiority we experience when faced with Western science and technology. I know you will point out that technology has no race and that several have entered its ambit who are not of European descent and who know no colonization. Yes I agree and would even add, "so have some erstwhile colonial peoples". Nothing prevents us from joining the latter.

You, our ancestors, have asserted your continued presence to make us work, so you can feel at home in global Christianity. No longer shall we join in demonizing you in translations and in theologizing. We realize today that cultural and religious pluralism is a global reality. We affirm therefore that taking this factor seriously demands that we take African religion seriously. Those of us who are Christians shall learn to be both authentically African and authentically Christian. The challenge is to strive to contribute to World Christianity and a Christian Ecumenism.

We crave dissent so while we take a critical distance from local cultures, which we find dehumanizing, we shall remain true to our African heritage. This means all externally stimulated change has to be minutely examined for we too have a responsibility to contribute to the changing and the shaping of world history and culture.

You heard the life stories that I heard today. We are faced with how to reduce the West's stranglehold over Africa. The market Euro-centrism of the past 500 years has meant that world-culture too bears its marks. We need to strive more intentionally to build on the values you crafted from your experience. We need a totally new vision of ourselves and a positive outlook that will generate innovative perspectives. Both Idowu and Mazrui describe Africa as a woman. I forgive their sexism. Mazrui describes Africa as a woman with the expression "the female continent – passive, patient and penetrable". In his *African Traditional Religion: a Definition*, Idowu compares what the powerful nations expect of Africa with what most societies expect of women:

> "Where she behaves herself according to prescription and accepts an inferior position, benevolence which her 'poverty' demands is assured, and for this she shows herself deeply and humbly grateful. If for some reason she takes it into her head to be assertive and claim a footing of equality, then she brings upon herself a frown; she is called names; she is persecuted openly or by indirect means; she is helped to be divided against herself..."

As women resent these stereotypes so Africa must refuse this female typology. We have participated in changing the world. We took part in evangelizing Africa, right from the inception of Christianity as well as during later centuries. It is our duty to identify our contribution to help posterity build up their self-esteem.

At the moment we continue bound under the western sphere of influence and seem unable to highlight our interdependence so as to build up the self-esteem of our children. The West continues involvement in how we run our economies and prosecute our politics because they need us for a market and for investment space. Our resources helped to develop their world so we can make them strengthen our regional structures. We can and must think Pan-African. We can and must think and work for change. We've done it in South Africa where we rescued our humanness from the jaws of racism. How will South Africa use this newborn dignity in Africa and globally?

The world extracts minerals from Africa and we have a numerical power in the UN. Should we not use this to make the transnational corporations more responsible? It seems to me that through the World Bank and the International Monetary Fund, the world community has secularized money and put it even higher than the political state. Could we in Africa keep our diamonds, gold and oil in the bowels of the earth, if we cannot make them speak for the good of Africa?

We have become heavily Christianized, could we engage in influencing the shape of global Christianity or at least develop our own distinctive African practice and articulation of the faith? Perhaps others may find ours speaking to them. At least we shall enhance and enrich the diversity and the variety of ways of living out the faith. We would be contributing to shaping the history of Christianity and demonstrate the universal import of the coming of Jesus the Christ. Western Christianity has in the main been a de-Africanizing power, but that does not need to continue. You our ancestors expect us to do better than that. So with you among the great cloud of witnesses I call upon my sisters and brothers of African descent to conversion and commitment; we cannot afford to do less.

A call to conversion and commitment

Return to ourselves as we turn to God so we can move forward with integrity. Never again shall we walk on tiptoe.

Never again shall we suffer humiliation.

Re-assert indigenous African ways that have seeds of humanization for all humanity. Refuse laws that serve the interest of lawmakers to the woe of the people.

Never again shall we be plagued with coups and religious strife.

Never again shall we condone the cultural de-Africanization from outside.

Refuse westernization that comes in the guise of Christianization.

Never again shall we be silent in the face of opportunistic foreign policies as in open markets and liberalization that sell our heritage to all bidders for a pot of porridge.

Never again shall we buy into the transplantation of foreign life styles without the appropriate soil in which they can make us prosper.

Recoil from inefficiency, mismanagement, corruption and our narrow definitions of who belongs and who is our community.

Never again shall we be satisfied with living as hunters and gatherers with no maintenance and creative culture and a resignation to death and decay of infrastructure.

We vow to you and to ourselves before this great cloud of global witnesses, seen and unseen. Never again shall we walk on tiptoe around the globe which is God's world and our common heritage.

Mercy Amba Oduyoye
Harare, Zimbabwe,
8 December, 1998

1. Journey of Hope to a New Africa

Africa is a religiously and spiritually diverse continent, with large populations adhering to Christianity and Islam, in addition to African traditional beliefs and practices and other world religions. There are great moral and spiritual traditions of wisdom that date back to antiquity and are consonant with the story of creation and its ultimate meaning. African spirituality is based on a common cosmology and understanding derived from a moral universe in which our relationship with God and the embrace of the goodness of life is at the heart of what it means to be human. This brings about the sharing of responsibility for the preservation and transmission of the vital force that sustains life as overseen by the great ancestors on behalf of God. The vital force is an invincible self-generating power in the universe that creates and renews life in all sentient beings. This force resides in all human beings and is brought to fruition in birth, sustained and nurtured in the rich network of communal relationships, and elevated back to the community in the spiritual realm through death. Accordingly when people die they don't fade out of the realm of what is considered the physical universe but become part of the web of cosmic dimension to human relationships that sustains life in the universe. Physical death not only brings a definitive end to the historical event of one's life but also is primarily the means by which the individual becomes present again to the community in the realm of the Spirit.

Despite preconceptions in the West, African Christian spirituality has deep roots in biblical history. In the Hebrew scriptures, Africans appear as part of the narrative of their love for God. In the New Testament record, Jesus has multiple encounters with Africa, including his sojourn as a child in Egypt and the African, Simon of Cyrene, who carried Jesus' cross on his Good Friday agony. Africa remains a place of pilgrimage for Christianity. Through Egypt it is part of the Holy Land because Jesus and his parents took refuge among these people and made it a sacred place. The first non-Jewish Christian was an African – the Ethiopian official converted by Philip the deacon on the desert road from Jerusalem to Gaza.

It is in Egypt where we find the greatest number of martyrs, spiritual leaders and theologians in the first centuries of Christianity. Insufficient links between faith and daily life in the cities of that time continued to influence the charismatic spirit of seeking God unceasingly in the desert. Hence monastic and hermitic spirituality has still today deep roots among Coptic Egyptians.

Yet this history is lost in the geographic expansion of Europe and its hegemonic designs as the protagonist of the Christian faith. Beyond the nostalgia of Egypt as the cradle of African civilization where Greek and Arabic alphabets were taught to the kingdom of Axum, one cannot surpass the glorious heritage of Carthage. Axum, an ancient almost mythical city state, existed about 2,500 years ago and was situated in the far northern plateau of modern day Ethiopia. Today massive ruins reveal the amazing civilization of this great kingdom south of Egypt. The discovery of the great walls of Zimbabwe further illustrate the fact that the African hinterland also excelled in architectural technology and that Egypt is not necessarily the epitome of African contribution to world civilizations.

Africa is not only the sacred home of humanity but also the custodian of the oldest of civilizations that ever existed and which gave birth to the ancient and modern world. It has been home to a multitude of traditions, values and spiritualities which predate Western civilizations. Not only did Western "civilization" seek to submit the world to its memory, it also sanctioned and produced unimaginable evils: the slave trade and its politics of "discovery" since the fifteenth century; colonialism; imperialism at the end of the eighteenth century and throughout the nineteenth; and fascism, communism, genocide, ethnic cleansing in the twentieth. Despite the violent changes that have taken place in Africa since the incursion of Western civilization (and in spite of all we hear about corruption and brutality among African leaders), today's African society is still closer to its spiritual roots than European or North American societies.

The vast majority of Africans are still poor peasants, who survive the harsh realities of life by holding on firmly to faith in the human person, in the human family, and in the human community. At the heart of African spirituality is the reality of God's omnipresence which is inherent in every human condition and a social landscape that is filled with the abundance of life. The presence of God is not an abstract idea; rather every spiritual experience is an existential prerogative to the very essence of life. God's blessings are often invoked during moments of encounter between two or more human beings. The generosity of God is so great that it is inadmissible for death to overcome life. It is through birth that life is replenished in the universe.

The first thousand years of the life of the church were immensely enriched by the social, religious and cultural milieu of ancient north-eastern Africa including today's Sudan, Ethiopia and much of North Africa. Christianity was in the north of the Sahara in the Maghreb and Roman North Africa by 180 AD. Egyptian Christianity, said to go back to St Mark, the evangelist, grew into a dynamic force and great theological systems evolved in the coastal city of Alexandria at its famous catechetical school producing theologians whose deep insights and interpretation of the meaning and spirit of the Gospels were amazingly articulated.

The works of such theologians as Clement of Alexandria, Origen, Arius, Dionysius and the great Athanasius laid the foundation for the growth of the early church in the Mediterranean world and in sub-Saharan Africa where the Ethiopian Orthodox Church remains predominant. Today the statistics of David Barrett's *Encyclopedia of Christianity* predict the shifting of the centre of world Christianity back to Africa.

The ancient Ethiopian and Egyptian churches are just as old as the rest of Christendom and must also not be forgotten. They have a rich spiritual legacy, which dates back to biblical times and has emerged intact from contacts with other cultures and religions over many centuries. (The Ethiopian Orthodox Tewahedo Church was the only indigenous sub-Saharan African church represented at the founding assembly of the WCC in 1948: all others were mission churches. It is still an active member.) Christianity in Africa is so full of vitality and charisma, such that the numerous new theologies of life and the varied interpretations of the gospel can hardly define it. If Africa is going to be the centre of Christianity by the year 2040 then one must begin to grapple with the kind of theology and ecumenism it is likely to bring to the world.

It was out of the public debates and controversies surrounding their teachings that the Christian faith was organized into a rational and ethical system. Doctrinal proclamations by Athanasius became the foundation of the ecumenical creed that is the heritage of Christianity even today.

The Coptic Church of Alexandria was the first church to be founded in the continent by St Mark in 42 AD. The Coptic Cathedral today stands at the spot where St Mark was martyred in 68 AD. The Patriarchate of Alexandria (the oldest of the four historic patriarchates, along with Jerusalem, Antioch and Cyprus) is Eastern Orthodox and the Coptic Church of Alexandria is Oriental Orthodox.

The Copts are authentic descendants of the Pharaonic Egyptians. It is a historical fact that the central doctrine of Christian faith, the Trinity, was first articulated and formulated by Africans. Preceding Judeo-Christian faith in 1500 BC a young Pharaoh, Akhenaton, first invoked the notion of monotheism. The doctrine of the Trinity was well understood and articulated by Egyptian theologians because it had common features with the faith of the ancient pharaoh triads. This is what helped the Egyptians to understand the idea of the Triune God, Father, Son and Holy Spirit.

St Mark was also the first Apostle to formulate a liturgy, as a regular church ritual to be followed in the celebration of the Eucharist. It was first done in Greek and later written out by Pope Athanasius in 330 AD. A copy was given to Formentius, first bishop of Ethiopia. The liturgy was revised by Pope Cyril the Great, and is now used in both Coptic and Ethiopian churches.

There was regular migration between Ethiopia and Egypt as the pharaohs pushed south along the Nile, the longest river on the planet, in search of gold and other treasures. They came across established kingdoms which they conquered and brought under Egyptian control. Near the modern town of Merowe, at the Fourth Cataract of the Nile, a city grew which became the centre of the empire the Egyptians called Kush. For 300 years they flourished in the Sudanese heartland, becoming one of the Old World's most significant trading centres.

The people were black Africans, either Nilotes or Kushites; it was probably they, historians say, who inspired the Greeks to call the *Aithiopiai* "burned faces", an early version of Ethiopia. Eventually the Kush began bumping against new rivals, from the Ethiopian kingdom called Axum, and in the fourth century AD, Ethiopia's King Ezana, the first Christian emperor of Axum, sent an army into Kush and sacked the royal city.

As Axum's power waned, two new Christian powers arose in the Middle Nile: the kingdom of Nubia with its capital at Dongola and the kingdom of Aloa, with its capital at Soba, near modern-day Khartoum. Both were powerful enough to resist the Arabs who had seized Egypt by 641. Sudan was a land blessed not only with minerals and spices but also with institutions of wisdom in which scholarship in mathematics and astronomy flourished and contributed to the architecture of the Nubian Pyramids in Egypt. The moral wealth and ingenuity of the Nuer people of the Sudan, for example, have remained one of the most awesome inspirations of a vision of life that integrates and harmonizes both the existential and metaphysical universe.

Sudan defines the northern and southern frontiers of the continent that is also connected by the flow of the waters of the Blue Nile north of the Limpopo. Sudan (*bilad as-Suda*, land of the blacks in Arabic) surely shares the dignity of Egypt and Ethiopia as a cradle of African heritage.

Then there was the other side of North Africa, the Maghreb, also with ancient links to the south which go back to Old Ghana, long before Mali the Great emerged to dominate the Sahel. The nomadic Berbers had been there in the Sahara desert a thousand years before the Phoenicians settled along the coast somewhere after 1000 BC and built Carthage in 841 BC, which in turn fell to the Romans in 146 BC. Rome itself fell to the Visigoths and for a brief while became part of the Byzantine empire before it was conquered by the triumphant armies of Islam, as the Arabs invaded all of North Africa.

In the Byzantine period at Carthage, great theologians and saints of the church such as Tertullian, Cyprian and later Augustine of Hippo, debated with eloquence the message of Christ in a world filled with claims and counter-claims about which was the authentic interpretation of the true meaning of the gospels. St Augustine of Hippo's autobiography *Confessions* has remained a spiritual masterpiece for centuries inspiring many people to embrace grace as the unconditional self-giving love of God to human kind. Augustinian spirituality was the epitome of biblical and philosophical inspiration.

When the Arabs invaded Egypt and then the Maghreb, sweeping across North Africa, some people remained Coptic Christians in Egypt but the majority converted to Islam. The wave of Islamization and transformation of North Africa into an Arabized world wiped out the significance of Christian heritage in the region for centuries to come. In the 16th century most of North Africa became part of the Ottoman empire and 300 years later, western European powers gained control.

And so it was that in 1976 the All Africa Conference of Churches' general committee met in Alexandria and adopted the "Confession of Alexandria", following an ancient Christian practice and conscious of their heritage in the ancient North African church. What they discovered did not just amaze them, they were also inspired by the cultural and spiritual heritage they found:

• the meeting facilitated direct contact between the churches in Egypt, the oldest on the continent, and the churches in Africa beyond Ethiopia and Sudan, the countries to which the Copts brought the gospel between the fourth and sixth centuries. The rest of Africa knew little about these rich and thriving Christian traditions in the midst of Islamic North Africa;

• members of the general committee marvelled at the history and tradition which had been hidden from them for so long. The AACC delegates saw in Old Cairo, in the streets and historic places of Alexandria and in the Valley of the Kings at Luxor, the vital link between Christianity and Egypt's ancient traditions. This provided them with renewed inspiration and courage to continue the search for identity in the African church, so that it too could make its own authentic contribution to the universal church;

- the expression of faith which flowed from the 1976 general committee listed the churches' current concerns as: "economic justice, the total liberation of men and women from every form of oppression and exploitation, and [a concern for] peace in Africa";
- they stated the churches' search for "authentic responses to Christ as Lord over the whole of our lives"; and
- affirmed that "the struggle for human liberation is one of the ways we confess out faith in an incarnate God."

The first millennium of Christianity was the period of consolidating the message of the risen Lord within and beyond the Greco-Roman frontiers of the Mediterranean world. The second millennium began with the great struggles for theological and ecclesial identity which first led to the divisions between East and West in 1054. And then later came the sixteenth century Reformation which saw western Christianity fragmented by the new enthusiasm of the movement that made the Bible a public document of faith and transformed the spiritual cosmology of medieval Europe.

With the missionary movement, Christianity came to sub-Saharan Africa, already divided within itself by the slave trade and the imperial colonial project. Around 1880, at a time when there was an emerging nationalism among European nation-states such as Belgium, France, England, Germany, Portugal and Spain, they began to jostle bitterly for the partition of the continent. The French and the British obtained parts of Congo, Central Africa and the West African coast. The French left to the Belgians the regions to the left of the Congo River, while they took the regions on the right bank. Great Britain united with Portugal to prevent Germany and France from "destroying world peace". Portugal grabbed Angola and Mozambique, while the British took the region around the Great Limpopo (modern-day Zimbabwe, Zambia, South Africa, Malawi, Swaziland, Lesotho and Botswana, and northeast, Kenya and Uganda).

The bitter rivalries between the European states led to the Berlin Conference (1884 to 1885) at which the Europeans agreed on the partitioning of Africa among themselves. The continent became a source of raw materials for European industrialization. With the partitioning of Africa into territories ruled and controlled by the colonial powers, a process of plundering of human and natural resources began from whose effects Africa still suffers. According to the Ghanaian historian Adu Boahen, the European states colonized Africa mainly to establish new markets for their finished products, to find a steady source of raw materials, to invest their surplus capital and to maintain prestige and power. The establishment of an infrastructure for the transportation of goods, an administrative system and even education were all meant to serve the economic gains of the colonial regime.

While making claims for universal suffrage and legitimacy of protest against oppressive regimes in their own backyards, the democratic ideals invented during the European "Enlightenment" were never applied during the brutal conquest of foreign lands. So the colonial Jesus was part of the intrigues of pacifying revolt against the capitalist interests of the imperial regimes.

As the Mau Mau freedom fighters in Kenya used to say, "when the white man came, he had the Bible and we had the land. He told us to close our eyes and pray and when we opened our eyes he had the land and we had the Bible."

In 1914, the first world war devastated and rearranged much of Europe. After a brief 20-year period of uneasy peace there came the most devastating world war in history. Europe was once again in turmoil and because of its colonial conquest of most of the planet drew almost the entire planet into a conflict that changed the course of human history forever. For Africa, the end of the second world war also meant the beginning of the end of the colonial enterprise. The fragmentation of Europe into East and West with the Cold War saw the emergence of new spheres of influence and competition from both sides for supporters in Africa. The always-floundering League of Nations became the United Nations, inspired to restore the promise of peace and unity of all humankind.

Various ecumenical initiatives interrupted by the second world war culminated in the founding of the World Council of Churches in 1948. This was the most vivid institutional expression and consolidation of the desire for unity among Christians. The basic biblical imperative for ecumenism is that even though there are divisions, Christ himself is not divided.

The forced contribution of African people to two world wars led to further impoverishment of the continent. After centuries of slavery, exploitation and colonialism, Africa sought liberation from the 1950s through 1994 when the last colony, South Africa, became free. It was in most cases a violent battle, for imperial powers did not give in easily and self-determination was a protracted struggle, which has yet to end. Most of the missionary churches with historical links to the colonial regimes were faced with a choice of loyalty to their colonial roots or solidarity with the local struggles for freedom. For many it was a difficult choice that also left behind its legacy of division.

However, there were already seeds of ecumenism among the historical missionary churches on the continent. One of the earliest was the International Missionary Council, which first met at Edinburgh in June 1910, regarded as the beginning of the modern ecumenical movement. Some 1,200 delegates placed at the centre of their work the obligation to make Christ known to the millions who had not heard the gospel. "Evangelization of the world in this generation" was their hallmark call. The 1940s saw local Christian councils arising in many parts of Africa.

From these came the idea of ecumenical schools for basic training and theological education such as Trinity in Kumasi (now in Legon), Ghana; Immanuel centre in Ibadan, Nigeria; St Paul's College in Limuru, Kenya; the Federal Theological Seminary of Southern Africa (FEDSEM) in Natal, South Africa and the Mindolo Ecumenical Centre in Kitwe, Zambia. Some of these ecumenical centres have been transformed into university colleges and Bible schools that offer degrees and diplomas in divinity, religious studies and theology. The missionary movement in Africa also brought with it access to modern European institutions including hospitals and schools which became the centres of western formation and socialization of a new African elite for public service.

The move to establish the Alliance of Missions as early as 1900 was also inspired by a vision to create a united "native church" in Kenya. Hence the emergence of the ecumenical movement was inspired by the desire not only for spiritual, but also institutional unity. These also led for example to the formation of national church councils such as the Christian Council of Kenya (CCK), which later became the National Council of Churches of Kenya (NCCK).

These national councils, many pre-dating the WCC, were associated with the IMC and, most of them, also older than the AACC, emerged as the public face of modern ecumenism in Africa. The NCCK, for example, was 62 years old in 2005, and others such as the South African Council of Churches have seen years of intensive prophetic engagement of the member churches in the formation of a just and democratic society.

The costs have been high. In the 1980s, the NCCK under the leadership of Samuel Kobia, then its general secretary, undertook intense educational work in political conscientization of churches towards democratic change in Kenya. This prophetic critique led to the banning by the government in 1988 of *Beyond*, the council's news magazine, and the imprisoning of its editor. Following the banning, the council revived *Target* which had been discontinued. Many church leaders became martyrs of this period of struggle for external and internal liberation from the end of colonialism to the present. The "road accident" that killed Anglican Bishop Alexander Muge of Kenya in 1990 recalled for many the martyrdom of Anglican Archbishop Janani Luwum of Uganda in 1977 at the hands of Idi Amin.

The role of SACC in the anti-apartheid struggle made the ecumenical celebration of the release of Nelson Mandela a landmark in interreligious relations in South Africa and a prelude to one of the most inclusive democratic national constitutional transitions that Africa has ever known.

But needless to say, other landmarks have been the refugees and mortalities of the struggle. The genocide of almost a million Tutsis and moderate Hutus in many of Rwanda's church compounds of all denominations in 1994, the maimings and massacres in Liberia and Sierra Leone in the same decade that saw South Africa free, declared wars of world proportions between Eritrea and Ethiopia and the millions killed in the Democratic Republic of Congo as the century ended, crossed all boundaries between denominations and faiths and even Christian councils, as failed states divided along ethnic and tribal lines.

The twentieth century saw enormous changes in Africa. Throwing off political colonialism and attaining self-determination was easy compared with the struggle to attain economic independence. As the then president (1980-98) of Botswana, Sir Ketumile Masire once reiterated, African leaders had become money-hungry, intolerant and selfish towards their own people after the attainment of political independence. Most of the leaders were ready to do anything just to attain their egotistical goals. Some leaders would drive their own people to ethnic animosity in order to stay in power. This was, however, political shortsightedness of the worst form because once ethnic violence had been stirred it could not be reversed easily. The Organization of African Unity (OAU) which was founded on the quest for unity among free African nations was now obliged to try to strengthen its mechanisms for preventing, processing and solving conflicts.

The president of Botswana simply told his colleagues that black Africa had now entered a different phase in its fight for freedom. The fight must now be directed towards internal structures of oppression.

The idea of freedom from colonialism was not to have a fox roaming freely in a chicken-coop. No, the fox must be tamed. A new era of second liberation had dawned upon Africa.

However, following the end of the Cold War in the 1980s and the ushering in of the so-called second liberation in Africa, the people turned to the church for guidance and direction. In a sense, history gave the church a push towards a new responsibility that it could not run away from. Yet, despite a prophetic vocation, the church was not fully prepared and much less equipped to adequately carry out this enormous task of providing spiritual and moral leadership in the process of reinventing Africa anew from every aspect of life and values of the people.

Africans have served the WCC, the AACC, the national councils of churches and other ecumenical structures in increasing numbers and in a variety of positions, making it possible for African perspectives to be aired in the global, continental and national arenas of decision-making. True, Africa's financial participation in the ecumenical movement has been far below that of Europe and North America, but in other ways African hospitality has never failed to facilitate ecumenical gatherings and encounters. Voices, votes and cheque books make it possible for ecumenism to be a movement but the spirit of ecumenism does not depend entirely on these.

When the central committee of the WCC was held in Enugu, Nigeria in 1960, Sir Francis Akanu Ibiam, the first African governor of colonial Eastern Nigeria, was a president of the WCC. The meeting brought the global ecumenical image closer to Christians in Africa and Africans saw themselves as a significant component.

Later, when Ibiam sided with his people during the Biafran war in the late 1960s and was forced into exile, he renounced his English knighthood and Christian name in protest against Britain's unquestioning support for Nigeria's inhuman treatment of the Ibo people. The WCC provided leadership in the Biafran humanitarian aid programme that placed the council squarely in the mode of ecumenical humanitarian aid regardless of the political tensions raised. The Nigerians who were present at the WCC's Uppsala assembly in 1968 came from a country in the midst of a bitter and vicious civil war. Biafra had seceded from Nigeria and declared its independence in 1967. The militarily superior Nigerians were using food and other sanctions as a weapon to starve the dissidents into surrender. Using newly developed mass media techniques and technologies, churches mobilized around the world. Those allied with both the WCC and the Vatican worked to feed millions of hungry Biafrans. JointChurchAid (JCA), the airline initiative that Scandinavians, Canadians and Americans set up to aid starving civilians by flying food into landlocked Biafra in the face of the Nigerian air force was an equal partnership under Geneva and the Vatican with a key role played by Eugene Carson Blake, second general secretary of the WCC at the time. JCA rapidly became known the world over as the Jesus Christ Airline.

Ibiam led the Biafran delegation to Uppsala to garner ecumenical support for a cause which the world had been erroneously told was a Muslim (northern Nigeria) versus Christian (Biafra) struggle but which was really a result of failed colonialism and western covetousness of Biafra's oil. Bola Ige came as leader of the WCC delegation from the federal Nigeria side, determined to counter this impression of Nigeria's corruption and instability. Both he and Ibiam came from the Student Christian Movement of Nigeria where they had been friends and colleagues. Whatever the merits of each side, the fact is that the Christians from war-torn African countries felt themselves accountable to the ecumenical family represented at Uppsala.

Many will point to the Uppsala assembly as a watershed and the preceding conference on Church and Society, held in Geneva in 1966, as the root of divergences that Uppsala introduced. "Behold, I Make All Things New" – the assembly's theme – signalled a significant change in the speed and intensity with which the ecumenical ship was entering new seas. The centre of critique was the roots of poverty in the third world and the need for developments that would uproot poverty.

Focus was specifically on the WCC's promotion of the Programme to Combat Racism (PCR) and other justice issues including women's rights, the politically oppressed, war and violence and self-determination. Youth played a noisy but influential role.

But it was also in 1966 that the World Council for Christian Education (WCCE) and the Sunday School Association merged in Nairobi in preparation for joining the WCC to become its office on education. For African Christians, Sunday schools were institutions in the mission structures which they held dear and which they struggled to maintain, with varying degrees of success. This became a point of commitment that the AACC was to inherit and promote through curriculum development programmes. From the African point of view there was never a paradigm shift. Challenges continued to pile up and the churches coped as best they could. If there was a shift at all, it was in terms of a more direct participation in determining what the challenges were.

The "moratorium" debate was at the heart of ecumenical discourse in the 1970s after AACC approved it in 1974 as "the most viable means of giving the African church the power to reform its mission in the African context." It became a bone of contention, misinterpreted by some western mission agencies – deliberately it seemed. Instead of embracing moratorium as a new relationship of mutuality enabling African churches to attain full maturity, certain mission boards forced the younger churches into submission by simply withholding all funds. For those who saw the liberation praxis as necessary for the church in society, moratorium was a positive contribution of the AACC to the ecumenical movement. It forced the churches and mission partners to rethink mission.

When the WCC's fifth assembly was forced to re-locate at short notice from Indonesia to Nairobi in 1975, churches in Africa rose to the occasion. They felt integral to the ecumenical movement. They were neither guests nor alms-seekers. It was the first time for such a meeting in Africa. Christianity was growing in Africa, faster than in any other part of the world. The assembly had shed fresh light on the many ramifications of the concept of, and the search for unity aided by the theme "Jesus Christ Frees and Unites." Rev. Philip Potter, a West Indian whose ancestors came from Africa as slaves, was elected general secretary of WCC (1972-1984) three years before and Nairobi was his first assembly in that position. Known for his soaring oratory and deep theological analysis, Potter's words had unique meaning equally for Africa then, and now: "...Through indifference, greed, envy, fear, love of power and short-sighted stupidity, [men] have created and developed a demonstrably unjust economic order."

And then he turned his attention to racism which was institutionalized at the time in white supremacist governments such as Rhodesia (now Zimbabwe), South Africa, Southwest Africa (now Namibia), Angola and Mozambique and openly practised in many other parts of the continent:

"The most frightening part of this dreadful human disease is the way in which the sale of arms, economic investments and bank loans involving individuals, groups and governments of many countries, maintain the oppressive racist structures, especially in southern Africa. Racism must be understood and tackled globally. Again, our investigations have shown that human rights are being violated everywhere and that we can no longer separate personal from social rights. They belong inextricably together and their violation is related to these threats to survival... We are not talking about abstractions. We are addressing ourselves to human beings who create and operate them... We are talking about human sin in all its protean forms. And that is what our biblical faith is about. It is... on the basis of this biblical faith that the churches which confess Jesus Christ, who frees and unites, are called to recognize their inescapable responsibility for humanity."

By no means was the fifth assembly a placid event that ignored the division in church and society; indeed, a good deal was heard about a new gap: that between the WCC and the churches. Nor was Nairobi a forum that merely repeated ideas without contributing new insights of its own. The PCR, by now a favourite target of WCC critics in western countries, was given a resounding commendation and renewed mandate. A major new undertaking was the beginning of a search for a "just, participatory and sustainable society". Again there was a gradual shift in theological focus from the liberation struggles of southern Africa to the global sources of oppression and the economic violence associated with them.

The developing world, especially Africa, was increasingly vulnerable because of the severe policies of the Bretton Woods Institutions – set up in 1948 at the same time as the UN – the IMF and World Bank, which produced an economic climate in which violence become so rampant that it was used as a systemic means of responding to the terrorism of capitalism and global forces of impunity. "It was significant that in this global situation of resurgence of violence and re-emergence of conflicts in the continent that the central committee of the WCC at its meeting in Johannesburg in January 1994 decided to launch a WCC programme to overcome violence," wrote Konrad Raiser, the then general secretary. The problem of violence was not confined to Africa since it was becoming a global trend and means through which minority and oppressed groups in society were addressing their grievances to the mighty and powerful. The Decade to Overcome Violence (DOV) process was born in Africa in 1998.

The eighth WCC assembly in Harare, the second to be held in Africa, was also its Golden Jubilee – a glowing reminder of 50 years since its founding in 1948. "Africa is God's gift to the world, to hear his word incarnated in a special theme invitation to 'Turn to God, Rejoice in Hope'. This is, above all, God's appointed opportunity for his church and the world, to act anew, break with the past and its destructive ways of constructing and reconstructing the face of the world. It is God's appointed Jubilee for a fresh start, for acting creatively, with compassion, especially to the vulnerable."

Harare was a call for healing and renewal of the soul of Africa, so that the mother continent may be the witness to the transformative power of the Spirit that brings a new humanity and life to a wounded and disfigured world.

The oikoumene is designated as the whole inhabited world whose members include the whole of creation. The oikoumene is God's household in which humans are called to be stewards. Hence the ecumenical movement signifies an openness to a variety of expressions of faith in God and commitment to solidarity which fully includes all the weak and vulnerable members of the household.

2. The Origins of Pan-African Ecumenism

> *Ecumenism has to do with the visible unity of the church and with demonstrating the spiritual unity of Christians, unity not only for its own sake but also because it is the mission of God entrusted to the church. Ecumenism has to do with the integrity of the whole human race, its unity and well-being as much as with the integrity of the whole creation. With a fresh understanding of ecumenism and unity, it seems clear that the churches have entered a phase of mutual respect and a higher level of cooperation. It was therefore not surprising that where churches did not act together, it was to deal with the unity of humankind and justice in human relations.*

Mercy Oduyoye

Africa's long life has been the story of the ebb and flow of kingdoms and dynasties, some great, some small, some exceptionally wealthy and powerful. Like empires everywhere they rose and fell, flowered and decayed. Waves of migrants, conquerors and peacemakers, swept across the continent for century after century. There were great migrations of peoples, Kushites and Nilotics up and down the Nile, the great boiling out of what is southeastern Nigeria of the Bantu people west and south and east and then north, then south again until they filled up the continent. The old empires (Kush, the Zanj coast, Mali, Benin, the Ashanti, the Kabakas of Uganda, Kanem-Bornu, the melancholy ruins of Tuareg Timbuktu, the Songai of Gao, Monomotapa,) cut across modern national boundaries. They also cut across tribal boundaries. They were fluid, expansive, organic, explosive – one of the great engines of African change. These empires were never tidy – what empires are? – with immutable boundaries.

Immutable boundaries are un-African. Like the cloud patterns, Africa is always changing. Sometimes, of course, the continent seems chaotic, formless, tragic. Rwanda and Burundi are horrid examples for all. Liberia and Sierra Leone deteriorated into murderousness. Zaire crumbled into the corrupt and deadly anarchy of the Democratic Republic of the Congo. Nigeria is called a nation of thieves. And there are the great stinking slums of Lagos and Nairobi.

But to understand Africa we must understand the timeline and the pattern. Africa must be seen in the long view, understood as a work in progress, in always-unfinished evolution.

Often tyrants rose, and equally there were wise kings and chiefs. There were long periods of peace and decades of decay and warfare. There were periods of savagery, periods of marvellous artistic flowering, music and prosperity. African history contains its own sources of optimism.

It is utterly obvious that Africa is far more than warlords and tyrants and bloodshed played out in the stultifying embrace of tribalism. That is the outsider cliché. Africa is going in many different directions at once. There is great political subtlety in which Africans are working out new ways of governing that are African. Among the people there is a great yearning for education and political democracy that is infectious and spreading, maybe not as fast as the dreadful scourge of AIDS, but as relentlessly. Despite crisis after crisis, all over the continent in unexpected ways, the rule of law is taking hold – now coups are condemned by other Africans in ways that are new (only outsiders have failed to notice).

Tribes are not what outsiders think, the central fact in African lives. In the long view, tribes have shifted and mutated, changed and evolved, been absorbed by others, with new tribes emerging. That's the key: over Africa's long, very long, history, new tribes have been emerging all the time – it is another of the great engines of change. It is a myth that in pre-colonial Africa political boundaries coincided with tribal boundaries; Africa was never that static. Only in the modern period has the notion of "tribe" taken on a quasi-permanent meaning.

As noted, the worst effects of colonialism, worse by far than the devastating economic exploitation and thundering racism, are the stultifying notion of the sovereign nation-states (the idea of a fixed boundary) and the ratcheting up of the technology of murder. No remaking of Africa's boundaries could have come close to satisfying the complex and ever-changing demands of Africa's ethnic minorities. It is said there were somewhere between 6,000 and 10,000 discrete political units in pre-colonial Africa, ranging from simple chiefdoms like the one inherited by Lesotho's founder, Moshoeshoe, to sophisticated empires run on federal lines by layered bureaucracies. It's true that the borders of today's nation-states took no account at the Berlin Conference of geographical, ethnic or commercial realities, and very small account of ancient kingdoms. But there is no ethnic group split by national boundaries in Africa demanding reunification. African leaders always assert the sanctity of borders, peculiar as they may be, but all the alternatives, in their view, are worse. New power bases are emerging that cut across national boundaries and they very much include church and religious movements. There are regional economic communities and free-trade zones.

It is impossible to underestimate the deadly effects of the European traffic in slaves. Hard as it may be to believe, there have been many attempts to "justify" the slave trade by pointing out that Africans occasionally enslaved each other. But nothing – *nothing* – has ever equalled the European theft of 13 million Africans, to say nothing of the two to three million who died on treks out of the bush and on the stinking slave ships across the Atlantic.

Hardly anyone in Africa any longer believes Africa's problems can be blamed forever on colonialism. New African leaders are weaning their countries from the addiction to foreign aid and foreign-designed development. Africa is an emerging market entirely capable of profiting through its own energy and efforts from global trade, provided they have a level playing field.

The richness of African culture – music, dancing, art, storytelling – brilliant writers and thinkers describe beyond words the cross-rhythms of the continent.

What outsiders rarely understand is just how *old* Africa is and how ignorant is the outsider view that ancient Egypt somehow sprang up fully formed in Africa and is yet somehow now not "African". Outsiders saw the complex stone structures of Great Zimbabwe and looked around for foreigners who must have built this most unique of stone *kraals* without mortar far south of Egypt.

Africa changes invaders more than invaders change Africa. Even Islam, that most infectious of religions, had trouble with tradition-inoculated African cultures. Africa *endures*. And how much more deeply spiritual Africa is and was and how much deeper than the dismissive "animism" of western anthropologists.

For the last five centuries Africa has largely been defined through successive historical events clearly determined by the mercantile and imperial domination of Europe. The exotic metaphors used to describe the continent and her people were much more a reflection of European fantasies and ignorance about a 'dark' world that was distinct and mysterious.

Even today with the frequent packaging of foreign aid to Africa, the connotations of helplessness are a reflection of the underlying racial attitudes that continue to undermine the peoples' dignity.

Colonialism

Africa was 'discovered' in the fifteenth century. That, at least, is what the old history books say. Professors teach it, students accept it. The media propagates it. Taken at its first meaning, this discovery meant, and still means, the primary violence signified by the word.

The slave trade narrated itself accordingly, and the same movement of reduction progressively guaranteed the gradual invasion of the continent. This historical distortion paved the way for centuries of abuse to the extent that it was not easy later for African leaders to come together with a common agenda of unity.

Indigenous languages and local values had been suppressed and replaced with exotic European ones. The continent was torn apart with impunity, so much so that the recovery process would not only take centuries but also demand a high degree of tenacity and courage in coming to terms with the negative facts of history. This called for the need of a very serious self-assessment among peoples of African descent both in the continent and the diaspora in order to respond to the inner cry for renewal of the reclamation of African heritage and identity. But this would not happen if Africans continued to be divided along the boundaries of European politics and faith, hence the resurgence of the spirit of Pan-Africanism both as a political ideology and ecumenical movement within and outside the continent. The political and spiritual version of the movement can aptly be established within two frameworks, i.e. the movement towards political and spiritual unity in Africa. These are the two sides of the same ethical paradigm.

The term Pan-Africanism was originally used by a West Indian lawyer, Henry Sylvester Williams, who practised law in London at the end of the nineteenth century. Africans had begun to face the consequences of systematic colonization and exploitation of land by settlers. Many South and West African chiefs went to England to protest against this deprivation of their rights. As the ideological embodiment of Black struggle, Pan-Africanism can be traced back among the freed slaves in the Americas and West Indies. Specifically this idea can be associated with W.E.B. DuBois, among others, until 1957 when Ghana regained independence. "But it was finally born here on the soil of Africa at this conference of independent African States in 1958 at Accra", wrote Kwame Nkrumah, the meeting's host.

There was the yearning among the ex-slaves to come back to their motherland. Pan-Africanism was initially associated with the "Back to Africa Movement". Marcus Garvey then founded the universal Africa Legion whose motto was "One People! One aim! One destiny!" There was also the underlying desire to establish a spiritual movement with the same ethic of unity based on the values and heritage of Africans. Garvey went ahead and established his own Africa Orthodox Church which would be led by a black patriarch. He adopted the motif of the "Black Christ". These movements did not find their way to Africa due to inhibitions by colonial powers which included the banning of his publications in all colonial territories.

On the continent the leading African proponent of Pan-Africanism was Kwame Nkrumah, the first president of Ghana, Africa's first country to gain independence (from Britain) in 1957. It was Nkrumah who translated the words of Jesus into a political slogan: "Seek ye first the political kingdom...". For him, that was part of the passionate appeal for unity: "The most important fortress we can build to counter the dark threats and the many sketches of the neo-colonialists is our political unity. If we want to remain free and enjoy the blessings of our African resources, then we must unite for the sake of our people and plan our defence as well as the exploitation of our material and human wealth."

The desire to attain political unity in the continent and economic self-determination led to Nkrumah hosting more than 60 nationalist organizations at the All Africa Peoples Conference in Accra which was to give birth to the OAU in 1963, the same year (and only a month apart) as the All Africa Conference of Churches was inaugurated at Kampala, Uganda under the theme "Freedom and Unity in Christ".

The first major world ecumenical conference to be held in Africa was the IMC at Accra in 1957 which actively encouraged regional and national ecumenism. But at a deeper level the meeting reflected the African churches' inextricable and often ambiguous link with European and North American churches and mission agencies. By 1961 Ghana, the first African colony to become independent, had been joined by 18 other nations.

Would the missions become churches even as colonies were becoming nations? The mission-to-church transition was often just as painful. Forming the AACC did not deter many western mission agencies from dominating "daughter churches" by sending money and personnel through new structures that often dwarfed Africa's national and regional ecumenical organizations. Later, proliferation of church-sponsored projects in Africa often meant that the ecumenical movement was only seen as one among many "donor agencies" from which outside funds could be sought. The difficulties of achieving independence from powerful overseas churches led some African church leaders in the early 1970s to call for a moratorium on sending overseas money and personnel to Africa. An African theologian has said that "Africa tends to be assimilated to the North. Even when it is left alone, it is not allowed to be itself." And, says another African church leader, "the strategy of determining Africa's priorities from outside Africa is the bane of the ecumenical movement on our continent."

The proliferation of activities by the secular and spiritual leaders in Africa reflected the mood of the times which were filled with both anxiety and hope for the continent. As in 1963, the AACC and the ecumenical movement in Africa continued to help member churches by accompanying and encouraging them in their attempt to remain faithful and relevant. There was interaction and crossing of boundaries from the spiritual realm to the political arena, inspiring a profound sense of enthusiasm for a new dawn of freedom and dignity for the African people. Every ecumenical gathering in the continent drew the attention of the political leadership. There was obvious synergy between the AACC and the OAU in the formative years. The definitive moment came when Dr Akanu Ibiam said in his opening speech at the first major consultation of African theologians at Ibadan, Nigeria in 1966 that "in the process of time we (Africans) hope by the grace of God to achieve something which will bring churches in Africa together in our efforts to build up the great countries of this continent upon him." The consultation predicted that "the continent of Africa will see unparalleled events and changes during the rest of the [twentieth] century." They could not have foreseen that many of these events would take the form of civil wars and carnage among Africans.

Ibiam's important statement captured the vision of the ecumenical movement at its inception in Africa. Mercy Oduyoye writes that "at Abidjan, Cote d'Ivoire in 1969 the churches, through AACC, showed their determination to engage in the effort of the development of the continent of Africa. The oppression under which millions of African people suffer was recognized as the context in which the churches' mission was to be carried out. The churches of Europe and America had co-operated with the AACC in work with refugees; the pointed question was would they stand with Africa in the fight against racist regimes in southern Africa? Would they work side by side with liberation movements that were called marxist and communist?" By the time of the third assembly of AACC in 1974 at Lusaka, the African churches' response to the challenges facing them was a clear determination to support liberation movements seeking to rid Africa of white supremacist governments. "Why restrict themselves to supporting refugees without having also endeavoured to tackle the social, economic and political factors that make people refugees?" Oduyoye asked.

She continued: "As a prophetic voice, the AACC has served Africa well. As a reconciling movement, its role in the Sudan and the oil it poured on the troubled waters of Nigeria has been crucial. At other levels too, the basic accomplishments have been registered. The village polytechnics started by the National Christian Council of Kenya and the Malawi Rural Improvement Programme illustrate development efforts. But for me it is the Programme to Combat Racism which is the core of our involvement. All pronouncements which the WCC has issued concerning racism since 1948 have to be verified, justified and put into practice. We do not need ecclesiastical marionnettes nor do we have any use for Christianity that is a tranquilizer rather than a stimulant."

Gatu and Carr

One of the most significant turning points in the ecumenical movement in Africa was the election of Rev. Canon Burgess Carr, a Liberian Anglican, to the position of general secretary of AACC in 1971. His legacy, often perceived as militant and radical, provided an atmosphere in which a new vision of the selfhood of the church was deeply embedded in the prophetic vocation of the ecumenical movement being in solidarity with people of Africa against all forms of oppression. At the 1974 Lusaka assembly the churches were called to self-reliance and self-determination for their economic and spiritual well-being. From the political independence movement, the ecumenical movement went further and summoned the churches to lead by example by de-linking their dependency on missions.

Not long before the AACC assembly in Lusaka, Rev. John Gatu of Kenya, then vice-chairman of the AACC general committee, shocked an ecumenical gathering in Bangkok in 1972 with his radical call for a moratorium on sending and maintaining missionaries in the South. At the heart of the moratorium was a profound sense of a spirituality of self-reliance and dignified living. It was often deliberately misunderstood in Europe and North America as an anti-missionary movement. However, the underlying theme was that the churches in Africa had reached a stage where their dependency on resources from the north was becoming an impediment to growth and identity.

In Lusaka, the churches were called to allow Christ "to set them free from easy dependence upon foreign money and men." Clad in a colourful monkeyskin robe, Gatu called for a realistic theology which strives for the salvation of the whole person. He declared: "We need to challenge the narrow conservative theology that seems to suggest that all that is necessary in man's salvation is his soul, forgetting that other material needs are part and parcel of this same person. The opposite is also false, when we think that all that is necessary are the material benefits without reconciliation of the person to God through the living Christ. Today," he said, "we must challenge those who are colonizing those who are unable to defend and liberate themselves. We must challenge powers of white racism in Africa. We must also challenge those who exploit the illiterate labourers in their houses, in the mines or any other places of work, whether they be white or black."

The combination of John Gatu and Burgess Carr inspired and sustained this new vision of Pan-African ecumenism that was anchored in the quest for justice and dignity of the African people. They both had a conviction that their mission of ecclesial and ecumenical self-determination was essential to the proclamation of the good news to the world. And for Carr, this had to begin with theological reflection on the selfhood of the church. He once said "nothing exposes the weakness of the church in Africa more than the absence of a relevant theology to deal with the situation of injustice so rampant in our continent." Even General Yakubu Gowon, military dictator of Nigeria and chairman of the OAU at the time, hailed the AACC for its courageous stand against oppression and injustice in all oppressed parts of Africa which, he said, "is still fresh in our minds and must be condemned."

"The churches in Africa, particularly those operating within territories still under colonial and racial regimes," Gowon said, "must not relent in their efforts to sustain the struggle against social injustice, oppression and human indignity in Africa, which constitute a rape of the world conscience." He went on: "As you continue the search for authentic cultural renewal in Africa as part of your programme of activities, I have no doubt that you will strive to promote those aspects of our tradition and culture which enhance the image and dignity of the African everywhere in the world."

General Gabriel Ramanantosoa, head of the Malagasy Republic, assured the AACC of constant support "in the just combat in which you are unceasingly engaged on the continent of Africa for the liberation of humanity and for the development and cultural renewal of Africa". He added: "I am convinced that your totally Christian action is an effective contribution to our common struggle." President William R. Tolbert of Liberia declared that the AACC, like the Church of Christ, "must be militant in order to be triumphant" in the execution of the great tasks which lie ahead of the organization. "I earnestly entreat you...to regard yourselves as a noble army of Christ which must climb the steep ascent to heaven through peril, toil and sacrifice, as the Son of God went forth notwithstanding foes, and executed his mission."

Since the moratorium, churches and the ecumenical movement in Africa have continued to take turns with their partners in hosting annual roundtable consultations to share the problems and prospects of Christian ministry in their respective countries, and explain what support may be needed from the other partners.

The end of official apartheid in South Africa in 1994 clearly marked a new era for institutions associated with Pan-Africanism and internal self-determination. Creative and definitive alternatives are now at the top of the agenda of the ecumenical movement in Africa. This is already symbolized by the ongoing synchronization of regional ecumenical instruments and the AACC. While the transition of the OAU to the AU (African Union) in 2002 was heralded as a major step in the direction of Kwame Nkrumah's original vision of a united Africa, it signifies an effort in the direction of consolidated regional cooperation which could not be ignored by the ecumenical movement in the continent.

The emergence and growth of regional ecumenical bodies such as the Fellowship of Christian Councils of Eastern and Southern Africa (FOCCESA), the Fellowship of Christian Councils in Central Africa (FOCCICA), the Fellowship of Christian Councils in West Africa (FOCCIWA) and the Fellowship of Christian Councils in the Great Lakes and the Horn of Africa (FECCLAHA) are signs of a process of renewal and consolidation of ecclesial relationships around new ecumenical frontiers that bring the search for unity, peace and justice closer to home among Christians. These regional ecumenical bodies provide a new model for regional consolidation with linkages and structures that synchronize relationships between official ecumenical instruments such as AACC and the churches in Africa.

The search for unity within the sphere of faith does not, therefore, ignore major secular developments, however frustrating or illusive they may seem. Institutional ecumenism in Africa would not thrive, survive or serve the world ecumenical family without the reading of the signs of the times and translation of such signs into new insights of what it means to be the church as a living organic community of faith. Hence the emerging alternative paradigms of ecumenical engagement that are unique and not based on competition for meagre resources from the north but rather on the local renewal of commitment to unity in the household of God signified in the prayer of Jesus.

3. Forgiveness and Healing of Memories

We have not sung because we were happy.
We have sung even when we cried.
We have sung so as not to allow ourselves to be broken.
We have sung to survive.

WCC worship, Johannesburg, 1994

When the Church of Jesus Christ on Earth by the Prophet Simon Kimbangu (the Kimbanguist Church of Zaire, now Democratic Republic of Congo) became a member church of the WCC in 1969, it brought a manner of praying that was unique. Other African Instituted (Independent) Churches (AICs) like the Church of the Lord (Aladura) from Nigeria offer songs that move worshippers. African spirituality is the authentic source of courage in the midst of historical dilemmas between the choice of enduring poverty and suffering and revolutionary violence. This spiritual courage has always been expressed by invoking God in song and dance.

The survival of the inner soul of Africa has been exemplified in the singing traditions of its people even in the diaspora: South Africa during apartheid and African Americans in the aftermath of slavery, and wherever Africans are, they are a singing people. South Africans sang away their oppression to the amazement and consternation of those who tortured and treated them with great inhumanity and degradation. A people who lived their history as if it was no longer their own did not seek retribution as the basis for correcting that history.

The terrible crimes against the Jewish people by Germany and the Axis powers leading up to the second world war are widely remembered under the slogan "never again". Public apologies and vast compensation have rightly been made by Germany and the international community for the genocide of six million Jews. Yet, the tens of millions of African slaves who were removed from Africa and suffered and died and those who lived and were sold as objects have received little in the way of public apology, let alone reparations from Europe and America and others who benefited from the traffic in human beings in the most brutal act by "civilized" Christians in the world's history. There are no memorial monuments in the wealthy and powerful western cities that were once slave markets and are now centres of global exchange of goods and ideas.

While Africans seek reparations, not only on the basis of crimes committed against them but also the massive resources that were stolen, African nations receive demands for repayment of dubious debts. The US alone spends 25 times the amount on its military than Africa receives annually in aid from the whole world. The World Bank suggests that poor countries could earn $350 billion in additional income by 2015 if subsidies in rich countries were scrapped, thereby levelling the playing field for African trade.

One of the greatest gifts of authenticity the church and its leadership in Africa has given to the world and the ecumenical movement is a way of healing the wounds of nations through a spirituality of justice and forgiveness.

When the struggle against apartheid was successfully accomplished in South Africa, a culture of tolerance, imbued with skills of dialogue and negotiation through the Truth and Reconciliation Commission's (TRC) process was achieved. Reconciliation and healing of memories took place in the context of a safe space for discernment and authentic dialogue. Stories of struggle and triumph against oppressive forces with the accompaniment of the ecumenical movement must be celebrated by all Africans.

Archbishop Desmond Tutu, retired Anglican archbishop of Cape Town and long-time ecumenist, who was chair (1995-98) of the TRC, says: "True forgiveness deals with the past, all of the past, to make the future possible. We cannot go on nursing grudges, even vicariously, for those who cannot speak for themselves any longer. We have to accept that what we do for generations past, present and yet to come is what makes a community a community or a people a people – for better or for worse." And, writes Ernst Lange, in his book *And Yet It Moves: Dream and Reality of the Ecumenical Movement* (Eerdmans, 1979), "The ecumenical movement is a movement for peace. Far wider than the Geneva association, it is in fact the way in which the Christian churches really serve the cause of peace."

And again Tutu says: "We do not usually rush to expose our vulnerability and our sinfulness. But if the process of forgiveness and healing is to succeed, ultimately acknowledgement of the truth and of having wronged someone is important in getting to the root of the breach."

Nelson Mandela, one of Africa's most towering figures – he gave a moving account of the contribution of the WCC and its Programme to Combat Racism to the struggle for freedom in southern Africa during the fiftieth anniversary celebrations of the WCC at Harare in 1998 – has been described by Tutu as a man "who emerged from prison not spewing words of hatred and revenge. He amazed us all by his heroic embodiment of reconciliation and forgiveness. No one could have accused him of speaking glibly and facilely about forgiveness and reconciliation. He had been harassed for a long time before his arrest, making impossible a normal family life. By the time of his release on February 11, 1990, he had spent 27 years in jail. No one could say that he knew nothing about suffering."

Through its "Reconstructing Africa" programme of dialogue and study, culminating in an event held in May 1997 in Johannesburg with the theme "Jubilee and the African Kairos", the ecumenical movement sought to engage creatively in solidarity and learn from the legacy of struggle in Africa to stimulate a new way of looking at the world. This has already generated renewed hope in the African churches that the world could learn from the struggles for dignity and well-being. Participants at the Johannesburg meeting expressed their conviction about the future of Africa:

"We are proud in seeing a vision of the journey of hope of African churches for the development of the continent for the 21st century. We are determined to work out this vision that promises life with dignity for the African people. We see such a vision grounded in the spirit of *'ubuntu'* the embodiment of African spirituality and moral integrity lived in sustainable communities."

During an African Christian-Jewish consultation held in Cameroon in 2001 which was sponsored by the Decade to Overcome Violence, a profound correlation between the Jewish *shalom* and the African *ubuntu* was revealed. "It is *ubuntu* to love and care for others. It is *ubuntu* to be just and fair. It is *ubuntu* to be compassionate. It is *ubuntu* to have good morals. A country which practises *ubuntu*, is the closest thing on earth to the kingdom of God. And so it is with *shalom*; to pursue peace is more than to love peace, anyone can love peace, but to pursue peace is to create peace. *Shalom* has to do with the verb *shalem*, which means to pay."

Rwanda and Burundi

A recent ecumenical covenant, *For a New Africa: with hope and dignity*, reiterated the solidarity in which the churches in Rwanda and Africa, together with government, civil society, African institutions and the international community, became part of the healing and reconciliation movement in the traumatized and genocide-scarred country.

WCC General Secretary, Samuel Kobia, spoke at the tenth anniversary marking the Rwanda genocide in 2004, saying vigorously: "There is hope for Africa. On this very day we shall endeavour to transform the memories of genocide into an occasion of the rebirth of a new spirit full of equanimity that overflows to bring healing to the past and reinvent a new future with confidence and hope. Christians killed and were killed, Christians must speak about what really happened, confess and ask for forgiveness. We must ask constantly, where did we go wrong? Where were we as Christians when the atrocities were being planned and executed? What must we do to ensure that such events are never repeated again?

"The crisis of vengeance will refuse to be silenced so long as we choose to allow our violent past to reclaim our consciousness of the future. When we think about the new rebirth of the spirit, let us never forget that memory is not just about a chronological record of social reality. By memory, in a theological sense, I am referring to the moral capacity to reinterpret events and organically relate them to the life of the community. Therefore we affirm the resolution to work together and to say once again with the people of Rwanda, 'never again'."

The bleached skulls and bones are a mind-shattering vision of evil that tests the visitor's senses at all levels. One is simultaneously in the midst of innocence and demonic crime. The physical remnants of the genocide, amidst the neatly piled cadavers, are faded, dilapidated clothing, bits of sandals and shoes among meagre personal belongings of babies, children, youth, women and men (although most *genocidaires* were men). It is a poignant display and an unending reminder of the horrific 100 days in 1994 when a million Rwandans were slaughtered.

The Ntarama Memorial (formerly a Roman Catholic chapel) as well as the Kigali Memorial Centre hold these stark reminders for all to see and never forget. The beautiful green hills with their banana fields, rivers and forests, turned into mass graveyards. "People who fled the scourge of the machete occasionally returned home to bury their dead. One could smell violence in the air. It could come anytime, like rain." There are so many stories of the women of the genocide who were raped endlessly in an orgy of violence – rape as a weapon of war, not sex – and who are today living with HIV and AIDS as are their children, the offspring of rape. There are too many child-headed and single parent households and totally disabled persons.

The depth of the horror is a challenge to the ecumenical movement in Africa for deep and profound introspection and reflection not just for the sake of the future of peace in Rwanda but for the rest of Africa. The abuse, ethnic hatred, anger, tension, humiliation, trauma, pain and tears remind us of the crucifixion of Jesus Christ. The false accusations and torture of the innocent are truly degrading, and an affront to the gospel. Hence, like Peter, the Apostle, the human response would be for survivors to draw their swords in revenge; and yet Jesus ordered

Peter to sheath his sword. Christ, the master warns that those who kill by the sword die by the sword. The Rwandan government, together with churches, the UN Criminal Tribunal on Rwanda, the traditional local *gacaca* courts and humanitarian agencies, have been engaged in acts of justice, healing, forgiveness and restoration of peace and order among the people. This is at the heart of the very biblical understanding that justice and truth must be embraced if real healing and forgiveness are to take place.

In neighbouring Burundi, it is evident that the people still live with the memories of atrocities and ethnic massacres committed by minority Tutsis against Hutus for more than three decades and especially since the assassination of their first elected head of state, President Melchior Ndadaye, in 1993 by elements of the Tutsi-dominated military which sparked an endless round of violence and open civil war, much of it also based on ethnic torment. Since then more than 300,000 Burundians have been killed in a population of just over six million. The achievements of a negotiated agreement under Nelson Mandela and South Africa's leadership opened a tenuous beginning of a new chapter for peace in the tiny country adjoining Rwanda which has the same political and ecclesiastical history of ethnicity and Belgian colonial barbarity.

Burundi's government still faces violence in a sporadic low-level civil war. The last remaining rebel group, the Hutu Forces for National Liberation (FNL), remains unwilling to negotiate with newly-elected President Pierre Nkurunziza

Most Burundians believed their country was on the path to peace after a series of polls led to the swearing-in of a government in August 2005 under a UN-backed plan to end ethnic civil war that has never stopped since 1993. Tutsis have held sway in Burundi since independence from Belgium in 1962 and have committed many of the worst massacres.

Nkurunziza's inauguration has produced a fairer share of power. He is a former guerrilla leader from the majority Hutu ethnic group. The struggles for political power since then have continued to undermine the need to embark on a serious programme of nation-building. In 1998 a provisional government took power and by 2004 a provisional constitution was approved but its implementation has been often delayed and elections postponed until 2005. During the initiative which led to the declaration for peace the churches were not only represented but also urged to create an atmosphere of mutual trust and reconciliation between warring leaders of various political parties.

The Arusha Accord (2004) provides a framework for a long-term solution to the problems of representation and power-sharing facing both the minority and majority groups in the country. The churches realize that given the historical circumstances facing Burundi there is need for urgent establishment of non-partisan instruments of democratic change and good governance. Churches are called to work together ecumenically and with all initiatives of public goodwill to ensure that every external intervention for peace becomes part and parcel of the local instruments of mediation. The problems in Burundi are by extension the problems in the Great Lakes Region and hence the process of demobilization, disarmament, reconstruction, reintegration and resettlement includes the realities of the whole region, the DRC, Uganda, Rwanda and Burundi.

The struggle to heal wounded memories and traumatized spirits can happen, not only in the context of justice but also in rebuilding trust through confession, forgiveness and honest reflection on the entire history and events that give rise to human tragedies. It is imperative that a regional approach to peace-building and conflict management be employed because the economy of war in this area has to do with resources and people who share ethnic boundaries. For this reason the WCC suggested to AACC and the sub-regional fellowships to consider a wider regional body, the Great Lakes Ecumenical Forum, (GLEF) that would bring together the civil society, ecumenical partners and other stakeholders in the region.

Peace means more than a mere silencing of the guns in the region. While cease-fires and a relative return to calm are good signs, they are not the realization of peace. They offer an opportunity for a more comprehensive and lasting political solution to national and regional questions that may enable the parties concerned to put behind them their history of war and get rid of the culture of violence as they face possibilities for a new future of lasting peace.

Speedy implementation of the cease-fire agreements, as in the case of Angola, testifies to courage and a profound sense of determination to end war in the region. Durable peace and economic reconstruction also require that peace be considered as a process of social and political transformation. This means that in order to keep hope alive, the churches in Africa are called to promote a deeper sense of belonging and solidarity that transcends ethnic categories of identity.

Sudan

The long-awaited peace for Sudan seems finally to be coming to some state of fruition, although the sudden death in a helicopter crash in southern Sudan in July 2005 of newly-appointed Sudanese Vice-President John Garang, the long-time southern Sudan liberation leader, has been a serious blow. Garang was a gigantic figure with the personality required to bring the warring Arabs and southern blacks to a just peace. He has been replaced by Salva Kiir, a trusted deputy in the Sudan Peoples Liberation Movement (SPLM) who has been sworn in as first vice-president of Sudan.

Shortly after independence from the British in 1956, the non-Muslim south Sudan, disappointed that the promises for a separate independence had not been kept, revolted and the country sank into civil war which was to last 17 years before a peace deal was brokered in 1972 at Addis Ababa with the churches playing a major role in the peace-making, especially the AACC and WCC. This agreement provided for relative autonomy and self-government for the south. However, it was soon undermined by the strategies of the north which increasingly was engaged in its project of Arabization and Islamicization of the nation under the growing influence of strict *shari'a* law. War broke out again after six years of faltering peace and lasted until the present fragile peace deal was achieved in 2002. More than two million people, mostly southerners, have been killed since 1956 and millions more are internal and external refugees. Sudan's is the longest civil war in African history.

Recently, under the auspices of an African regional grouping, the Intergovernmental Authority on Development (IGAD), peace talks between the Sudanese government (Khartoum) and the SPLM which controls most of the south, reached historic agreements after a long and difficult negotiating process. The signing of the Machakos (Kenya) Protocol in July 2002 marked a historic turning point towards a just and lasting peace for Sudan. This protocol has brought about a cessation of hostilities and provided for recognition of the right of self-determination for southern Sudan. As part of that deal, Garang became first vice-president of Sudan and his deputy, Riek Machar, second vice-president in 2005, with the expectation that SPLM may eventually form a government of South Sudan of which Garang would have been president.

The protocols are one manifestation of the resilience of the churches in southern Sudan and the accompaniment of the ecumenical movement for the war-ravaged country. The Sudan peace, like South Africa, is reminiscent of the new gains in ecumenical social responsibility in Africa. However, the ongoing state-sponsored starvation, displacement and hideous tribal violence against Muslims in Darfur (western Sudan) poses a major challenge to both the New Sudan Council of Churches (NSCC), based outside the country in Nairobi, and the Sudan Council of Churches (SCC) headquartered in Khartoum.

The Sudanese churches (particularly within the NSCC in the south) initiated a grassroots-based peace process – peace from below. A series of strategic conferences organized by NSCC provided the space and mechanisms for the local churches and civil society involvement in peace-building and reconciliation. Through strategic conferences, the Sudanese churches and local groups gained experience and knowledge in peace work.

Sudan Ecumenical Forum

Widely representative of the churches in Sudan, both councils include Roman Catholic, Orthodox and Protestant communions. For purposes of security, NSCC moved its offices in 1989 to Nairobi, while the Khartoum-based SSC continued to provide care to displaced southerners who had moved to the north to escape war and on whom the north continued to impose its tactics of discrimination. The two are not separate councils but extensions of each other and have been relentless advocates for peace and transformative justice in both southern and northern Sudan.

The WCC-initiated Sudan Ecumenical Forum (SEF) has provided a framework since 1994 through which the two councils, churches, the AACC and church-related humanitarian agencies were able to become part of a regional and global network that is engaged with other ecumenical bodies, the United Nations, the European Union, IGAD, the African Union and international NGOs with a special focus on the Sudan question.

The World Council of Churches, the All Africa Conference of Churches, Caritas Internationalis, Norwegian Church Aid, Bread for the World of Germany, Church World Service, the National Council of Churches of Christ in the USA, the Lutheran World Federation, Christian Aid and many other Christian agencies became actively involved in the Sudan. Their involvement also included providing humanitarian services such as food relief to the refugees and displaced people, medical care, water and scholarships to Sudanese in the diaspora.

The fellowship of churches in solidarity with the ecumenical movement in Africa rejoiced at the new-won peace in Sudan. The world community of donors and civil society institutions whose primary concern is a smooth transition in Sudan met in April 2005 in Oslo to deliberate on the country's future of Sudan after the peace agreement. Donors pledged up to $4.5 billion over the next two years to cover Sudan's humanitarian and reconstruction needs.

The ecumenical movement in Africa, including the World Council of Churches, has had a long history of solidarity with the people of

Sudan and continues to accompany the churches through the SEF and the two councils so that the country will never again slip back into the horror of the past armed struggle and civil war. With the implementation of the aid package, Sudan could begin to recover. The signing of the peace accord remains the dawn of hope in ending one of the longest and most protracted struggles of modern history.

Global estimates indicate that southern Sudan and other marginalized areas in the nation would require at least US$500 million for infrastructure rebuilding alone – not including the de-mining of hundreds of thousands of anti-personnel landmines. Transformation of the land to provide nourishment and support for both humans and the ecology of life in the region is needed. There are so many ex-combatants and victims of war in Sudan who still live with the nightmares of atrocities that haunt villages in the south. More than a million are in urgent need of assistance to return home from various corners of the world and more than four million internally displaced are in urgent need of resettlement.

The genesis of the SEF came from a stated need by the churches and agencies working in Sudan for a transparent and systematic approach among all the actors and agendas for a coordinated church network. The success of SEF over more than 10 years is often seen as a model for other ecumenical church action and advocacy in situations of conflict in Africa. Prior to the Forum's foundation, there was a plethora of bilateral actions and initiatives with little or no space for sharing. The churches and aid agencies in particular pushed the idea of a forum to act as a clearing house for peace and reconciliation advocacy work in Europe, North America and Africa, to assist in clarifying issues and actions and to help avoid overlap and establish divisions of labour.

The WCC was asked to convene the first meeting in Geneva in 1994 with Samuel Kobia as chair. It would focus on peace promotion, leaving individual partners to make their own decisions and actions within the framework of the Forum, but it was understood they would inform and consult before taking decisive steps. They would meet annually but would not take partisan positions beyond advocating urgently for peace itself at all levels and sectors in Sudan. Information-sharing was considered vital to peace and advocacy work both from the scene of the conflict and from the region to partners in Europe and North America.

It was a successful attempt by the widest possible partnership of churches – the Roman Catholic Church was fully involved – to impose on themselves what Clement John of WCC calls "ecumenical discipline" in a forum situation without establishing a bureaucracy or limit on the freedom of partners to act. John was the SEF's first secretary. A unique plan which exists to the present was to establish "focal points" in Europe and North America, as well as at AACC for Africa. Focal points were designated to do advocacy for peace and reconciliation, and to analyze and synthesize information for dissemination to partners.

After two years, the SEF decided it needed to articulate a common position on the war and the work of the Forum. The churches were aware that despite their "peace from below" work with civil society and local communities, they had little participation in resolving the conflict, even though peace-making was a matter of faith and an important mission of the church. This lack of participation was especially noticeable given that the ecumenical movement in 1972 was responsible for signing the Addis Ababa Accord that first brought an end to the fighting in South Sudan. Because of their deep concern that the churches should actively participate in peace-making efforts the SEF produced a seminal paper called "Here We Stand United in Action for Peace" on 25 September, 1996 at a church leaders of Sudan consultation at Morges, Switzerland. The statement, supported by all the partners, was issued on behalf of, and speaking to, all the people of Sudan who, by then, had endured more than 40 years of destructive internal conflict with huge loss of life, displacement and destruction of almost all institutions of society including churches. The vision of SEF for Sudan's future was clear.

"Whatever political solution is chosen by the people, we believe that peace and harmony will depend on the following principles:
- recognition that all human beings are created by God and are precious and equal in [his] sight;
- acceptance that cultural, linguistic and social diversity is a gift of God's creation, and not to be suppressed but rather to be celebrated and recognized as a national richness and resource;
- freedom of religious expression, worship and witness;
- a lasting and true peace must be based on justice and full and equal rights for all Sudanese;
- participation in political, social and economic life should be open to all irrespective of racial, ethnic, social and religious background;
- steadily widen the effective participation of all people in political processes and decision-making;
- political and social conflicts should be solved peacefully; and
- an openness to trusting dialogue between alienated political, social and religious groups within society."

The vision, however, had to be translated into practical steps and, while the churches and their agencies could not prescribe a particular or specific political solution, SEF did call for the war to stop because it was daily increasing the suffering and there was no hope of decisive resolution. SEF also called for a popular expression (referendum) of the people's wishes, as soon as hostilities ceased, to resolve the many political problems and a similar referendum for self-determination by the marginalized areas (i.e. the South). In the meantime, humanitarian agencies like the airlift, Operation Lifeline Sudan, and other relief, development and educational activities by the churches should be allowed to continue.

It would be another eight long and deadly years before the war stopped in 2004.

In 2002, Konrad Raiser made a pastoral visit to Sudan and told the Sudanese government in Khartoum that the peace talks had become "endless" and stressed the WCC's commitment to conflict resolution and reconstruction of war-ravaged southern Sudan. He described the 18-year religious conflict as a kind of "deceptive façade" used by Khartoum's Muslim government while actively engaged in exacerbating all kinds of inequalities. He stressed the WCC's commitment to the SEF process which it had helped to set up and told an ecumenical gathering organized by the Sudan Council of Churches that the SEF was doing all it could to monitor the conflict and mobilize ecumenical support for both Sudan's councils, along with overseas partners. Concern was expressed during Raiser's visit that the war had expanded into an oil war especially in the Upper Nile region where oil leases had been granted to foreign companies causing increased violence in that region which was creating a worse situation. Raiser replied that one of the SEF perceptions was that the root cause of the war "is uneven socio-economic development" caused by "unfair distribution of wealth. Oil exploitation is aggravating that imbalance and contributing to the underdevelopment of the marginalized areas."

In 2003, Kobia was named as a special ecumenical envoy to monitor and contribute to the peace process. His appointment made visible the support and input from the churches and partners in SEF to the peace process and enabled dialogue between the parties in conflict who did not trust each other but who had confidence in the on-going work of SEF and the envoy. The result was that involved governments invited the WCC to be one of the international organizations to witness the peace agreement which finally came about in 2004.

The work of the SEF does not stop with the end of hostilities and it will continue to accompany the Sudanese people in reconstructing their shattered country as the members acting as a forum have done since 1994, especially in the areas of peace, reconciliation and democracy. The SEF, by establishing its "Here We Stand United in Action for Peace" position and adhering faithfully to that process throughout the long, frustrating and enormously destructive ten years of conflict, war, death, displacement and many setbacks, established a model for ecumenical work in conflict areas that could be used in many other situations.

Decade to Overcome Violence (DOV)

At the same eighth assembly where the journey of hope was launched, the WCC, well aware of its long history of involvement in issues of peace and justice dating back to the destructive divisions of two world wars, affirmed the Decade to Overcome Violence (DOV). The assembly believed that its previous Programme to Overcome Violence which grew out of the hugely successful Programme to Combat Racism (PCR) should continue past its mandate in 1998 for another decade. It is a process and development of networks, focal points and wide ecumenical fellowship that follows in many ways the pioneering model of the Sudan Ecumenical Forum.

The Decade to Overcome Violence: Churches Seeking Reconciliation and Peace, to give it its full name, calls churches, ecumenical organizations, and all people of goodwill:

- to work together for peace, justice, and reconciliation at all levels – local, regional, and global;
- to embrace creative approaches to peace-building which are consonant with the spirit of the gospel;
- to interact and collaborate with local communities, secular movements, and people of other living faiths towards cultivating a culture of peace;
- to empower people who are systematically oppressed by violence, and to act in solidarity with all struggling for justice, peace, and the integrity of creation; and
- to repent together for our complicity in violence, and to engage in theological reflection to overcome the spirit, logic, and practice of violence.

DOV formally began in 2001 with an international launch in Berlin.

We live in a world pervaded by the culture of violence expressed and experienced in different ways by all people in every part of the world, so DOV addresses all forms of violence, not only physical and visible when death and destruction take place, but also structural when people are forced into poverty, subjugation, and denied basic human rights on account of unjust social, political and economic structures. Today, violence cannot be seen merely as an expression of enmity or hatred or as a retaliatory act, but also as a means of becoming and remaining wealthy and powerful. Culture, traditions, and religion play their role. Wars, civil wars, armed conflicts, communal clashes and terrorist attacks on the one hand and violence within homes, against women, children and young people, racially oppressed groups and ethnic, linguistic and religious minorities, and against nature on the other, overwhelm life in the world today. Violence is also entertainment and teaches violence to children. The profits from the weapons' industries keep the economies of some countries strong.

Violence is a problem common to all human communities. Christians attempt to seek reconciliation and peace with the inspiration and resources of their faith in the God of life. Peace-making is crucial to the affirmation of this faith. Forgiveness is also central to the Christian understanding of peace and reconciliation.

The vision of a new world order based on the value of justice is one that gives a sense of direction and purpose to the Christian vocation of peace-building. Violence as an expression of irresponsible assertion of power over the powerless denies and abuses life. The churches are compelled to be in solidarity with its victims in judgement and in hope of a new order, which ensures life for all – free from fear and aggression.

DOV does not claim that it will overcome all forms of violence. At the end of the Decade (2010) undoubtedly there will still be violence, but the churches as they participate in this global movement for peace hope to become sensitive to situations of violence within and around them and to participate in the task of healing the brokenness. But what it does is to call the churches to contribute to cultivating a culture of peace in the world. It attempts to do so by giving visibility to people-based, non-violent ways of resolving conflicts and dealing with differences with the hope that these will inspire similar initiatives elsewhere.

An important motivation for this commitment is the determination to stand alongside certain sections of people who always seem to be the victims of most forms of violence on account of the unjust values that dominate structures of human relationships in our world today.

The Decade is really an invitation to an open space where people of all faiths, races, languages, and walks of life, work together for peace and churches find the possibility of discovering the meaning of shared humanity as they work with people of other living faiths and movements for the sake of a better world.

Because the DOV is a process shaped by the initiative of the churches, the role of WCC is to assist and support the work of the churches in their efforts towards overcoming violence. The WCC attempts to facilitate the emergence of a global movement of churches for peace by lifting up new and ongoing responses of churches and people around the world to various manifestations of violence. WCC is also committed to analyzing and interpreting these responses to come up with creative responses. As a part of this process, the WCC has identified four themes to focus much of its own theological and ethical work in the coming years:

- the spirit and logic of violence which also include anthropological and cultural legitimizations;
- the use, misuse and abuse of power;
- the issues of justice; and
- the crucial role of religious identities.

DOV is a movement that attempts to strengthen existing networks as well as inspire the creation of new networks for peace worldwide. As such, it is not limited to any institutionally organized network but is a process facilitated by the WCC.

4. Reconstruction of Africa

Unless it participates actively in the rebellion against those struc-
tures and organizations which condemn people to poverty and
degradation, the church will become irrelevant.

Mwalimu Julius Nyerere,
first president of Tanzania.

As Africa moved into the twenty-first century, poverty became the
burning issue both on the continent and, belatedly, in the North, especially among the eight wealthy industrialized nations that make up the
G8. For the churches it was a fundamental issue and clearly it was the
eradication of poverty, not some mealy-mouthed alleviation. As Kobia
put it in his book, *Courage to Hope* (WCC 2003) "For Africans, our
goal should be to eradicate poverty because this goal is noble, and it is
the right course to chart and pursue...It is also possible."

How best to organize the economy for the sake of sustainable and
inclusive development remains a pressing issue. The last decades of
the twentieth century saw a shocking and steady decline in the living
conditions and livelihood of the peoples of Africa. There was also a
gradual decline in volumes and returns on trading primary commodities which have been Africa's economic mainstay since independence.
This, coupled with neo-liberal economic policies, the scourge of HIV/
AIDS and other diseases and violent conflicts, have made life in
Africa more precarious than ever. This situation has been summarized
by the World Bank as the African Development Crisis. Indeed, it is a
crisis on two interconnected planes: ideology and practice. As a crisis
of thought (ideology), it has been partly due to lack of a relevant
coherent theory that is sensitive to the indigenous knowledge systems
and informed by the empirical needs of the people in rural communities, argues Thandika Mkandawire in his book *The Crisis of Economic
Development Theory* (Africa Development).

The crisis of practice has been the problem of how best to implement the abundant natural resources in the continent to create wealth
and provide basic services for the majority of its people. This crisis
touches on questions of governance, competence, corruption, equal
trade opportunities, human rights and the ecology – how best to manage the politics of allocation and use of the vast resources in Africa to
create wealth and sustain national economies.

Encounters with world financial institutions

In this context the WCC sat down, no less than three times, once at the highest levels, with the so-called Bretton Woods Institutions (BWIs), the World Bank and the International Monetary Fund (IMF), between 2002 and 2004, twice in Geneva and once in Washington. The dialogues, which the WCC called "encounters", involved trying to find critical areas of common ground in the fight against poverty although WCC perceptions of the BWI policies were generally negative of the ideologically neo-liberal framework of the IMF and the World Bank.

The meetings culminated in a high level encounter at the Ecumenical Centre in Geneva where, for half a day on October 4, 2004, the leaders of the three organizations held a round-table discussion. Representing the BWIs were Augustin Carstens, deputy managing director of the IMF and James Wolfensohn, president of the World Bank and from the WCC Samuel Kobia, general secretary, and Agnes Abuom, WCC president for Africa. Their respective staffs had worked hard at preparations which, incidentally, had been initiated by the BWIs back in 2002 before Kobia became general secretary.

Speakers from the three organizations addressed such topics as poverty eradication, human rights and social justice and the democratic deficit: how developing countries can have greater and more effective voices in decisions made by the BWIs.

It fell to the President from Africa to deliver a principled and straightforward paper linking directly how poverty can only be eradicated when it is seen as an issue of lack of justice and human rights. Dr Abuom, who is an active member of the Anglican Church of Kenya and served on the NCCK as chair of the programme committee, was elected President of the WCC at the Harare assembly to represent Africa. She is a historian and works as executive director of TAABCO Research and Development Consultants, based in Nairobi. She is also the regional coordinator of the "Building Eastern Africa Community Network" (BEACON).

Her work on justice issues in her own country led to her detention by the Kenyan government for a period in 1989. She has been committed to the ecumenical movement for many years, has been a member of a number of international ecumenical delegations and has been particularly prominent in debates on the effects of economic globalization in Africa.

In her presentation she quoted from a Russian proverb: "My own bread is a material question for me, the bread of others is a spiritual question." The huge economic gulf in the world, she asserted, cannot be bridged by economists' tools. "We need the tools of ethics and the teaching of 'love one's neighbour'."

The WCC looks critically at any economic system from an economic justice perspective which calls for another way of doing economics and development. The WCC calls for abandoning current economic orthodoxy and a search for non-classical methods aimed at resolving poverty, inequity and environmental destruction which are increasing, especially in Africa, at an "alarming rate." Abuom, as the major speaker for the WCC, argued strongly for biblical standards of trade-justice and firmly taking the side of people in poverty as a measure of development.

"An economic system in which the fruits of economic growth mostly benefit the rich, leaving millions of people struggling in ever-deepening poverty is 'ruthless growth' and was described as such by the UN's *Human Development Report for 1996*. Under these circumstances," Abuom charged, "it is cynical to speak of 'equal opportunities for all'. To what extent do people in poverty possess equal opportunities to produce, sell and buy products and enjoy the fruits of their production?"

She told the heads of the BMIs, whose failed development policies had left much of the world underdeveloped, that their emphasis on an unregulated market confronts the churches and the ecumenical movement speaking for the poor with "speculation, exploitation and inequality. We call it the 'champagne glass economy' where 20 percent of the world's population owns more than 80 percent of the world's wealth."

Then Dr Abuom posed the main question of the WCC for the IMF and World Bank: "How can our economic operations go beyond *homo economicus* to addressing a holistic view of the person and the earth?" The answer lies in the critical differences between the three institutions: "While we believe that poverty increases under the current world system, the World Bank and IMF believe the contrary."

Both sides said they wanted to get rid of poverty but disagreed profoundly on the need to eradicate inequity by qualitative regulation of markets in the name of justice. And here Abuom admitted that "we have not succeeded in convincing the BWIs to take seriously social, cultural and human rights as essential elements for development, nor have we been able to convince them that the current market systems need to be changed."

While the churches, indeed most world faith communities, have what Wolfensohn himself called "precious little relationship at all" with the BMIs, Abuom said they should both at least uphold the issue of human rights. "The WCC has said this many times. We need to ask ourselves, 'How do our operations lead to the violation of economic, social and cultural rights? Do our procedures violate peoples' rights to employment, food, livelihood, land water, freedom and dignity?' If the answer is 'yes' then we are far from doing justice."

She went on to outline the WCC's position and where it differed from the BMIs:

- Trade alone does not remove poverty and inequity, instead development of home markets is a precondition for people-centred growth in poor countries. Building just, participatory and sustainable communities which practice economies of solidarity, is what the WCC advocates.

- Policies must be guided by the principles of human rights and justice which are imperative once we recognize that gross inequalities threaten global peace. The WCC is committed to inclusive policies, including specifically improving the role of women.

- Environmental destruction caused by economic expansion (especially by rich countries) without adequate protection measures will have a devastating impact on the ecosystem. There must be limits to the carrying capacity of the earth. Figures on the state of the environment are shocking. Why are the BWIs not alarmed by this situation?

- Transfer of resources from poor to rich countries, the flight of capital, should be stopped. Instead of punishing countries that try to retain capital for their own development, the WCC wants to find ways to prevent massive financial and resources flows from South to North which means, of course, that the poor continue to finance the rich.

- Finally, the WCC President called for democracy within the BWIs, meaning that there must be economic power-sharing within the world. Membership in the two institutions now totals 184 countries but the industrialized countries have 40 percent of the votes, while Africa, at the opposite extreme, gets just four percent of the votes. The poorest continent has only two executive directors to represent 44 countries. If these institutions cherish democracy as one of the conditionalities for loans, they should be the first to show it.

Dr Abuom, flanked by Samuel Kobia, concluded her encounter with Wolfensohn and Carstens with a ringing call for transformative justice that goes beyond the mere fulfilling of rights set out in the UN Committee on Economic, Social and Cultural Rights (CESCR).

"[Transformative justice] will ensure we respect rights, but also work for the necessary conditions for their implementation and realization. In recognition of this constructive task, the WCC speaks of transformative justice as the guideline and instrument for change."

Wolfensohn of the World Bank responded with praise for a faith-based, cultural dialogue in view of the recognized links between poverty, peace and stability. But he turned immediately to the current world crisis "due to short-term fears and misplaced priorities", citing figures showing that rich countries spent US$60 billion on development aid throughout the world, while spending a staggering US$900 billion on defence and US$350 billion on agricultural subsidies. "In such a situation of crisis it is important we work together." But he then called on developing countries to face the problem of governance and corruption and agreed with Kobia that a human rights approach to development was essential at the World Bank. However, he admitted strong resistance from the bank's board of directors to such an approach.

The leaders of the three organizations agreed on the importance of the UN Millennium Development Goals (MDGs) in a joint statement issued following the encounter. While committing themselves to a continuing dialogue, no further encounters are planned and differences were openly admitted. These included development issues such as approaches to development, financial markets and the impact of globalization, along with economic policy issues such as those relating to macroeconomic stabilization, government budgets and international trade.

The rise of SAPs

The history of African societies since slavery has been the history of struggle for freedom and human dignity. The quest for self-determination in Africa was primarily a quest for ownership of resources that were taken from the people. This struggle was inspired by various contesting ideologies: capitalism, mixed economies, African socialism and, at times, the Marxist analysis of liberation. In each case, vested interests in the world of superpowers and former colonizers competed, without concern for Africa, for its political and economic soul. The results have been as varied as the African economies or as the miseries of the African people in various states.

Pan-Africanism informed much of the struggle for freedom and dignity of the African people in the early days of liberation: it sought to restore pride and confidence and that nurtured various nationalist movements and tried unifying the continent as a means to realizing a free and dignified Africa. Perhaps Pan-Africanism's greatest contribution was in laying the foundations for an Africa free of direct colonial domination. The movement left the task of how to organize economies to the various regimes in each new state. Most opted for nationalization and state ownership of resources, means of production and provision of services in the agriculture, health and education sectors as part of a political nationalism, including patronage as a system of rewarding loyalty. Some argue that weak governance, dependence on colonial systems – which, in themselves, were corrupt and inefficient – , mismanagement, bureaucratic ineptitude and corruption inhibited economic development. Many newly-independent states quickly became authoritarian, elitist and unconcerned with the plight of their citizens. Significantly, they lost autonomy over the policy direction of their economies with the ascendance of international financial institutions such as the BWIs and later, the World Trade Organization.

With these came "efficiency" and western-style democracy called Structural Adjustment Programmes (SAPs). These sought to redress the governance failures of African states and reduce the influence of corrupt or inefficient politicians and administrators in the economy, as well as selling off the ownership of parastatal institutions which provided services to the public sector.

The SAPs imposed horrendous restrictions on ordinary citizens, especially the poor, and did nothing to wipe out corruption. They were, and are, a dismal failure. Their emphasis on reducing essential state expenditures in health, education, social services and infrastructure led to high dropout rates from schools, drastically reduced access to medical care and reduction in productivity in the agricultural sector. This reversed the gains that had been made in the fight against poverty, ignorance, disease and smallholder agriculture. Indeed, reform in the agricultural sector such as the removal of marketing boards did not in any significant way redress the cause of low productivity and profitability as was optimistically predicted. On the contrary, SAPs exacerbated the misery of the vast majority of African people and made their livelihoods even more precarious than in the first decades of independence. The untrammelled imposition of free market economy and American-style democracy also helped to breed ethnic hatred, crime and violence.

The WCC Harare assembly instructed the central committee to carry forward work begun in 1997 in Johannesburg by the Africa Reconstruction Programme (ARP). This was a call for a new emphasis on dialogue and study, capacity-building and information-sharing, so as to develop solidarity within the ecumenical family, and enable Africa to make its unique contribution to the world ecumenical movement.

The September 1999 central committee meeting identified three broad areas as a basic framework for a revitalized ARP: war and conflict (including governance, micro-disarmament, children and women in armed situations); economic justice, including globalization, and debt (from the perspective of human rights and human dignity), and spirituality and ethical values that enhance life with dignity.

The programme's broad goals are to:

- discern the mission of the churches in peace-building, conflict resolution and reconciliation with a strong emphasis on repentance, forgiveness, truth and healing;
- address emerging and pressing issues such as globalization, trade, finance and debt; and
- promote a culture of life and peace with justice and respect for the integrity of creation.

The programme has energized and motivated existing church and ecumenical networks into concerted action towards formulating a new vision for Africa. These networks include: theological associations, uprooted people's networks (in central, eastern, southern and western Africa) youth networks, e.g. AACC Youth for Peace Institute, women's networks, national councils of churches, African sub-regional fellowships and the AACC urban rural mission networks (churches and leaders of community-based organizations).

Three critical challenges to church and society in Africa have been identified: the nature and role of the nation-state, violence, and corruption. It is becoming increasingly clear that the nation-state model is not working in Africa. Indeed, the very legitimacy of the current model is at stake. A concerted effort to re-imagine the nation-state in Africa must be built into the ecumenical agenda early in the twenty-first century.

In Africa, violence is structural and systemic (economic, social, cultural), as well as physical and self-inflicted. Of great concern here is the emergence of self-financing civil wars in Africa. The armed factions in the civil war in Angola which used "blood" diamonds, oil and other natural resources owned by the people to pay for the long-running civil war that was eventually reduced to banditry, sadly heralded a trend that was later repeated in several other countries in central and western Africa such as DRC, Sierra Leone and Liberia. Ongoing civil wars are fought, not on ideological grounds, but about who controls economic wealth. God's blessing of natural resources is being turned into a curse for innocent people. The ecumenical movement is called not only to advocate overcoming such forms of violence, but also to challenge the legitimacy of civil wars in Africa.

Corruption and graft exist in all countries of the world. What passes in some European and North American countries as sales commissions would be considered as corruption in others. Corruption, the western media asserts, only exists in the South. A society where corruption and graft are institutionalized and generally accepted as a norm cannot progress.

In many African countries corruption has become a cancer whose treatment requires nothing short of invasive surgery. Even more than the political and economic crises, this huge moral crisis poses the greatest challenge to Africa. Moral leadership is the most critical area in which the church is expected to play a specific role.

Through the Fellowship of Churches and Councils in West Africa (FECCIWA), the ARP has supported and facilitated churches to address the issue of corruption through a consultation that brought African national councils of churches together to deliberate on the ethical challenges posed by corruption to help the churches continue their efforts to overcome corruption at the national level.

An African renaissance calls for the people of Africa to rediscover their soul. An African renaissance is therefore a journey of self-rediscovery, and restoration of Africans' own self-esteem. Churches and ecumenical networks that have taken up the theme of African renaissance are seeking the specific input that Christians can bring to this imperative.

Dakar Declaration

Major attention was given by WCC in 2000 and the first quarter of 2001 by supporting African debt campaign initiatives such as *Africa Jubilee 2000*. National campaigns against debt and structural adjustment programmes (SAPs) culminated in a pan-African consultation from December 11-14, 2000 in Dakar. This consultation, known as *Dakar 2000*, issued a declaration, "Africa: from Resistance to Alternatives", which says in part:

"...The total and unconditional cancellation of the African debt is a demand based on undisputed economic, social, moral, legal and historical arguments, because the debt problem is not simply a financial or technical issue as the World Bank and the IMF are tempted to demonstrate. It is fundamentally a human, social and political problem."

Debt service and conditionalities associated with debt have contributed to the aggravation of poverty. Moreover, debt has been widely reimbursed to the North: for the past few years, Africa has been transferring more resources to developed countries than it receives. In addition, most of Africa's debt is odious, fraudulent and immoral. In fact, in most cases, debt has been contracted by non-representative regimes that have used the monies received for purposes that were not of much use to their peoples' interests. Often, this debt served to consolidate and even legitimize dictatorships that used it to oppress their own people, with the benevolence and well-known complicity of western countries:

- Debt has also been contracted to undertake mega-projects designed to stimulate exports at the expense of meeting people's fundamental needs.
- The reimbursement of that debt is immoral: its service is diverting resources essential in the struggle against poverty, illiteracy and disease.

Thus, from whatever angle the issue of Africa's debt is examined, it is unacceptable. It is all the less acceptable in the light of the historic debt that the West has incurred from Africa that is immeasurable.

The churches' Dakar Declaration demanded both the restitution of what has been taken from Africa for centuries by slavery, colonization and post-colonial SAPs and globalization, and reparations for all the crimes and damages inflicted upon its people.

The Dakar conference included representatives of women's movements, youth movements, rural and urban workers and international solidarity movements. It called again for the immediate and unconditional cancellation of the African debt, the end to Structural Adjustment Programmes, even as they are renamed Poverty Reduction Strategy Programmes (PRSPs).

An earlier consultation on Africa and globalization, held in Togo in September 2000 in conjunction with the World Alliance of YMCAs, focused on globalization and human rights in Africa, with a special focus on youth. The AACC was represented by its youth desk. It sought to engage African youth in the quest for a new vision for Africa so as to increase their capacity to participate meaningfully in the process of social reconstruction.

African youth have a huge stake in building more just, peaceful and ecologically sustainable societies, and their involvement in shaping such societies must be affirmed and facilitated by the ecumenical movement. A WCC-sponsored seminar on theology and globalization with young African theologians in Accra, Ghana, was a response to this challenge. In a statement drafted after a visit to the *El minah* slave castle near Accra, the 30 young theologians from 17 African countries declared that "*El minah* not only represents an oppressive system of skewed distribution of socio-political and economic power that persists to this day, but also echoes the failure of the church to denounce that system...

"Yet as we gathered outside and said with our hearts, 'Never Again' to the *El minah* of Ghana, we find ourselves confronted by the *El minah* of globalization. Like the *El minah* of 1482, the *El minah* of globalization stands unbowed over the world and drips blood over the peoples of Africa."

On a women-to-women solidarity visit to Liberia, an ecumenical team visited several refugee camps to talk with the women and children. Ecumenical women-to-women solidarity visits have become an important expression of support to women and children in conflict situations. Two such visits, organized by the WCC, the World YWCA, the Lutheran World Federation (LWF) and the AACC, were made by teams of five women each to Liberia and Sierra Leone in 2000.

Women, as women, are often targets of very specific forms of violence, and sometimes go on living in contexts of intimidation and fear after the conflict is supposedly resolved. As was said during the Sierra Leone visit, while violence against women is exacerbated in war situations, it exists even in the absence of war especially as globalization and debt make slaves of economies. Women need to feel safe to talk about the violence they experience; these visits created that space for genuine sharing.

"We went to these countries to offer international solidarity to the women; to listen and to bring back their concerns to the world. We affirm the role played by women in the peace, reconciliation and democratization process. We call on the global church to offer continuing support to women as they engage in the effort of healing and reconciliation, of reconstructing their own lives and those of their communities...," the visitors declared.

In this context, the churches in Africa have been asking hard questions and evaluating carefully the claims emerging in this century for the various visions for awakening Africa's economy such as the New Partnership for Africa's Development (NEPAD), the G8 poverty elimination programme, the UN Millennium Development Goals (MDG) and the Commission for Africa in 2005, chaired by UK Prime Minister Tony Blair

When the churches try to trace the problem of development in the last three or so decades they realize that the continent has never been left to develop its own models of economic growth that are relevant to the values and realities of life in Africa. In the 1980s and early 1990s, at a time when Africa was being faced by this new emerging global order, in which international financial institutions were gaining more visibility and clout, scholars and some leaders in the continent committed themselves to advancing alternative means of sustainable development.

Critical accompaniment

In a major speech, in 2003 in Johannesburg, Samuel Kobia spoke about the newly-formed NEPAD as a step in the right direction for African economic emancipation but said that it must also be accompa-

nied by spiritual emancipation, just as the end of apartheid had signalled South Africa's political emancipation.

"This denotes the fact that the African human condition is more
than just mere material deprivation. The mistake made at independence was to consider political emancipation an end in itself....The
challenge to the churches is to formulate what constitutes spiritual
emancipation to reinforce economic and industrial emancipation for
Africa."

The speech was addressed to an Ecumenical Consultation on
NEPAD sponsored by the WCC, AACC, and the SACC entitled "The
Quest for Common Understanding and Shared Vision for Twenty-first
Century Africa". Kobia referred to the 1998 Harare assembly of the
WCC which had anticipated the urgency and significance of a new
vision for Africa when African delegates promised:

- to reconstruct and rebuild communities so all may have fullness of life;
- to transform social and economic institutions;
- to pursue peace and reconciliation; and
- to cultivate ethical values of good stewardship of resources.

In this context, Kobia praised NEPAD as a framework for vision
and a programme for action. It does not shy away from the discourse
on democracy and good governance and it is open to engagement with
African society. "However, NEPAD cannot address the issue of partnership without addressing mutual respect as Africa's history of
exploitation has damaged the dignity of both oppressors and
oppressed. Partnership must include the restoration of right relationships between donors and recipients."

One of the strengths of NEPAD, Kobia said in his opening address,
is that it is forward-looking. "It does not dwell too much on the past,
nor does it wallow in self-pity."

The ecumenical movement should welcome NEPAD, but the
churches need to analyze its basic values, principles and methodologies. It is already apparent NEPAD is heavily influenced by neo-
liberalism in its approach to development. The people of Africa are not
yet fully involved in its process. It is essentially a project of a handful
of heads of state (Mbeki of South Africa, Obasanjo of Nigeria, Wade
of Senegal and Boutiflika of Algeria).

"How can NEPAD be built into a popular movement in which the
people are deeply involved? Collective ownership of the process will
increase African peoples' confidence and faith in its outcome. Yet
NEPAD has tremendous potential and hence the need for the ecumenical movement to dialogue with, and engage the leaders that have formulated the vision."

Kobia called for reconstruction of Africa "from below" and encouraged good governance and financial management, but he emphasized forcefully that the churches of Africa must consider carefully and deeply what values – including traditional values – they can bring to the process of democratization, so that they may give voice to home-grown democracy based on:

- integrity and wholeness;
- the relational dimension of democracy;
- consensus-building as a way of reaching decisions; and
- equality, considering the unnecessary suffering of the people as morally wrong.

Later the same year, the AACC assembly in Cameroon in 2003 agreed and resolved to accompany NEPAD, but not uncritically. The accompaniment would be based on definitive values of abundant life and justice, informed by the institutional and social memory of AACC's values of truth, justice and peace.

As the beacon of inspiration and a place of renewal, the mandate of the churches is anchored on the preferential option for the poor, the oppressed and the marginalized. The notion of justice is intrinsic to the biblical values upon which the work and calling is anchored. Every action and response by the African churches together to public issues is informed by the prophetic vision of the church as the moral conscience of society. In order for Africa to meet its peoples' basic needs, especially with regard to food, water and shelter, the churches in Africa are called to increase the peoples' capacity for self-reliance, advocate for debt cancellation, and seek solidarity with institutions and people in the North who share the same concerns.

That there is considerable global concern for the need for a better Africa is increasingly evident. These initiatives are welcome for they bring hope of renewed interest in the material life of a people dehumanized by poverty, disease and violent conflicts. What is not clear is whether NEPAD, the G8 and the Commission for Africa or the MDGs will make significant differences for the lives of God's people in the long term. The churches must examine and analyze carefully the claims and promises of these development initiatives against the quest for a free and dignified human life for all in Africa.

NEPAD's concept of development is vague and has been used to refer to a diversity of projects and processes that are based on notions of rapid modernization of the continent. Consequently, NEPAD borrows the key assumption – although in a somewhat subtle sense – of the global agenda of neo-liberal economic policies as the remedy to Africa's underdevelopment. It assumes that the crisis of development in Africa is caused by lack of investment in general and direct foreign investment in particular. NEPAD's programme also assumes that the lack of accountable and transparent governments in Africa account for the present situation; it sees good governance as requisite in turning around the present poverty, conflict and disease.

It seeks to remedy this crisis through a new partnership that will deliver investment and engender accountability and transparency in government. Insofar as it advocates for accountable and transparent governments through the *voluntary* peer review mechanism, it may be welcome. Indeed, there is need for the church to engage in and support such a move. Yet the mere fact that the process is voluntary and lacks enforceability makes it vulnerable to unstable or corrupt governments.

African development should not aspire to the atomized individualism or soulless capitalism of the West, which appears to be NEPAD's point of reference. The problem of development in Africa is not so much a lack of inclusion into the international political and economic systems as it is the nature of inclusion. Indeed, the problem with investment in Africa is not so much its shortage, as its nature which is too often the mineral-rich extractive type that relocates the other process of value addition outside Africa. In other sectors of the economy, it tends to de-industrialize African economies.

NEPAD's choice of neo-liberal policies as the remedy to African economic problems is questionable. These economic policies include privatization, commodification of public services and introduction of user-fees in health, education and agricultural services. Where these have been established poverty has been exacerbated, unemployment increased, economic and gender inequalities aggravated, resulting in deprivation of basic needs and erosion of basic human rights.

WCC's president for Africa, Dr Agnes Abuom has also been critical of NEPAD, despite its being hailed in the international and continental media as a major step on the part of African political leadership in search of a new vision for Africa. However, she is one of the eminent African church persons who believes the ecumenical movement is challenged to respond to NEPAD, and that it is also imperative for the church in Africa to contribute to the ethical component of the broader vision of Africa in the 21st century.

Abuom says the concept, implementation and ownership of NEPAD should not remain a preserve of a small political elite but should grow into a popular movement for the African people. She has said that privatization leads to a "total looting of people's investments" and that, for too long, poverty and development have been looked at in terms of "Lazarus seeking crumbs from the table".

The UK-initiated Commission for Africa could be a sign of hope despite its tendency to be diverted by Britain's involvement in the war in Iraq and on terrorism and reliance on high-profile international entertainers. Blair's initiative also seeks to eradicate poverty, disease and hunger. To achieve this, the commission proposes to address the twin issues of trade and aid. Its proposals on aid are laudable, rejecting "tied aid" in which the recipient has no autonomy over its use, and is often forced to buy equipment or employ the services of the donor country. The commission argues that Africa can come out of poverty if it observes good governance, improves its infrastructure and becomes self-reliant. Consequently, it advocates for debt relief and an increase in aid to Africa.

Blair launched the Commission for Africa in February 2004 saying: "Africa is the only continent to have grown poorer in the past 25 years; 44 million children do not go to school, millions, as you know, die through famine, or disease, or conflict, and Africa risks being left even further behind." He called Africa a "scar on the conscience of the world." Of the 17 commissioners appointed, nine were from Africa, including President Benjamin Mkapa of Tanzania and Prime Minister Meles Zenawi of Ethiopia.

The Commission for Africa reported in March 2005 with great hoopla and fanfare in the presence of many celebrities from the western entertainment business and called on wealthy countries to double aid to Africa while forgiving Africa's crippling debt and simultaneously challenged African nations to root out pervasive corruption.

The commission's support for a dramatic increase of aid echoes the recommendation of a team of experts sponsored by the United Nations Millennium Development Goals (MDGs) and led by Jeffrey Sachs, an economics professor at Columbia University in New York, who directs the Earth Institute which strives for an end to world poverty. To accomplish an end to poverty, Sachs says, aid should be doubled.

Britain was chair of the G8 group meeting in Scotland in July 2005. In that role, Blair pushed for his sweeping plan to diminish poverty in Africa. "Live 8" concerts were held around the world, drawing millions of fans, and holding governments' feet to the fire as the Commission for Africa's report was unveiled. But in the midst of enormous world-wide publicity and media-hype, there was also a contradictory atmosphere. The US, obsessed with Iraq and its war on terrorism, was lukewarm in its commitments, Canada was also unwilling to guarantee 0.7 percent of GDP for aid, although historically it had proposed this goal 30 years earlier. Other countries made key commitments but as the summer of 2005 drew to a close, Blair was himself preoccupied with domestic and Middle East terrorism and the "Live 8" celebrities were on holidays.

While the report of the commission said Africa was ready for a huge new infusion of aid and debt relief, it also sharply defined corruption and ineffective governance as critical issues which could delay implementing the commission's proposals.

Taken together, NEPAD and the Commission for Africa open an opportunity for dialogue on what needs to be done to help Africa. The churches are engaging with both, speaking with the distinct voice of the downtrodden.

The church should speak for the poor against privatization of utilities such as water, energy, education, health and agricultural services. The church must also speak against false dichotomies such as public versus private, state versus "free" market and trade versus aid. The church should encourage alternatives using the desired option for the majority poor as the guide to service provision, not simply its profitability. The markets should be made subordinate to basic human needs. To worship efficiency measured in terms of profitability is to worship a false god. The church should encourage the autonomy of various actors in the development process, making a case for the desire of dignified and free human existence.

In essence, according to the ecumenical approach, says Rogate Mshana, WCC's executive for economy and justice, "any programme that seeks to address the African problems of poverty, food insecurity and scarcity, declining production and lack of technology, must go beyond the false dichotomy of either state or market prescriptions on how to organize the economy. There are sectors in which state ownership and control of property are desirable, just as there are areas where private ownership and control of means of production are advantageous."

To create an enabling environment, in which the economy of African countries would flourish, developed countries such as the US and Europe should cancel African debts, so that these resources can be used to provide food, shelter, health and education to the people of the continent.

"The dynamic of debt creation is part of the dynamic of inequality. On the one hand, attempts to develop – whether through increasing exports or through nationally-oriented production – often result in rising debt. On the other hand, the very process of expansion on the part of the industrialized countries, led by transnational corporations and banks, has stimulated the creation of debt in the Third World countries," writes Marcos Arruda in *An Ecumenical Approach to Economics* (WCC Publications).

The burden of external debt-servicing weighs heavily on many developing economies. This is increased by the uncertainty of export earnings from commodities and the threat posed by the new protectionism to change structures of agriculture, manufactured goods production and trade. The ecumenical movement over the years, says Mshana, introduced a number of terms into the development debate within the Christian community to emphasize the point that development is more important than economic and technological progress. The stress on social justice, self-reliance, people's participation and sustainability has contributed substantially to new and creative action by the churches.

Poverty as violence

Poverty is the worst form of violence in contemporary Africa. However the root cause of poverty in Africa has to do with conditions arising from the negative forces of history and the contemporary unjust global economic system. Economic globalization is "the process of consolidation of wealth and power by the rapid integration and structuring of national economies into one global economic order through trade, liberalization, privatization, and deregulation. The aim is to remove the obstacles to the global movement of capital and production of goods that have accumulated in advanced, industrial capitalist countries. Its primary institution is the transnational corporation," writes the *"Women's International League for Peace and Freedom: Bread and Roses"*.

In this regard the surplus capital accumulated in the form of private profit crosses boundaries from one part of the globe to another regardless of how it has been acquired and the local conditions upon which it has been produced. Another critical aspect of economic globalization which the churches and people in Africa are facing is privatization of public goods in the name of corporate efficiency. This is the result of conditions for aid being imposed by international financial institutions. State-owned enterprises including telecommunication, public services such as health care and distribution of basic necessities such as water are being privatized and sold to foreign companies at subsidized costs.

The rapid increase in population, coupled with decreasing agricultural productivity and unequal distribution of national resources further exacerbated social tensions already inflamed by ethnic factors. Today about 44 per cent of the African population are living below the so-called minimal, and extremely low, poverty line. And without functioning economies that respond to the plight of the poor and vulnerable in society, it is virtually impossible to control crime and violence from the streets.

The agricultural sector is also important. The mismanagement of farmers' institutions of credit, the cooperative, has to a considerable extent contributed to low production of goods. There is an urgent need to redesign these institutions allowing farmers greater autonomy from the structures of bureaucratic control and abuse. The farmer, as the main producer, should have a greater say on his or her produce than is the case currently in the continent. The agricultural sector is also a significant player in food production as well as employment. At a time when drought, famine, and food scarcity is biting African economies there is a need to address the consequences of increasing landlessness among peasant farmers and the decreasing returns in farming activities.

The abundance of extractive natural resources in countries such as the Democratic Republic of Congo, Nigeria, Angola, Sudan, Sierra Leone and many others – perhaps with the exception of Botswana – often brought their people misery instead of prosperity. Responsible investment of natural resources can only be achieved if their use is negotiated and stipulated in the national constitution. It is also vital for African governments and the companies exploiting mineral or oil resources to make public the contracts or agreements between them. This way, the opportunity of abuse of revenues by the state, or elites, is limited. The remedy to the resource curse is putting in place inclusive institutions that govern the use and access to resources for the benefit of all. This is the Botswana experience. Consequently, the WCC and the church in Africa advocate for equitable and fair trade between the developed countries of the North and the developing countries of the South, in particular.

The National Councils of Churches' (NCCs) economic justice departments have developed public policy monitoring mechanisms for the purposes of lobbying governments and the donor community on economic issues. Indeed the churches together, through the NCCs, continue to focus on equitable use of resources between groups within the society, and between generations, paying attention to the inequalities wrought by the markets. The churches acknowledge that the material needs of the individual can be met through the market, however there are many human needs that are best provided for outside the so-called free market.

The church in Africa has yet to come to terms with the language of the market in order to engage it with a clear understanding. Theology must articulate a vision of life that comprehends and transcends the logic of the market. The church, through various ecumenical programmes, especially the economic and social justice witness at WCC and AACC, continues to point out that the market in its current form, characterized by exploitation and commodification is but one phase in the evolution of global capitalism. In its early phase, markets were socially embedded and responsive to the needs of the people. The property rights that existed in this market were tempered with ethical concerns, which regulated use and access to factors of production and reproduction. Consequently, the churches in Africa are called, as churches elsewhere, to support a market that is socially embedded, and which encourages solidarity in institutions such as the cooperatives and rotating credit associations.

Several prominent African women ecumenical leaders, advocates for economic justice and women's issues in the churches in Africa, have asked: "If globalization is so good, why are communities and especially women much poorer than before? Why is the gap between the rich and poor nations and persons within those nations getting wider and wider? Why do we have an urgent ecological crisis on our hands? Why do we have so much armed conflict and civil strife in Africa? Why is there an over-consumption by a few who have the financial resources and economic power and freedoms which have led to greed, exploitative systems of overproduction, marginalization and exclusion of the majority who are forced to live on less and less? Why is it that for the majority of the poor, despite the rhetoric of democratization and popular participation, the experience is that of exclusion from meaningful participation in the economic and political lives of their nations and communities? Why are less developed nations largely excluded from the global market place?"

The average per capita income in Africa today is lower than it was at the end of the 1960s when, in fact, most African countries were well ahead of today's wealthy nations of the Far East such as Singapore and South Korea. The 1980s and 1990s have been described as Africa's "lost development decades". Many African countries experienced either stagnation or a reversal of the gains made in the 1960s and 1970s. Between 1965 and 1985, sub-Saharan Africa's GDP per capita increased less than one percent a year. And, despite positive economic indicators in some parts of the continent since the mid-1990s, growth slowed again after 1998, and poverty is increasing. According to World Bank statistics in 2001, incomes for nearly half of the continent's 760 million people averaged less than 65 cents (US) a day. The average GNP per capita for the sub-Saharan region was US$492. But in 24 countries, GNP per capita was $350, with the lowest incomes found in Ethiopia ($100), the Democratic Republic of Congo ($110),

Burundi ($120) and Sierra Leone ($130). Reversing this decline is perhaps the most pressing challenge facing African governments and the international community in the coming years.

In *A Jubilee Call for African Women*, (WCC 1999) the African ecumenical women leaders emphasized that: "The consequences of economic globalization in Africa are often detrimental to the poor and vulnerable, women and the working class. With its emphasis on competition with winners and losers, the global market excludes millions of people from any meaningful participation in the economy. As corporations gain power over governments, governments have less ability to act on behalf of the people."

The ecumenical movement over the years introduced a number of terms into the development debate within the Christian community to emphasize that the agenda of development in poor countries transcends economic self-interest and technological progress of the rich and overdeveloped nations. There are numerous theological and scriptural resources developed and invoked by the churches in defence of the poor and for provision of alternatives to the forces of globalization.

However the biggest challenge to the faith community has always been how it can help enable Africa to overcome poverty. Often where there is a church there is some economic activity in the vicinity. There could be a church hospital or clinic and a school to provide healing to the sick and nourishment to the mind. Wealth, as in African traditional society, has always been perceived as the significant total value of the person to the community and vice versa.

And God has always been part of that equation, signifying abundance in the economy of life i.e. "I came that they may have life, and have it abundantly." (John 10:10) The economic activities of the church in Africa are often accompanied by the moral investment in people, regardless of their standing in society. Indeed, in order to replenish household economies which provide food and other basic needs to the people, many churches have initiated projects which show and teach people how to produce what they need to overcome hunger and sell what is surplus to the local markets. The churches, too, are equipping the faithful with analytical skills to discern, interrogate and accompany the people in dealing with the might of the global market. Together they revisit the question of food sovereignty contrary to the popular notion of food security which does not encourage domestic self-sufficiency in the local economy.

The world-wide church guided by the ethical principles of its social teachings does indeed have a responsibility to contribute to the public discourse around globalization. All retrenchment programmes to cut down the size of government and increase efficiency without corresponding social safety nets remain dangerous and have led to social crisis and political upheavals. It is therefore imperative that the churches together develop clear policies and negotiate with governments on behalf of the poor with regard to the question of retrenchment programmes.

The Millennium Campaign

The poverty debate peaked, but weakly, in September, 2005 when world leaders gathered at the United Nations to measure progress toward its Millennium Development Goals (MDGs) to reduce poverty, which were set to be completed by 2015, barely 10 years away.

The main aim of this inter-agency initiative of the UN was to create awareness that would lead to action on the goals which were adopted by the heads of state at the Millennium Summit of September 2000. At this summit 189 countries pledged to achieve the goals of human development. In partnership with the WCC, the All Africa Conference of Churches has set up a coordinating mechanism that incorporates initiatives by the sub-regional fellowships, NCCs and member churches in Africa. The ecumenical campaign is inspired by the Lord's Prayer, seeking God's mercy in being free from poverty and gaining the power for production of daily bread in Africa. The UN Millennium Development Goals are:

1. To be free from extreme poverty and hunger.
2. To ensure that all boys and all girls complete primary school education.
3. To promote gender equality and empower women.
4. To reduce by two-thirds the mortality rate among children under five.
5. To reduce by three-quarters the ratio of women dying in childbirth.
6. To halt and begin to reverse the spread of HIV/AIDS and the incidence of malaria, tuberculosis and other major diseases.
7. To ensure environmental sustainability.
8. To build up a global partnership for development.

Five years later, the heads of state were told during the UN general assembly's sixtieth anniversary meeting in October, 2005 that the goals have fallen back due to lack of commitment inside and outside Africa, lack of funding, lack of infrastructure, lack of investment in women and a "business-as-usual" attitude in North and South across all eight goals, according to a recent study by the International Food Policy Research Institute (IFPRI).

Unfortunately, the United Nations was focused on many issues other than poverty and the major states especially preferred to discuss other things such as terrorism, alleged corruption, the Iraq war etc., instead of poverty. On its sixtieth anniversary, the UN general assembly produced a weak and divided vision of the world which was roundly criticized by many, including the Secretary General, Kofi Annan. The US was accused of scuttling both the MDGs and a much-needed reorganization of the UN's infrastructure and administration.

The churches and social movements in Africa, accompanied by the WCC, are endowed with a far-reaching network of people in both rural and urban locations. The theological self-understanding of the church does not alienate it from being engaged on social, economic and political questions. On the contrary, the church has a moral and ethical duty to empower people to comprehend the trends in society and enable them to be effective participants in transforming the conditions of life. The church is a custodian of hope in the midst of human affliction. This creates a formidable challenge to both the churches and social movements with the responsibility for discernment and radical engagement that must lead to alternative ways of thinking and responding to the dilemma of development in Africa.

The church has always been involved in critical areas of development such as the establishment of mission schools and hospitals. More recently, churches across Africa have been engaged in civic education and peace-building initiatives. The church is called to become the conscience of the people and lead them by example. Hence the ecumenical movement supports the need for home-grown models of economic development that are owned and managed by the people themselves.

5. Health and Spirituality of Africa

In the African world-view there is a fine connection between human experience and the value of life. Africans are called to embrace life with all its vicissitudes because at the end of every epoch, God has always given the final verdict of hope that reigns over every negative force in history. And HIV and AIDS are not an exception because they are one of the major afflictions upon the people in Africa. When one looks into the eyes of orphaned children or dying mothers, one sees a future filled either with bitterness or forgiveness towards a world that is at best indifferent. The orphaned children of Africa carry the banner of hope and compassion that transcends the anguish brought about by HIV and AIDS. They are the custodians of a new future for the continent. Africa must invest in their future health, education, empowerment and support. The adults remain inspired by their resilience against the fear and current state of gloom.

Africans, being a people on a journey of hope bound by historical dilemmas, constantly turn to God whose presence among the poor bestows on them the gift of courage and wisdom. God receives the suffering of the people of Africa as part of the reality of the cross, and reinvents the negations of that history into projects of liberation. The church in Africa is therefore admonished to see in these times a new moment of grace in which God is inviting the whole of humanity to embrace the spirituality that transforms human suffering into a narrative of living hope.

The outbreak of this, as yet medically incurable, HIV and AIDS pandemic that has afflicted the world for more than three decades, challenges Africa to rethink the intrinsic value of abundant life. Church leaders in Africa are called to a journey of discernment. Such a journey must lead to a re-celebration of human sexuality as a divine gift of love for the flourishing of life. The tendency of too many Christians to stigmatize human sexuality and blame the AIDS pandemic on immorality, especially in the name of church standards, is not only no solution, "it is a major contributor to rejection, discrimination, misunderstanding and loss of trust that HIV people have to live with," says Canon Gideon Byamugisha of the Anglican Church of Uganda. "HIV is a virus and AIDS is the disease it causes; neither is a sin."

HIV and AIDS have occasioned a new *Kairos* moment of truth about what it means to be alive in a world where life and death struggle for reality in Africa. The eerie denial caused by the deafening institutional silence of some churches and governments in facing the reality of sexuality and the fact of HIV and AIDS have caused further unnecessary loss of life in the continent. HIV and AIDS cannot be considered an epidemic in the classic sense – a disease that appears, affects people in a community or region, and then disappears. It has become a pandemic that has come to stay in human communities and that acquires global proportions in terms of its reach and consequences.

By 2005 nearly 40 million people world-wide were living with HIV and some 25 million had died. Worst hit is sub-Saharan Africa and especially eastern and southern Africa where nearly 30 percent of all people have been affected with the virus and more than 14 million children orphaned. Countries especially hard hit include Botswana, Kenya, Lesotho, South Africa, Swaziland, Uganda, Zambia and Zimbabwe.

Statistics show that in an advanced country like South Africa, between 1,500 and 2,000 people are infected with the human immuno-deficiency virus (HIV) every day, more than 600 people die daily from acquired immune deficiency syndrome (AIDS)-related causes, some 800 babies are born to infected mothers every month.

A child born into a poor family also inherits all the ills associated with poverty. Few can improve their situation, and HIV and AIDS intensify their suffering. Many are infected by mother-to-child transmission of the virus. In 2003, South Africa had at least 88,500 orphans, and three percent of all households were headed by children less than 18 years old.

This trend is aggravated across the continent by the economic demands of child labour, especially in rural communities. Throughout rural Africa, children become involved in farming and domestic chores at an early age. Boys herd livestock, and girls assist their mothers with preparing food and collecting water and firewood. West African children are estimated to be net contributors to the household by the age of 10.

To make the situation worse, the pandemic across Africa has left innumerable children orphaned, especially in rural areas. Because the extended African household economy that supported affection and compassion towards such children is often no longer viable, they have nowhere to turn. Communities, families, and individuals in Africa are helpless as they watch their sons and daughters bound in hopelessness without medication or facilities to combat the disease. The young give up on life early when they see their parents helpless and their communities engulfed and ravaged by fear of the unknown. One must enter into the world of orphaned children to comprehend the degree of anguish that HIV and AIDS bring to their lives. The misery that accompanies the death of parents and loved ones leaves many children helpless and with unanswered questions about life.

The vicious tendencies to stigmatize people living with HIV and AIDS are often based on social and religious taboos and attributes of human sexuality which children do not understand. Churches, especially in rural Africa, are still struggling to develop a theological vision and interpretation of human sexuality that is coherent with African values and cosmology.

The most chilling nightmare of HIV and AIDS are the inevitabilities associated with it. This includes a culture of fear and a profound sense of misery that negates the promises of love and joy in the gospels. There is the terrifying tendency, based on bad theology, that feeds into a sense of hopelessness and anguish that claims the virus and disease as an apocalyptic event, thus naming it as God's curse upon humankind. This kind of ignorance is dangerous and only serves to alienate and spiritually stigmatize people living with the illness.

A disease that speaks multiple languages

Nyambura Njoroge is a Kenyan theologian and global coordinator of the WCC's ecumenical theological education programme. She describes HIV and AIDS as "a disease that speaks multiple languages and thrives on other pandemics".

This reality of Africa has been depicted by Musa Dube, a leading New Testament scholar and global HIV and AIDS theological educator by dramatically retelling the story of the Samaritan woman (John 4:1-41).

"In this re-telling, the story of the Samaritan woman is our story. Her experience of many husbands is our experience. In short, the economic and political crisis of African countries, under foreign and local political powers alike, is a story that we share with the Samaritan woman."

One can hardly describe this most materially- and humanly-endowed of all continents, filled with mineral resources and beautiful landscapes and hard-working, hospitable and deeply spiritual people who were determined to reclaim their dignity and repossess their wealth. Tragically, the continent concluded the twentieth century with a disease that was first associated with gay men in the US which led Christian fundamentalists to link the disease with sexual immorality and sin. Consequently it was believed by too many that AIDS must be a punishment from God and so from the onset it spoke a religious and moral language.

By 1986, the World Health Organization (WHO) leaders approached the then WCC general secretary Emilio Castro to inform him that churches must look into this disease because it spoke a religious and moral language. The WCC responded by holding the first global ecumenical consultation on the AIDS crisis (by then HIV had not become a household name). Later the WCC executive committee noted that "the AIDS crisis challenges us profoundly to be the church in deed and in truth: *to be the church as a healing community*" (WCC 2001: 96, emphasis original). Since 1986 the ecumenical movement became part of the conversation in various ways. But within a very short time, whatever the African "fighting and stubborn spirit" had managed to salvage after a century of exploitation, AIDS slowly and miserably began to destroy human lives in their thousands.

Says Njoroge: "Wherever the disease went it claimed 'shame, guilt, denial and silence' as its code of conduct followed by stigmatization, discrimination and rejection as well as millions of graves, shattered dreams and communities and a paralyzed church and other religious communities. Many Africans learned to live with a deadly secret and the political and religious leaders (except in a few cases) perfected the art of silencing those around them. Unfortunately the religious and moral language of 'punishment and sin' gained prominence in African pulpits before the spirit of courage and truth (prophetic voice) found its rightful place. Even some westerners claimed that Africans are naturally promiscuous, hence Africa south of the Sahara was hit the hardest."

Nevertheless, the conspiracy of silence and secrecy was too much to bear and a few prophetic and pastoral voices were heard crying out because Africa's beautiful robust children were no more. Once again, Musa Dube dramatically retold the biblical story of the bleeding woman (Mark 5: 24-43) and spoke for millions of African women.

"Still bleeding and searching for healing, Mama Africa has been struck by a new disease: HIV/AIDS. She is now a nurse. She runs home-based care centres for her dying children and people. She washes them, feeds them, holds them in her arms, and rocks them, singing a little song, while she awaits their death. And when they finally die, she rises to close their eyes, to wrap them and bury them. Mama bears in her own flesh the wounds of their suffering. And they die in her loving arms. …At this moment, Mama Africa is nursing a sister, an uncle, a brother with one hand; with her other hand she is holding a dying child and feeding many, many orphans." (Dube 2001)

Fortunately, African women theologians' voices that emerged during the global HIV and AIDS era had identified African religion, culture and scriptures (Bible and Qu'ran) as the site of theologizing and insisted on using a "gender lens". The first publication (1992) by the Circle of Concerned African Women Theologians: *The Will to Arise: Women, Tradition, and the Church in Africa*, attests to this awakening. "Even though most of us did not write on the HIV/AIDS pandemic in the early 1990s, the work we had done on African rituals and practices that are harmful and degrading to women's lives and bodies, on sexuality, creative and contextual Bible studies and gender analysis paved the way for us to join the battle against the pandemic," Njoroge says, and adds, "I believe that by insisting and demanding that women's experiences, perspectives and social location must be given their rightful place in theologizing and in theological education is beginning to yield results in Africa.

"By the time of the third Pan-African Conference of the Circle in 2002, we could with confidence theologize on the theme 'Sex, Stigma and HIV & AIDS: African Women Challenging Religion, Culture and Social Practices'."

During this conference in Addis Ababa, the Circle was not only theologizing on the global pandemic but learned first-hand from women living with HIV and AIDS. The late Brigitte Syamalevywe, a woman living with AIDS, addressed the plenary: "I am not a statistic, I am a woman living with HIV/AIDS…I am a spiritual being having a human experience …HIV and AIDS must become a priority on all national and international agendas".

Circle members (individually and communally) are bringing the culture of silence, secrets, denial, guilt, shame, social death, and trauma to its knees. "But it is so catastrophic that it is the deadliness of HIV/AIDS that has intensified the awareness of women's powerlessness and many more secrets in our lives," writes Njoroge.

A recent research on women, war and peace sponsored by the United Nations Development Fund for Women (UNIFEM) has revealed that the huge amount of violence against women in conflict areas is the greatest kept secret. Unfortunately, this has increased HIV infection for women and children.

Certainly, the research should not ignore the devastation and hopelessness that extreme poverty has caused Africa and especially how it impacts the reproductive lives of poor women. HIV and AIDS is a disease unlike any other because it has not only devastated the whole person but has almost managed to destroy family units, the strong bonds that make the African extended family and the economic system.

Many have not begun to fathom the magnitude of Africa's orphan crisis now that many children are growing up without the supervision of adults. Sibling or child-headed homes are a reality in many households and yet few churches have any pastoral theology, care and counselling that speaks to this generation of orphans. Unfortunately the conflicts in Darfur (western Sudan), northern Uganda, Ivory Coast, Democratic Republic of Congo and the political instability in Zimbabwe will only increase the number of orphans and traumatized adults.

Says Njoroge: "We have made the choice to battle against the HIV/AIDS pandemic and much more. We now know the disease speaks multiple languages and thrives on multiple pandemics. Providentially, we are beginning to see a change of heart in the churches that stood paralyzed for many years as AIDS claimed many lives. Nonetheless we also know that churches and theological institutions and programmes remain paralyzed on many other fronts as people struggle against the pandemics of abject poverty, chronic hunger and malnutrition, gender-based violence, bad governance and abuse of trust and power among religious and political leaders, rampant corruption and civil wars and genocide."

The good news is that finally in Africa there is an acknowledgement that institutions and programmes of theological education and ministerial formation are powerful forces at work in educating generations of church leaders, theologians and theological educators and influencing the directions churches move or do not move in mission, evangelism, diakonia, ministry and ecumenism. Theological education and ministerial formation have become the new site for the struggle for life and healing as they act upon "the testimony, analysis, hopes and vision of these ordinary but extraordinary women – survivors, leaders and heroines".

At the heart of HIV and AIDS is the encounter with vulnerability, weakness and frailty of a part of humankind in the face of those who are endowed with resources and power to alleviate human suffering in the world. There are already enormous resources being earmarked globally towards strengthening responses to the pandemic. However, most of these resources are hardly invested in the transformation of the conditions that make people susceptible to infection through the poverty found in most parts of Africa. There is a real danger that the pandemic has been transformed into an industry of misery in which highly profitable northern pharmaceutical companies, condom manufacturers and expensive western mass media versions of HIV and AIDS education are monopolized by the North at the expense of impoverished health institutions in the South.

As a spiritual response to this dilemma, the churches in Africa are now grappling with the question of how to affirm faith in the abundance of life, in the face of a culture of fear and death. HIV and AIDS has become more than just a pandemic, it is now a system with its own language of resource mobilization. It is often forgotten that beyond the statistics and figures there are real human lives.

The ecumenical response

No other calamity since the slave trade has depopulated Africa at the rate AIDS has done. It is a plague of genocidal proportions. The African churches, indeed all churches, were faced with the need to change language, policy, and behaviour and mobilize their own resources to reverse the epidemiological trend and give to those infected. Churches in particular have the capacity to influence the behaviour of people so as to render them less vulnerable to HIV, and to promote an attitude of care and love. Uganda is a prime example where close cooperation between government, churches and NGOs has led to a reduction of the infection rate by nearly 50 percent. The joint efforts resulted in delayed sexual intercourse among young people (abstinence), reduced numbers of casual sex partners (fidelity) and an increase in condom use (prevention).

Participants in a church leaders' consultation in November 2001 in Nairobi perceived the event as a breakthrough in the opening up of African churches, and serious commitment of northern churches and their funding agencies, to the case for HIV work in Africa. In the Plan of Action adopted by the consultation, the participants made commitments to ways of transforming their message into action, combating stigma and discrimination to giving life and becoming centres of welcome and knowledge. In its conclusion, the plan stipulated that the Health and Healing Programme of the World Council of Churches (WCC) would launch the Ecumenical HIV/AIDS Initiative in Africa (EHAIA) within the framework of the Journey of Hope, as a separate administrative unit. The purpose of EHAIA is to help African churches implement the Plan of Action; the term "AIDS competent church" was coined to express the overall objective in three words.

Recalls Kobia: "EHAIA was the most comprehensive programme on HIV and AIDS. The conceptualizing designing, planning and implementation were done by the wider ecumenical movement – WCC specialized ministries, AACC and the African churches."

Today, EHAIA is working throughout Africa and can be most easily reached through four Regional Offices (in Accra, Nairobi, Kinshasa and

Harare). Regional coordinators plan, facilitate, often fund, and implement conferences, workshops, and training courses, leading towards the
five objectives of EHAIA, that make for an AIDS competent church. In
addition, there is a theological consultant who works with church leaders
and institutions of higher theological education all over Africa to reread
the Bible in the age of HIV and AIDS and make the resulting theology
accessible in the messages and ministries of churches to their member
women, men, and children. EHAIA is not restricted to WCC or AACC
member churches; in fact it cooperates substantially with the Roman
Catholic Church as well as churches that can be categorized as Evangelical, Pentecostal, African Instituted and their umbrella organizations.

Achievements

EHAIA started in April 2002 with one Regional Office and the
Geneva Support Office managed by Dr Christoph Mann; the last
regional coordinator started one year later. Since then, thanks to staff
enthusiasm and the readiness of churches to respond to the services
offered, the achievements are amazing by everyone's account. Such
achievements include:

- *Participation of people living openly and positively with HIV in
  EHAIA conferences and workshops brought church leaders for the
  first time into contact with people living with HIV and AIDS
  (PLWHA), resulting in a complete turn-around of attitude, a resolve
  to tackle the problem, repentance and a plea for PLWHA forgiveness
  on behalf of churches.*
- *The Plan of Action was used as a basis for churches to develop
  their own, and therefore owned, HIV policies – including work-
  place policies that gradually remove stigma and discrimination
  inside the churches.*
- *Capacity-building courses responding to a broad range of felt needs
  were organized to upgrade and expand church services so that
  responses to HIV and AIDS may finally reach proportions commen-
  surate with the epidemic. Depending on the area, themes covered
  pastoral counselling, training of pastors in general, rereading the
  Bible in times of HIV, gender violence and HIV, human sexuality discussions among youth, introduction of HIV into the curricula of
  theological training institutions.*
- *Local audio-visual productions were organized (that have been
  shown on national television stations) and music albums were produced to reach people in the faith community more broadly.*
- *In addition to involving people living with HIV and AIDS in nearly
  every meeting, EHAIA has an agreement for mutual cooperation and*

administrative back-up with the African Network of Religious Leaders Infected or Directly Affected by HIV and AIDS (ANERELA).
Quantitatively the statistics kept through participants' lists estimate conservatively that by the end of 2004 more than 7,000 persons have been reached through just over 100 meetings that had at least one full day of discussion about HIV or training on the agenda (more than half of them with EHAIA as the main funder also). The number of people reached in the churches is even greater where EHAIA staff were presenters or facilitators at events planned by others.

The result is best captured in typical statements from participants:

"We rely on you as a resource for further HIV information," general secretary of the Evangelical Church Alliance in Chad, (where most churches strictly reject WCC and all its publications), speaking to the EHAIA central Africa coordinator after he had helped the development and adoption of an Action Plan based on the EHAIA Plan of Action;

"This is the first major initiative from WCC that really takes the disadvantaged position of churches in lusophone countries seriously," general secretary of the Mozambique Council of Churches, after learning that EHAIA will have a lusophone coordinator for the five Portuguese-speaking countries in Africa in late 2005;

"The instruction booklet for soldiers has travelled with the chaplains and soldiers of our ECOWAS troops to all countries where they operate and even to Haiti," Army general and doctor-in-charge of the Togolese army in August 2004 about a booklet facilitated by EHAIA West Africa;

"I cannot imagine that we would have had the consultation without this emphasis on HIV and AIDS. Clearly it is perceived by all (mainline churches, Roman Catholics, Evangelicals, Pentecostals) as the number one issue on the agenda of the churches in Africa. It is not an item of controversy between "ecumenical" and "evangelical", at least not in the discussion we had with so many Evangelicals, Pentecostals and African independent churches around the table," Global Christian Forum Coordinator after a conference in August 2005 with EHAIA input.

An independent evaluation report of the first two years summarized its findings: "EHAIA is contributing to a 'culture change' in churches in terms of how people living with HIV and AIDS are viewed and embraced in their communities. EHAIA is also helping churches to strengthen their technical understanding of HIV and AIDS; increasingly, churches are developing the capacity to understand the magnitude of the epidemic and its potential impact on their communities:

- just as the virus has no denominational boundaries, EHAIA works with all churches and beyond;
- if a church feels a need to respond to an aspect of the crisis, EHAIA starts its support from there; cooperation is not based on

theological preconditions or alliances; instead, rereading the Bible together in these times of HIV can be part of the process;
- the most suitable way forward for a church is sought; EHAIA is not restricted to a certain sector of HIV work or fixed on certain methods; however it links churches to suitable other players inside and outside the faith sector;
- where perceived useful, EHAIA invites churches to courses, consultations, workshops or retreats, almost always with contributions from sero-positive Christians, that raise awareness and encourage behaviour change, individually and institutionally; and
- EHAIA fills gaps in HIV-related teaching tools from a Christian perspective through suitable publications.

Due to the broad response by churches, the existing staff cannot meet the growing demand for cooperation and consultation any more. Thus the International Reference Group (EHAIA's Board) has agreed to a moderate staff growth, if the funds can be mobilized:
- a lusophone Africa coordinator;
- a second theology consultant to intensify mainstreaming of HIV into the curricula of theological training institutions;
- a locally hired assistant coordinator for each of the four regional offices, whose professional training and experience complements the special skills of the respective regional coordinator and to provide more continuous office presence considering the frequent travels of the coordinators.

With the Plan of Action, the churches committed themselves to:
- ensure that, as an essential resource, people living with HIV and AIDS are supported and become involved in church activities;
- promote accurate information on HIV and AIDS, revise curricula for theological institutions, develop participatory educational programmes, empower women and girls, educate men to change their behaviour and take responsibility for containing the spread of HIV;
- develop curricula and training materials on the pandemic at all levels within the church; equip a new generation of church leaders to engage the churches on issues related to HIV and AIDS;
- promote effective means of prevention and practices that save lives; promote voluntary testing and counselling;
- support existing care and counselling structures and build a movement of care that originates from communities;
- encourage congregations to make available buildings and property for the support, training and care for people living with HIV and AIDS;

- support local congregations in caring for vulnerable groups, especially children, orphans, widow(er)s and caregivers; encourage and support networks of HIV-positive clergy;
- advocate for access to health care, anti-retroviral drugs (ARVs), and prevention of mother to child transmission.

During the last two decades WCC has developed a wide range of HIV/AIDS-related statements and tools. Some are not in use any more, others are remarkably timeless and still in high demand. EHAIA has since added publications which are certainly relevant and not only for African settings.

The material includes basic studies and policy statements of church leaders' consultations for reflection in the churches and the wider society. Over a three-year period, the churches' response to HIV has been mapped in on-going country studies because fast-changing fields of work require updating of some of the early reports. Practical training and teaching as well as liturgical materials are provided as they are presently available; production of more tools for everyday church life will receive emphasis from EHAIA over the coming years.

The four regional coordinating offices in west, central, east and southern Africa, and soon the lusophone, whose work is to accompany and support churches in their regions through:

- advice on how to start or intensify their own implementation of the Plan of Action in denominational or local policy papers;
- special HIV and AIDS retreats for church leaders;
- courses to include HIV in the curricula of clergy and lay training institutions;
- training of trainers for church group leaders (women, youth, men);
- capacity-building for planning programmes and resource mobilization to implement them;
- exchange visits with churches for sharing of good practice;
- resource persons for HIV and AIDS discussions in synods, assemblies, and gatherings; and
- printed and visual material for work with the congregations and communities.

Since the churches ended their denial and became involved in the pandemic, the work of the average church leader has grown beyond measure. Much is laid at the feet of the local church in the HIV/AIDS struggle. Few come into the pastoral work with skills to deal with HIV and AIDS: there are more orphans than extended families can absorb; more widows grieving and impoverished; more grandparents burdened with the care of grandchildren; many more people are dying and need the compassion of a caring church, many of these are dead and need to be buried, and thousands need counsel. There are the majority who are not infected and need to be helped to keep safe.

Role of pastoral care in healing and health

Musa Dube has written widely and powerfully on the subject and in the introduction to her book *AfricaPraying*, which is a handbook of HIV and AIDS-sensitive sermons and liturgies, now in its third printing since the Harare assembly, she writes:

"Most ministers who are serving now, never learned about HIV/ AIDS in their theological training programmes. They were not taught about counselling, prevention and care. They did not learn to read the Bible from an HIV/AIDS context. They were not instructed in preaching from an HIV/AIDS perspective. They do not have a liturgy that specifically addresses the origin and meaning of HIV/AIDS. How should they deal with the stigma? How should they address the needs of the affected? How should they minister to the infected? In short, a minister is challenged to learn a whole new way of doing ministry without the time for any meaningful research, studying and learning."

EHAIA, through its programmes, regional groups and materials provides a resource and accompanies African churches in exploring how the Christian faith can use its resources in the HIV and AIDS struggle. *AfricaPraying* is designed for all who have to handle situations created by this relatively new pandemic – church leaders and workers, Sunday school teachers, youth leaders, the laity. The five sections give sermon guidelines and worship outlines for services ranging from weddings to funerals; such key moments of the church's year as Christmas and Easter; attitudes of compassion or discrimination; congregations peopled by youth or grandparents; and social realities like poverty and gender inequality.

What Dube is saying in her writings (another of her books is *HIV/ AIDS and the Curriculum: Methods of Integrating HIV/AIDS in Theological Programmes*, WCC Books, 2003) is that the pandemic faces church leaders at all levels and places in the ecumenical movement with their greatest challenges because stopping the spread of the infection involves more than simplistic answers like abstinence and faithfulness. It requires the healing of all relationships: those with one another, with God and with the environment.

"While abstinence and faithfulness are no doubt effective moral values which must continue to be encouraged, the church has been forcefully brought face to face with the fact that individuals are not islands. Real people live within particular economic, cultural, political and social institutions and structures that determine the decisions they make and implement. Consequently, even when people know and wish to abstain in order to protect themselves, when confronted with hunger, they may choose to get involved with sex work to raise money for food. Even if some women wish to abstain from unfaithful partners, they have to think about losing shelter and support in cultures that still remain patriarchal. Even if women are faithful, in cultures where unfaithfulness is culturally tolerated from men, they will still be at risk of infection.

"Also, many families are separated over a long time by labour migration, displacement through political and economic oppression, and many raging wars, thus making faithfulness in marriage into an impractical ideal. Further, in war-torn zones, abstinence will not protect women from rape which is used by warring factions as a weapon of war. Family, health and education systems do not work in war zones. But worse, rape is not confined to war zones, and is on the rise due to myths surrounding HIV/AIDS. With the loss of control that characterizes the HIV/AIDS atmosphere, rape has become a symptom of men's desperate search for control over women's bodies. Young girls, children and infants are raped in their homes, in the streets, by both strangers and their own relatives. Within such a social context, how does it help for church leaders to carp on abstinence and faithfulness as the key to preventing HIV/AIDS?

"Clearly, we also need to address the social diseases and injustices of poverty, violence, gender inequality, human rights abuse, child abuse, ethnic conflict and cleansing, international injustice, discrimination in sexuality, race, age and physical and mental ability. Our liturgy must insist on, and celebrate, justice."

The churches' healing ministries were first introduced to Africa during the era of colonialism and foreign mission and they have been continued ever since with hospitals, clinics and care-giving by churches in ecumenical cooperation. From the 1970s ecumenical endeavours shifted to community health and to the participation of people in their own health-care provisions. The application of community-based health care to the HIV and AIDS pandemic has been a significant arena of ecumenical cooperation. The WCC programme "Health, Healing and Wholeness" signalled the need for churches to pay more attention to primary as well as preventive health care.

The receding role of governments in Africa in providing basic health care, much of which was inherited from colonial churches and taken over by the states, and the growing involvement of private and NGO sectors, demand an urgent response from the ecumenical movement in Africa. An alternative institutional framework needs to be established to meet pressing needs and consolidate the links between the socio-economic realities and health-care demands, especially for women. With the feminization of poverty in Africa there is an urgent need for affirmative action in health-delivery systems. Contemporary medical training in most African countries does not equip care-givers with skills for dealing with the consequences of domestic and other forms of violence, especially rape and sexual assault on children. Domestic violence and its consequences have become a continental public-health issue, profoundly linked to HIV and AIDS.

The need for global partnership in facing the crisis of HIV and AIDS is critical indeed. But churches and people of faith must always return to the values and norms of experience with living communities in Africa. The people of Africa have always cherished an integrated vision of social reality. It is this connection between human experience and the structure or systems that yields an integrated understanding of the value of life.

It is important that churches continue their mission of health and wholeness as part of their mission service. Nearly 40 percent of all health care service delivery in sub-Saharan Africa today is offered and maintained by the churches and hence there is already an infrastructure of delivery that invites collective strategies for the ecumenical movement. Global partnership is critical and the resources available must be linked to local conditions and capacities for faith communities to provide preventive care and healing to people living with HIV and AIDS. New approaches to health that are based on local resources and cultural values must be employed in the models of care-giving and advocacy.

6. The Quest for Justice and Human Dignity

The origin and demand for democracy is deeply rooted in the traditions of participatory decision-making and consensus-building among African communities through time immemorial. Another name for democracy, as a humanizing process in the world view, is dignity. African democracy, as an ethical way of making public choices, was exercised long before the colonial enterprise. Moral space emerged when people sought collectively among themselves solutions to issues and questions with regard to their needs and social well-being. It was not specific to, nor confined by, periodic election of leaders in the community. Rather, it was the whole life of the community, taking into account the interests and rights of minority groups as well. Communal aspirations were decided through a process of open consent by consensus. It is a process long upheld and practised in its highest councils and committees by the WCC, including at the ninth assembly at Porto Alegre, Brazil. The process does not detract from, but rather upholds, the moral authority of the people to express both their singular and collective consent on any particular issue affecting the well-being of the community.

"What is important is *not* that a state be democratic, but that it provides justice, equality and dignity for its citizens. Democracy, after all, is *not* a solution, *only* a method." (Author unknown.)

What would Africa have become in its struggles to keep culture and identity intact in the midst of persistent encroachment from outsiders and what might Africa have become if larger, better-organized ethnic groups had been afforded the geographical space or other means to resist foreign domination?

Think of ancient kingdoms like Kongo in Central Africa, or Dahomey (famed for its bronze sculpture, called Benin today) and the Ashanti in West Africa, or Monomatapa in southeastern Africa, just a few of the numerous examples of African peoples who created large, well-structured states, with codified legal systems, diplomats and many other kinds of bureaucrats and a range of public services from customs to mail delivery. One can easily imagine proto-states like these taking their place among today's modern nation-states, if only the invaders had given them an opportunity to develop. Instead, they were willfully and utterly destroyed by the colonial powers, as were invaluable cultural resources and much of Africa's self-confidence.

Historian Basil Davidson writes that Ashanti, the kingdom that once controlled most of present-day Ghana, was "manifestly a nation state with every attribute ascribed to a western European state, even if some of these attributes still had to meet maturity. It possessed known bound-aries, a central government with police and army, consequent law and order, and an accepted national language... What might have happened if indigenous development could have continued, and pre-colonial structures had remained free to mature into modern structures, can indeed be anyone's guess. Suppose the sovereignty of Asante [a widely used alternative spelling for Ashanti] had not been hijacked.... Could the resultant Asante nation-state have answered to the needs of the twen-tieth century? Would it have acted as a magnet for its neighbours?"

Regrettably history provides no answer. We are left instead with a humiliating picture of Africa and Africans, such as the images that endure in popular fiction like *Tarzan*. How many Westerners today realize, or are even capable of imagining, that it took most of the nine-teenth century for the mighty British colonizers to overcome the Ashanti, after a series of bitter and closely contested wars? Ultimately, the West African kingdom was undone by superior technology, espe-cially the Enfield rifle, which was accurate at 800 yards, and later machine guns such as the Maxim, which allowed the British to mow down their opponents.

"But it is important to recall, especially since such things are not taught in schools, that the British-Ashanti wars were struggles between two proud civilizations that shared similar concepts of nobil-ity, courage and duty to the sovereign, but were separated by radically different notions of fair play and ethics," writes Davidson in *Africa in History* (1991).

At the end of World War II, Britain had a mere 1,200 senior colo-nial service officers in all its African colonies combined, meaning that London had assigned a skeleton crew to run more than a dozen colo-nies covering more than two million square miles, with a population of 43 million. Then in 1957, barely half a century after wiping out the Ashanti state and imposing colonial rule, an astoundingly fickle Brit-ain changed its mind again and granted Ghana independence under a state structure that London copied directly from European blueprints. The question that goes unasked in the western media's news coverage of Africa, and in most of the other ritualized hand-wringing over the continent's plight, is why anyone should be surprised that the extremely violent European hijacking of Africa's political development resulted in misery and chaos.

It has become fashionable in discussions of the European slave trade to object that Africans were great slave traders long before the white man ever set foot on the continent. But seen against the failure of western education to give generation after generation of students a clear picture of the horrors of Europe's imperial conquest, this is simply an attempt at justification. The prior existence of slavery in Africa is a fact just as slavery existed in much of the world. But there can be little comparison between the age-old institution of slavery, in which captives were typically absorbed and assimilated into the culture that captured them, and the industrial scale of Europe's triangular slave trade and even less with its impact and brutality.

By the 1700s, each year some 60,000 slaves were being shipped across the Atlantic from West and Central Africa. This figure does not take into consideration the tens of thousands killed in the violent slaving raids and long treks through the bush or the many thousands who died of starvation in the ships. The slavers depopulated a huge stretch of the African coast from present-day Angola in the south to Mauritania in the north. Some demographers calculate that, by 1850 the total population of the continent would have been about 40 percent higher than it actually was at the time.

"But the most damaging legacy is that the Western slave industry, like its Arab-run twin concentrated in East Africa, fueled mass confusion, pitting neighbour against neighbour, society against society, damaging almost beyond repair the intricate social codes that prevailed in one African society after another.

"For Africans, enslavement was a threat that compounded the uncertainties of existence – a fear at the back of the mind, dulled by familiarity perhaps, an ache that induced a lingering fatalism in society as it passed from generation to generation. Kidnapping, capture, enslavement threatened villagers in various parts of West Africa for up to 400 years …. The pre-existing political economies in which chiefs and leaders commanded the respect of their subjects were transformed into systems controlled by warlords who obliged indebted chiefs and leaders to collect slaves as payment against forced loans." (*Africa: A Biography of a Continent* by John Reader, 1997).

The role of NGOs

The proliferation of international NGOs as the arena of activism in Africa in the modern era would not have been possible without the social deficits created by the African nation-state. International financial institutions began making policy demands on good governance after the end of the Cold War as conditions for multilateral and bilateral aid. SAPs were doled out to African countries with conditions that were an invasion of sovereignty and loosened the economic basis of state authority. The new climate of globalized politics negatively affected the new and fragile internal political arrangements in most African nations. Such developments became especially destructive when they created an environment in which "democracy" was used as a tool to legitimize new elite power takeovers at a time when relationships between African countries and the international financial institutions were not subject to the consensus of the public.

Internal democratic arrangements were overshadowed, overtaken and overwhelmed by a global international oligarchy: the BWIs and the hundreds of bilateral agreements with governments and NGOs. Africa is the stage of one of humankind's greatest tragedies and yet, the world remains largely inured to it, all but blind to the suffering and deprivation of one-ninth of the world's people.

Today, the pickings are just as "exotic" as ever but have been updated to meet the needs of the modern era. Africa interests the West for its offshore oil reserves in Angola, Libya, Nigeria, the Gulf of Guinea and Sudan's liquid gold which are seen as one alternative to supplies from an explosive and unstable Middle East, or for rare minerals like coltan in the DRC, which powers our cellular phones, and always the glittering demand for gold and diamonds and the industries demanding copper, bauxite and other base metals. Rip it out of the ground and ship it north and west for processing. There is one new twist to western self-centredness, however – a driving interest in Africa driven by fear of disease and immigration.

Democratic Republic of the Congo

The tragedy of Africa's third largest and potentially, one of its wealthiest, countries, the Congo, began decades before the height of the independence era, in the time of King Leopold of Belgium. When independence occurred and democracy was presented to the people they voted overwhelmingly. But their chosen leader was unacceptable to the US, well aware of Congo's enormous natural resources. The tragedy begun during colonialism simply continued when the Central Intelligence Agency (CIA) helped to engineer the overthrow and death of Patrice Lumumba, Congo's first, and only, democratically-elected prime minister, in September 1960, after a mere two months in office. The coup was just one of dozens that would contribute to making Africa the world's least stable continent. And during the Cold War era, lurking behind every coup and every undemocratic regime change or dictatorship could be found this tragic pattern that was set in place in Congo, as elsewhere, by what author John Le Carré once called, with appropriate scorn, "the global architects, the world order men, the political charm-sellers and geopolitical alchemists who in the Cold War years managed collectively and individually, to persuade themselves – and us too, now and then – that with a secret tuck here and a secret pull there, and an assassination somewhere else, and a destabilized economy or two or three, they could not only save democracy from its defects but create a secret stability among the chaos." (*The Constant Gardener*, 2003).

Congo, sometimes known as Zaïre, whose geographical position astride the equator, in the very centre of Africa, still suffers from Lumumba's ghost and restless spirit and years of corrupt, misguided, pro-Western policies driven by guilt rather than genuine care, that have resulted in the last three years in the largely unpublicized deaths of at least 3.3 million Congolese, the largest civilian toll of any conflict since World War II.

Africa's long, long history has been the story of the ebb and flow of kingdoms and dynasties, some great, as we have seen. All these rose and fell as they did when Europe was engaged in hundreds of years of war, savagery and brutality. They flowered and decayed. Waves of migrants, conquerors, peacemakers, swept across Africa century after century. The old empires were fluid, organic, explosive – one of the great engines of African change.

The trappings of independent statehood were introduced very late in the day, and sometimes not at all. Today the African state remains largely bifurcated and is vulnerable to a personalized infrastructure of delivery of power in exchange for the unquestioned loyalty of its subjects and ethnic clients.

In 1986, the noted Kenyan scholar, Ali Mazrui wrote that the African state, since independence, "has been subject to two competing pressures: the push towards the militarization of politics and the pull towards the privatization of the state; and the competition between capitalist greed and the quest for naked political power." Even while grievances against the state would remain legitimate, the state itself is also under siege by a new sophisticated form of global capitalism. Market economies driven by private enterprise, the protective trade blocs of Western-style democracy, all dominated by a single global power infrastructure, crush the local scene with impunity. Hence the African state, under international siege, cannot then turn to its own people in order to be rescued from global tyranny. Instead the state is under double jeopardy from both ends: the international sphere and from the local polity, which is deeply disenfranchised by the global forces.

"It was no coincidence that the debate about Africa's 'second liberation' took place once the major powers no longer needed to compete for Africa's international support in the Cold War. The East-West conflict had provided the first generation of post-colonial African leaders with their means of survival. In the early 1990s, domestic support became more important than foreign patrons for the first time since independence. African leaders had to confront the inherent weaknesses of their regimes and consider sharing power with others. The early 1990s were an uncomfortable time for Africa's rulers and their clients, for all this happened at a time of deep structural economic crisis. The driving force behind Africa's second experiment with democracy came both from ideological conviction and the growing impatience of an ever-bolder public consciousness, and from the related matter of the continent's prevailing economic crisis," Masrui wrote in *The Privatization of Security in War-Torn African Societies*.

On the other hand, the new technologies facilitating the rapid movement and sharing of information have created a new climate in which public dissent against tyranny has led to alternative forms of solidarity beyond the state, and even, global manipulation. And here new seeds of hope are being planted in the continent. From the use of fax machines in the late eighties to the Internet revolution in Africa in the nineties and beyond, tools of information-gathering have become part of political organizing that elude state censorship systems. The free flow of information has continued unabated despite the security apparatus and diminished the capacity of the state to control and manipulate public opinion.

The growth of a fervent urban-based civil society has been nourished by the aspirations of middle class values in many countries. The social sphere is collective action that is voluntary rather than compulsory and persuasive rather than coercive. It provides a basis for criticizing the excesses of both the state and the market – a realm in which neither direct state power and compulsions nor considerations of efficiency are dominant. Non-state civil associations are now becoming generally accepted components of civil society. Religious institutions are also included among these, especially where the church is divided from the state.

The role of the "accompanying" church

Only the church ecumenically has had the capacity to mobilize the community and initiate dialogue on areas of possible conflict. Following on from the visions of her predecessor, the late Aaron Tolen of Cameroon who demanded that the WCC "begin to look at Africa with new eyes", and the outspoken courage of the late Kenyan Anglican Bishop Henry Okullu of Maseno South diocese who challenged churches to radically change, Agnes Abuom, the Kenyan Anglican who is Africa's current WCC president, says: "The church is the only solid organizational structure outside government since the colonial era. During this period of social transformation it is active in peace-making and advocacy for good governance, health and education but it is weak on economics and gender. Economics is too technical and there are not nearly enough women in decision-making."

Abuom says the WCC "is committed to accompanying the churches and the ecumenical movement in Africa through a process in which conscientization becomes part of collective reflection that will strengthen the church as the effective instrument of radical social transformation." Speaking in Kenya during an official visit by WCC to AACC, in April, 2004, Dr Abuom said the ecumenical movement must be transformed into "an organic space of reflection and dialogue that serves to enlighten leaders, including policy-makers." She reminded the church leaders that their organizations must "reclaim" their place as a "sanctuary of unity not just for churches but also civil society and other instruments of governance which include the nation-state in Africa."

She referred to the Programme to Combat Racism in southern Africa set up by the WCC in the late 1960s which accompanied the liberation movements and the anti-apartheid struggle in South Africa until that white supremacist ideology and its horrendous attempts at decades of social engineering was overthrown peacefully in 1994.

In her address to the Nairobi meeting, Abuom described the faith-based Ufungamano Initiative as "a shelter for forces of change under the auspices of the ecumenical movement in Kenya." The Ufungamano Initiative consists of more than 52 religious and secular organizations formed in 1999 at Ufungamano House with the aim of reviving an earlier unsuccessful constitutional process in Kenya. It has been described as the most high-profile and widespread attempt to right the country's constitution from the grassroots level.

"The reason why the religious community was entrusted with this is because people still have trust in religious institutions in Kenya," she said, adding that this multi-faith partnership – particularly between the Christians and Muslims – is the first of its kind in Kenya's history. And that is what made the Ufungamano Initiative especially vulnerable. Violence used by some political opponents to a new constitution was a direct attempt to start a religious war by turning Christians and Muslims against one another, according to Ufungamano leaders in a joint statement and press conference by representatives from religious bodies such as the Kenya Roman Catholic Episcopal Conference (KEC), the National Council of Churches of Kenya (NCCK), and the Supreme Council of Kenya Muslims.

"We believe that the churches and the mosques have a big role to play in correcting the evils and wrongs that we are seeing in society today."

Abuom told the WCC and AACC leaders that the common challenge in the ecumenical movement today is "to develop alternative methods and methodologies for a comprehensive understanding of the prevailing conditions that lead to conflicts on the continent."

Poverty and disease in most parts of Africa mean that struggles for the well-being of the poor and the weak must be at the top of the agenda for ecumenical accompaniment in Africa. But the WCC president challenged the churches above all to develop a capacity for "truth-telling" as essential to the healing of memories, asserting that truth was the only way to "facilitate an honest and confident approach to healing and forgiveness".

"Reconciliation is based on forgiveness, and forgiveness is based on confession. We at the WCC do not believe in cheap forgiveness and reconciliation. The truth must be told and accepted and then, and only then, memory shall be respected," she said. Abuom was referring to the tensions which had to be dealt with following the end of apartheid in 1994 in South Africa, the genocide in Rwanda the same year, the Sudan peace-making and other crises in Africa in which the churches have accompanied efforts to restore harmony. "We must begin with a process of facing the truth of the events as they took place. And there is no place other than the church where this process can begin and come to fruition."

The pastoral visit by the most senior officers of the WCC which continued on to Rwanda for the memorial of the tenth anniversary of the genocide was, Abuom said, "an affirmation that the whole ecumenical family not only walks with Africa but also learns how God continues to do wonderful things among her people."

The churches together with the people have begun to enter a new decisive and historical stage in the renewed struggle for freedom and human dignity. It is increasingly the role of ecumenical accompaniment in the African reality to be involved in building democratic institutions beyond the sphere of electoral politics. Peace-building activities are also being made part of the ecumenical discourse. Skills of dialogue and negotiation, which were part and parcel of the institution of social wisdom, are being used by the churches to engage women and men in a painstaking exercise. The art of consensus-building has become a dignifying act of community-building. It is also the integral process by which communities and people's movements begin to internalize the values of holistic participation.

Interfaith dialogue and civil society

Relations between Christians and Muslims in Africa are more often than not painted by the mass media as distant, mistrustful and violent – a history of religious clashes. Politicians are not above fomenting trouble by stressing differences for their own ends – but, as in the example of Ufungamana, the contrary often prevails and a history of interfaith dialogue in Africa goes back many years.

The Project for Christian-Muslim Relations in Africa (PROCMURA) was established by the churches in Africa with support from partners in Europe and North America as early as the 1950s. Its origins link into the political and religious climate in those heady days when leaders of African nationalist movements in their agitation for independence advocated the need for constructive relationships and cooperation across the diverse linguistic, ethnic, religious and cultural frontiers.

On the religious front, African churches were considering how they would become self-governing, self-supporting, and self-propagating once independence was attained. It was in the area of self-propagating that the seed of PROCMURA was sown. The churches were conscious that in post-colonial Africa, nation-states would evolve and nationals of a particular country would be made up of Christians and Muslims among others. They therefore advocated the need to:

- develop a programme for constructive Christian-Muslim engagement as co-citizens in the emerging African independent states; and
- evolve principles of faithful and responsible Christian witness that would respect the spirit of good neighbourliness

A series of consultations with churches and mission bodies in Africa, Europe and North America led to the establishment of the Islam in Africa Project (IAP) in 1959. In 1987, the name was changed to its current PROCMURA to make it clear that the project was aimed at fostering constructive relations with Muslims and that it is a Christian project. The project currently works in 18 countries in Africa.

When the people gathered together under a tree and convened a "palaver" or an "indaba" or a "town meeting" largely to address an issue or issues integral to the life of the community, every voice could be heard. In this communal jurisprudence the process of legislating the outcome of the people's choice is because everyone irrespective of gender or social status must be included.

The churches realize that the moral duty of democracy transcends every notion of competitive power politics, for even in times of dispute and retribution the people still have to live together and share the resources of the community. And in times of conflict, democracy can be a tool of peace-making. Even justice can be overwhelmed by the fact that there is no future without forgiveness and no forgiveness without truth, says Archbishop Desmond Tutu, former head of the Church of the Province of South Africa and former president of the AACC (1987-97). The WCC and the churches in Africa struggle to accompany one another in this journey.

The raison d'être for the African churches' engagement in the democratic project within the civic public realm is not only grounded on moral and theological imperatives but also on the distinctive ecumenical claim of the church as the household of God amid the pilgrimage of creation. All human institutions and peoples of good will are welcome to be part of the ecumenical journey of hope for the whole creation. The churches, through the NCCs and regional fellowships in Africa, have provided shelter to civil society institutions facing hostility from the state.

New theological insights and methods of understanding the complexities of global and local political arrangements are increasingly becoming essential. In the absence of elections there is on-going moral formation of the youth especially on the values of responsible citizenship. The ecumenical movement in Africa provides that environment and space for sustained social inquiry on the meaning and functions of good citizenship upon which the moral foundations of good governance rest. And finally, peace-building initiatives must translate into moral communities of people living in peace with one another towards the new ecology of life.

Most of the countries in which ecumenical social responsibility became the guiding paradigm after the Harare assembly of the WCC in 1998 were either going through democratic transition or were on the verge of political and social upheaval. Involvement in civic education expanded beyond mere response to specific events in the electoral process. Democracy was not just an episode but an ongoing process that encompassed all spheres of human life.

The NCCs in Africa have accompanied the work of advocacy groups within civil society, in some cases dating as far back as pre-independence days, in promoting and supporting democratic change in Africa. A look at some of their activities is revealing:

- **The Council of Christian Churches in Angola** has been involved in activities relating to democratic change since 1985. The council perceives its role as historical in shaping the destiny of the nation whose 27-year long civil war (1975-2002) left 1.5 million dead and another 4 million displaced before peace slowly came about in 2002. The council knows how the population of 11 million needs to be nourished by the values of good governance and democracy. However, first poverty must be eradicated in a potentially wealthy nation where today 70 percent of its people live below the poverty line on less than a dollar a day. Although endowed with many rich resources of oil, diamonds and fertile land, Angola's economy is badly skewed. Its infrastructure outside the capital is destroyed. Human rights advocacy and peace-building initiatives occupy much of the civic mission of the council. The Angolan churches, including the council and the dominant Roman Catholic Church, organized campaigns for peace between the warring factions in the civil war to try to avert further escalation of conflict. In 2003 the then WCC general secretary, Konrad Raiser, led a delegation of accompaniment and solidarity to the struggling country and its churches. The prestigious business magazine, *The Economist* (2000, p. 42) conceded that the "Angolan churches have a larger support base than any other organization in the country".

- **The Malawi Council of Churches** allowed its offices to become a safe space for political pressure groups since 1990 when it supported the Roman Catholic Bishops Conference pastoral letter critical of the oppressive regime of the late Life President Hastings Kamuzu Banda, along with the Muslim sheikhs. Successful political transition from a one-party dictatorship to multi-party democracy has largely defined the activities of the council which include civic education around good governance, anti-corruption and reforms in the public sector and election monitoring. The MCC has asked what sort of governance is required for a people made in the image of God? What is the theological basis for political engagement? How does all this fit in the mission of Jesus of providing abundant life? Malawi has now held three successive democratic elections since 1994 but its 12 million people are among the poorest in Africa, facing recurring drought due to human-made climate change, HIV and AIDS and a massive deficit in food reserves. The council and the other religious faiths work tirelessly to try and help meet the needs of its members but poverty and disease are rampant.

- **The Christian Council of Mozambique's** involvement in democratic changes in its southern African country starts as far back as 1983 when it encouraged the then one-party government to engage in conversations with the South African apartheid regime that supported the destabilizing and violent RENAMO rebels. The CCM initiated and sustained dialogue between the warring factions during the long civil war (1975-92) by: establishing contacts with South Africa to cease support for RENAMO and persuading its leadership to begin dialogue with the Mozambican government; engaging in massive civic education to prepare citizens for peace and democracy; and supporting the negotiations leading to the 1990 cease-fire implementation through the Rome Peace Accords, which led to the first general elections. The talks were at first informally facilitated by the Roman Catholic lay movement, Sant' Egidio, which led to formal resolution of the civil war. The council later initiated a process of disarmament which, since 1995 has collected and destroyed more than 260,000 weapons. In 2004, a delicate transition of power occurred when President Joachim Chissano stepped down. The churches helped prepare the transition. While Mozambique, once the poorest country in the world, has made some rapid strides forward economically, the living standards of most of the 20 million people living outside the capital, Maputo, are still extremely poor, requiring the churches to try and influence the badly skewed economy and support the poor.

- **The Council of Churches in Sierra Leone** (CCSL), first established in 1924, began a new programme in 1996 to conduct civic and voter education to prepare for elections that same year, after years of coups and civil war since 1991 had ravaged the country, with "blood" diamonds at the centre of much of the conflict. Tens of thousands of people were killed and maimed and two million of a six million population displaced. The churches faced a massive challenge to bring about reconciliation after the elections of 1996 were held. But the peace broke down until British forces under UN command brought about a ceasefire and ultimately democratic elections to a ravaged country in 2002. The council has been preoccupied with establishing a transition from war to peace and creating understanding among religious leaders and religious communities to remain impartial in politics. The CCSL's credibility enabled it to come face to face with the government on national socio-economic and political issues. The ecumenical movement, working within movements towards democratization and good governance based on moral principals, became a guarantor in conflict management and peace-building.

- **The Christian Council of Zambia (CCZ)**, working with other civil society organizations, became part of a reform movement for pluralism in the 1990s when the government finally held a Constituent Assembly which, in 1991, led to the first of three consecutive multi-party elections to date. Accompanying dialogue and providing moral direction has always been the council's major area of intervention. The council has been engaged in various projects for nearly 21 years on matters of socio-economic and political life. In Zambia it goes without saying that the church should and must continue its prophetic voice and say no to injustice in its various forms. The churches' skills of non-violence helped prevent the second president of the republic from manipulating the constitution in order to seek re-election for an unconstitutional third term. With 11 million people, Zambia's churches have long worked ecumenically and regionally as voices for liberation and democratization, a difficult task as corruption has hampered improving living standards for the people.

- The reason for the formation of the Rhodesian Council of Churches in 1964 (in then white supremacist Rhodesia) was linked to the struggles for liberation. Some churches supported quite openly the Second Chimurenga, as it was known; others were split along racial lines, but the council was ecumenical. In 1980 it formally became the **Zimbabwe Council of Churches** (ZCC) when Zimbabwe attained independence. Samuel Kobia, current WCC general secretary, was given the job of reorganizing the council in 1980-81 to prepare the newly-named ZCC for the challenges in a newly liberated country. Specific areas of engagement today are: human rights awareness and advocacy; mediation during and after the liberation struggle; civic education; voter education and election monitoring; constitutional reform; and economic justice, linking domestic and global policy issues. In recent years, as the political leadership of Zimbabwe has become more autocratic, failed land reforms have led to economic failure and elections which WCC/AACC/ZCC monitors said in 2002 were not free and fair. Groups of Christians inside and outside the ZCC have upheld the Christian stance on human rights and good government, led principally by a loose coalition of some Roman Catholic, Anglican and Evangelical church leaders. Here again, wherever possible, WCC and AACC have accompanied the churches of Zimbabwe as they struggle to be faithful amidst difficult times.

- **The National Council of Churches of Kenya** (NCCK) for more than 60 years has had intensive socio-political and economic involvement as a mirror through which church and society can ethically evaluate themselves and the state. Civic education programmes, for example, endeavoured to promote a well-informed, spirited, and responsible citizenry but also sought to create corridors of dialogue with the state, among aggrieved political parties, between private and public sectors, and finally among communities living in conflict. NCCK offered choices for self-governance in order to promote a moral sense of self-worth with dignity among the citizens as a way of complementing and filling the void where the state had become morally dysfunctional. Some of the most articulate criticism of former President Daniel arap Moi came from Anglican and Roman Catholic bishops as well as Presbyterian and Methodist leaders and the leadership of the NCCK. The council continues in this mode and was deeply involved in the Constitutional debate of 2004 and 2005 through the interfaith Ufungamano Initiative.

- Following the death in 2004 of the President of Togo, the dictator, General Gnassingbe Eyadema, and the unconstitutional imposition of his son, Faure Eyadema, by the army, as successor, the ecumenical movement welcomed the call by the African Union for: "respect for the nation's constitution in the provision of interim leadership for Togo, that will lead to the democratic election of a president of Togo in accordance with the constitution". The AACC on behalf of the churches in Africa and in solidarity with the people of Togo affirmed the call for a return to constitutional law in the country. Both AACC and WCC expressed the need for vigilance and resilience of the people and the accompaniment of the churches in the region. Subsequently elections were held in April 2005 amid allegations of fraud and violence which affirmed Faure Eyadema as president who has promised "transparent" elections "soon".

The self-understanding of the church as having its origins in God and that all human beings are created in the image and likeness of the creator makes its place in civil society distinctive. The ecumenical movement, while in critical solidarity with the poor and the oppressed, has always through its institutions maintained a critical distance from partisan politics. This is a policy position derived from a common theological vision shared by most NCCs in Africa.

NCCs and democratization

The role of the church in the process of democratization is a sign of its serious presence in Africa. In a number of countries, churches have participated as independent observers of free elections. During the first multi-racial elections in South Africa in April 1994, the South African Council of Churches (SACC) participated in the Ecumenical Monitoring Programme on South Africa (EMPSA) as election-observers.

The NCCK and the SACC have recently paid attention to questions on Christian ethics in African politics with some success. The churches are aware of their role in the society and wanted to contribute towards creating conditions under which people would utilize their freedom in a responsible manner and strive to live in dignity. As institutions, the churches in South Africa (the SACC and the South Africa Catholic Bishops Conference) have remained in critical solidarity with the oppressed and suffering people.

From the time Africa was swept by a wave of western-style multi-party elections in February 1990, which began with the national conference in Benin, the independence and multi-party elections in Namibia, the release of Nelson Mandela and the unbanning of the African National Congress (ANC) and other liberation movements and the Malawi, Mozambique, and Zambia multi-party elections, the number of democratic regimes has risen sharply. Botswana has had multi-party elections since independence, as has Senegal. Kenya, although sometimes fractured and violent, has been multi-party since 1992 and Tanzania since 1995.

The immediate constituency of the NCCs in Africa are the churches themselves who can make a unique contribution to the democratic transition; some have mediated and complemented this process through their member churches. Their duty is derived from the very nature and essence of what it means to be church. The NCCs, while providing the nexus for the local and national experience of the oikoumene and koinonia, bring the good news of change in society by facilitating what the churches may not achieve on their own.

Devolution of power to the geographic regions only addresses the territorial dimension of group identity and may increase the stakes of groups to be isolated from the state or to seek new alliances outside the nation-state. It is vital that institutions within civil society and the churches in Africa put in place early warning systems that will safeguard the society and equip the stakeholders for rapid response. The church must remain vigilant and awaken the society to focus on the present situation of poverty as the sure basis for resurgence of endless violence in the streets and the elite corridors of power. Neutrality in mediation as the consequence of preventive diplomacy is critical indeed.

Peace-making cannot be separated from reconstruction, rehabilitation and reconciliation. One of the critical issues in order to find long-term solutions to recurring conflicts in the continent is the form and structures of governance and how these relate to the realities of life in the continent. The constitutional form of the state and how power is organized around delivery of services to the people is crucial for sustainable peace. Each country must democratically develop its own forms of constitutional government with mechanisms of enforcing, protecting and promoting the rule of law.

7. Renewing African Ecumenism

Africa today is still among the most studied and least understood regions of the world. Many of those investigating the African reality are located in university faculties, specialized institutes, study centres, think tanks and other policy-oriented institutions in the West. All the turmoil of the last few decades confirms that neither imperialism nor colonialism was a simple act of accumulation or acquisition but related historical events in which the memory and identity of a continent's people was maimed and mutilated. Yet, as the shrine of human origin, the place where humans first stood upright, Africa bears the historical burden of ancestry that has a deep and most profound implication in the ecumenical motif of unity within the household of God.

Samuel Kobia referred to this heavy responsibility during his first official visit as WCC general secretary to his home country, Kenya, in 2004: "As the birthplace of the human race, the ultimate destiny of Africa ought to be reconfigured around engagement with contemporary global realities. By about 20,000 years ago the transition to Late Stone Age industries was virtually complete all over Africa. And then there was Axum, which had become a city state by the first century AD, and had its first encounter with Christianity in the fourth century. I conclude that Africa is not only our primordial home but essentially the spiritual home of Christianity. It is now generally accepted that by 2040 the centre of Christianity will have shifted to Africa. The question we have to ask is what kind of Christianity it is going to be. And what kind of moral responsibility will Africa bear towards the rest of Christendom and the world by virtue of being the centre of Christianity?"

As the mother continent, Africa is intrinsic to the cultural and social memory contained within the whole ecumenical creation in the pilgrimage of time. In the context of encounter between churches and spiritual movements, the ecumenical movement embraces this pilgrimage of hope. The World Council of Churches, through its work of accompaniment with the churches in Africa, endeavours to be part of this new reality of prophetic engagement of the churches and the peoples of Africa.

Kobia continued his 2004 lecture at St Paul's College, Limuru, Kenya with a powerful challenge to the churches and their continent, telling Africans to cease "agonizing and apologizing... or even reminding the world about your need to be affirmed through the history of those who enslaved you and oppressed you by the very cruelty of their own ideology and institutions!"

The WCC's sixth general secretary, the first from Africa, predicted a future when "Africans in the diaspora will accompany us... and together we will affirm that Africa, as the primordial home of humanity, will rise to the occasion and take leadership in the struggle to create a new world in which all will live as good neighbours to each other. With confidence, with intellectual and theological competence, we shall work hand in hand with one another to prepare for the new dawn of the kingdom of God upon the people of Africa."

The themes of AACC

Authenticity and relevance have always been concerns for Christians of Africa but much more so since the Western missions became churches. For the AACC, this was not new: its inaugural assembly at Kampala in 1963 reported in drumbeats, its theme "Freedom and Unity in Christ". The second assembly at Abidjan in 1969 had sent out the same signals but these emphases were seen by some Christians, both African and non-African, as extra-ecclesial and therefore not the proper business of the AACC. The third assembly at Lusaka in 1974 signalled the movement from theological conservatism to a fresh empowering gospel and criticized rigid and timid church structures inadequate to the challenges of the continent. The watchword at Lusaka was "The Struggle Continues" (*A luta continua*" from its Portuguese liberation movement origins in Angola, Mozambique and the West African colonies).

The themes of AACC assemblies continued to reflect the concerns of ecumenism and those of many churches as well as the majority of humanity in Africa: fourth assembly, Nairobi 1981, "Follow Me... Feed My Lambs", expressing faith and hope that God would hasten the liberation of Africa (John 21: 15-19); fifth assembly, Lomé 1987, "You Shall Be My Witness" (Acts 1:8); sixth assembly, Harare 1992, "Abundant Life in Jesus Christ", held in the context of deep crisis on the African continent; seventh assembly at Addis Ababa in 1997, "Troubled but not destroyed" (2 Cor. 4:8-9) when the AACC itself was in dire straits; and the eighth assembly, Yaoundé, 2003 "Come, let us rebuild" (Neh. 2:17-18).

These themes, messages to the churches, other ecumenical events and deliberative sessions are reflected in the efforts of other ecumenical bodies. The best-known is the radical anti-apartheid statement of the South African Council of Churches (SACC) called *The Kairos Document* of 1985. It arose out of the struggle to discover how to be Christians in what the SACC called a situation of death. The "moment of truth" (*kairos*) is defined as "the moment of grace and opportunity, the favourable time in which God issues a challenge to decisive action". Since that historic date in which the churches criticized "state theology" which justified theologically the status quo and called for "prophetic theology" as an alternative, *Kairos* documents have been emulated worldwide but rarely again – and certainly not often enough – among ecumenical families in Africa.

This powerful statement is still regarded as a theological watershed, which called for Christians to take action against any repressive or illegitimate state, in this case, the apartheid state of South Africa, which it described as having "no moral legitimacy" and which had become "an enemy of the common good". For the church to be the church, it must stand "unequivocally and consistently with the poor and the oppressed". The document also critiques "church theology", which in only "a limited, guarded and cautious way… is critical of apartheid". Instead the document promotes biblical teaching on suffering and oppression in relation to a social analysis of the structures of oppression in South Africa. But not all churches in South Africa were prepared to accept this "Challenge to the Churches" (the subtitle of the Kairos document).

Shortly before the WCC's eighth assembly in Harare in 1998, a group of ecumenical Zimbabwean Christians published a *Zimbabwean Kairos Document*, denouncing "poverty, ill-health, bad governance, corruption, fear and hopelessness" in their country. The document was produced by Ecumenical Support Services (ESS) using a similar methodology as the South African document, arguing that the Zimbabwe nation "had been plunged into a political, economic and, above all, moral crisis shaking its very foundation". It particularly criticized the ruling ZANU PF party of President Robert Mugabe (having been in absolute power at the time of the assembly for all 18 years of the country's independent existence) claiming: "Despite our hopes and expectations [at independence and the end of white minority rule] in 1980, today we find new black political and economic elites within the same structures". The Zimbabwe churches – this statement aimed directly at the ZCC – were also criticized, since "while some have constantly challenged injustice, both before and after independence, many have failed to educate their members about abuses of power by authorities".

During the WCC assembly itself, the plenary session on Africa returned to *"ubuntu* and the African *kairos"*. *Ubuntu* refers to an African sense of belonging and sharing and finding identity. The plenary ended with a liturgical act of "commitment to a journey of hope" by all Africans "from the continent and the diaspora" to work for a better Africa, saying "never again" to many forms of suffering and humiliation that the continent's people have known, and joining in an act of "covenant with God". The assembly was called to accompany the African churches on their journey of hope and the delegates sang *Nkosi Sikilel'i Afrika* (God Bless Africa) as a symbol of mutual ecumenical solidarity.

The (South African) Kairos Document

There can be no doubt that our Christian faith commits us to work for true reconciliation and genuine peace. But as so many people, including Christians, have pointed out, there can be no true reconciliation and no genuine peace without justice. Any form of peace or reconciliation that allows the sin of injustice and oppression to continue is a false peace and counterfeit reconciliation. This kind of "reconciliation" has nothing whatsoever to do with the Christian faith.

Church theology is not always clear on this matter and many Christians have been led to believe that what we need in South Africa is not justice but reconciliation and peace. The argument goes something like this: "We must be fair. We must listen to both sides of the story. If the two sides can only meet to talk and negotiate they will sort out their differences and misunderstandings, and the conflict will be resolved." On the face of it this may sound very Christian. But is it?

The fallacy here is that "reconciliation" has been made into an absolute principle that must be applied in all cases of conflict or dissension. But not all cases of conflict are the same. We can imagine a quarrel between two people or two groups whose differences are based upon misunderstandings. In such cases it would be the two sides. But there are other conflicts in which one side is right and the other wrong. There are conflicts where one side is a fully armed and a violent oppressor while the other side is defenceless and oppressed.

There are conflicts that can only be described as the struggle between justice and injustice, good and evil, God and the devil. To speak of reconciling these two is not only a mistaken application of the Christian idea of reconciliation, it is a total betrayal of all that Christian faith has ever meant. Nowhere in the Bible, or in Christian tradition, has it ever been suggested that we ought to try to reconcile good and evil.

We are supposed to be against injustice, oppression and sin – not come to terms with it. We are supposed to oppose, confront, and reject the devil and not try to sup with the devil. In the situation of South Africa it would have been totally un-Christian to plead for reconciliation and peace before the apartheid injustices had been removed.

There is nothing that a tortured world wants more than true reconciliation – the peace that God gives and not the peace the world gives (John 14:27). The peace that God wants is based upon justice, peace and love. The peace that the world offers is a unity that compromises the truth, covers injustice and oppression, and is motivated by selfishness. At this stage, like Jesus, we must expose this false peace, confront our oppressors, and be prepared for the dissension that will follow. As Christians we must say with Jesus: "Do you suppose that I am here to bring peace on earth. No, I tell you, but rather division." (Luke 12:51). There can be no real peace without justice and repentance.

AACC Strategic Renewal

The AACC is increasingly a key strategic instrument for rallying together the church and the community in Africa, committed to unity, healing and restoration with the justice and repentance that the *Kairos Document* calls out for. The ultimate ecumenical vision must be translated to all spheres of life in the continent. The AACC is currently undergoing a number of structural reforms, strategic and operational changes which can be traced back to policy shifts of the general assembly in Yaoundé, Cameroon, November 22-27, 2003. This involved moving the organization strategically so it could play its part in the reconfiguration of the ecumenical movement.

Early the next year, in January 2004, a wide representation of NCCs, sub-regional fellowships, AACC, theological institutions, church publishing houses, laity, peace and reconciliation groups and the WCC met in Nairobi to hammer out a Common Statement of Purpose and Action for the next three years, accompanied by WCC on this common journey. According to Dr André Karamaga, executive secretary of the WCC Africa Office, it was to be a process of revitalization for the churches in the new Africa. This process Karamaga sees as a model for any ecumenical organization in crisis.

As the Ecumenical Focus on Africa (EFA) mandated by the Harare assembly in 1998 moved into the twenty-first century, the viability of the AACC – and most other regional conferences of churches – was in serious question, much as was the OAU which went on to revitalize itself as the African Union. The OAU had been formed just a month before the AACC in 1963 and they were sometimes seen as twins. How could there be a new Africa if the regional church body was not viable? Were the sub-regional fellowships in competition with AACC? What steps could the WCC take to accompany AACC in its revitalization process while continuing to respect its autonomy and identity? What were the best steps of accompaniment?

The AACC was in serious difficulties both financially and organizationally. The elected leaders decided the organization needed time to reflect on its future plans, identify and prepare for new staff leadership and get ready for Cameroon in 2003. They did not want to be rushed into taking hasty decisions and needed time and space to reconfigure. As an act of specific accompaniment, the WCC seconded one of its most senior African staff, Melaku Kifle, to AACC for a year to act as interim general secretary so a transitional period could prepare for new elections and the assembly. Kifle was able to stabilize the situation, prepare for the Yaoundé assembly and prepare the organization and staff for the arrival of a new general secretary. This was true accompaniment. The eighth general assembly was held in Cameroon, where critical decisions were made; Bishop Mvume Dandala of South Africa was elected general secretary and the space was created to develop a common purpose and action.

Karamaga says that in terms of vision, WCC and AACC "walked hand-in-hand" to translate their various covenants into action. Accompaniment did not stop when the crisis ended and WCC was with the new structure of the AACC as it moved to shape itself to be effective and viable in the reality of the new Africa.

A transitional advisory team was appointed to accompany the general secretary in implementing a new vision and mandate of the ecumenical instrument in Africa. There is a yearning to re-vision the memory and calling of AACC which requires a new form and expression of what it means to be African and ecumenical in today's world.

The Cameroon assembly had committed itself to internal reforms through a panel of 12 "disciples", comprising representatives from the main ecumenical agencies in Africa. The main focus of the panel is the renewal of the movement in Africa through a consultative process by the AACC, NCCs, and sub-regional fellowships, accompanied by the WCC.

The challenge was to envision and manage various ecumenical expressions of faith in order to facilitate good stewardship of resources and become more efficient in the delivery of services to the churches in the continent. The outcome of these consultations led to the identification of members of the panel of 12, guided by management experts, to look into consolidating the structures of ecumenical institutions in the continent. Equipped with new commitment, AACC is destined to become part of the self-renewal in the twenty-first century, as the ecumenical movement prepares, together with the churches of the world, for the shift of the centre of Christianity to Africa.

Today, more than ever before, Africa is experiencing a need for institutions with a sustainable and predictable future and the AACC is no exception.

The AACC continues to be part of the cutting edge discourse on issues pertaining to the impact of globalization in the South. In order to equip the churches for their prophetic ministry in society, the AACC engages in an ongoing process of discernment of the political and economic forces operating in Africa to develop a coherent understanding of the contemporary trends in the world that affect the continent. This should provide the framework of engagement in all spheres of public life. All initiatives on public issues would be informed by the prophetic vision of the church as the conscience of society. The AACC will make every effort to become the hub of inspiration, the place of synergy and organic space for reflective dialogue among leaders and policy makers on the ecumenical life and prophetic mandate of the churches in Africa.

There is continuous policy review forecast on the events in the continent in order to equip the churches to speak with one voice. Pastoral visits by the general secretary and staff of AACC in collaboration with, and accompanied by, the WCC continue.

An example of this has been the on-going crisis in Zimbabwe which was forcibly brought to the attention of the ecumenical community at the 1998 WCC assembly in Harare with the presentation of the *Zimbabwe Kairos Document.* Not long after the assembly delegates had returned home, President Mugabe launched a controversial land reform programme which, however long overdue, was badly implemented and contributed to an economic and political crisis which has steadily worsened until by 2005, Zimbabwe, once the self-sufficient breadbasket of southern Africa, was on the brink of bankruptcy and chaos; it requires massive amounts of food aid; its economy is in tatters and a series of elections (both presidential and parliamentary) have been marred by vote-rigging and intimidation. Human rights abuses and corruption are widespread.

Within this difficult situation, however, some churches and their leaders have borne courageous witness to the gospel values of justice, peace and reconciliation and have found support within the ecumenical movement and the WCC.

In 2004, the ZCC convened a retreat for heads of Zimbabwean churches at the resort centre of Lake Karibe and were accompanied by AACC and WCC representatives.

The new general secretary of AACC, Bishop Mvume Dandala, pleaded with officials of the Zimbabwean Council of Churches to be faithful to their mandate as the conscience of their nation. He said that, as church, they did not derive their mandate from the nation state but from God who called them into service for the sake of the good news. The struggle to heal wounded memories and the traumatized spirits of the landless and those whose land was confiscated without compensation brought the following reflections from the AACC:

In rebuilding trust through confession, forgiveness and honest reflection on the entire history that gave rise to the problems facing Zimbabwe and as their ecumenical sojourners the AACC shall:

- accept the commitment to a fair and just redistribution of land in Zimbabwe, as desired for all of Africa. We urge you to clarify for yourselves and for the benefit of the continent the principle that should enable land to be the bedrock of an equitable economy in Zimbabwe. This will form the basis for our visioning together not only for Zimbabwe but for Africa as well;

- accept with humility your sadness at the circumstances that have surrounded recent land reclamation in Zimbabwe. We urge you humbly, to be deliberate in truth, your focus not to offend what amounted to violations of human rights. Please consider ways by which this process of land restoration to the people will be marked by honour, justice and dignity. The ecumenical family is ready to think with you on these as far as possible;

- it is only the church that can assist Zimbabwe to find the higher ground of common nationhood, as it lifts the people above the politics of partisanship to the plane of values that should inform everybody, including politicians; and

- we pray that you will be given wisdom and strength to de-racialize the future of a country that has been marked by a colonial legacy of racial bigotry. As church, we believe you have the tools more than anybody else in Zimbabwe to come to the moral rescue of the people of Zimbabwe so that they may rise above the politics of partisanship.

The WCC also publicly and officially condemned the violent displacement and destruction of homes and stands of poor urban dwellers by the Zimbabwean army and police in mid-2005 and pledged its solidarity with the churches and people of Zimbabwe. The WCC expressed its deep sadness at the events that led to more than 700,000 poor urban families being made homeless and deprived of their places of business during Operation Murambatsvina (Operation Clean Up Rubbish). It said the government had committed an act of cruelty when homes and market stands were destroyed by government decree which violated the most basic principles of human decency and dignity.

The operation was carried out during the winter months and at a time when the rural areas were particularly unable to absorb those expelled from the urban areas because of the effects of drought and Zimbabwe's chaotic land reform programme. The government embarked on this urban cleansing with orders from the highest level at a time when the Zimbabwe economy was near collapse, suffering from high unemployment and inflation, increasing poverty, acute food shortages and high levels of HIV and AIDS.

The WCC said "it is difficult to ascertain why the government has embarked on this inhuman campaign. To carry out such acts of cruelty with impunity against its own people shows clearly that the government is losing the moral and ethical ground for leadership, healing and reconciliation."

The churches were shocked that the government would not allow churches and civil society groups to assist the homeless, hungry, jobless people whose homes were destroyed and the local market economy, their only way to eke out a living, was dismantled and driven away.

"There is a moral, ethical and theological imperative to assist those who are suffering. The Gospel asks us to assist the poor, the vulnerable, the hungry, the homeless, and the sick. 'Truly, I say to you, as you did it to the least of these, … you did it to me' (Matthew 25:40). The Church has a commitment to provide support and assistance.

"WCC affirms and supports the messages of the Zimbabwe Council of Churches (ZCC) and the Zimbabwe Catholic Bishops' Conference (ZCBC), which underscore the dire nature of the situation."

As the ZCC statement of 20 June 2005 notes, "The clean-up operation has resulted in untold suffering where families are left in the open air in this cold wintry weather. The misery that this operation has brought upon the affected people is unbearable. We are witnessing the total loss of livelihood for whole families for some people who were operating within the parameters of the by-laws."

The ZCBC pastoral letter of 17 June points out that: "Any claim to justify this operation... becomes totally groundless in view of the cruel and inhumane means that have been used. People have a right to shelter and that has been deliberately destroyed in this operation without much warning. While we all desire orderliness, alternative accommodation and sources of income should have been identified and provided before the demolitions and stoppage of informal trading. We condemn the gross injustice done to the poor."

Operation Murambatsvina was segregation against the working poor and denial of the long-suffering Zimbabweans' right to make a living in an ailing economy. It was seen by many analysts as an act of revenge by the ruling ZANU-PF because urban poor supported the opposition in parliamentary elections immediately preceding the mass evictions and demolitions. Said the WCC: "The church is not only called to care for the poor, but also to question the structures of injustice that lead to poverty. The churches in solidarity with one another are called to seek God among the poor, the vulnerable, the hungry, the homeless and the oppressed people of Zimbabwe.

"WCC hereby calls on the government of Zimbabwe to suspend with immediate effect Operation Murambatsvina and to urgently address the pressing needs – shelter, food, health, etc. – of the evacuees. Churches and relief organizations should also be given unrestricted access to the displaced persons."

As part of WCC's continuing accompaniment with the churches of Zimbabwe, it called on the government to initiate dialogue with the opposition, churches and civil society groups and begin the process of addressing the real needs of suffering Zimbabweans. "Zimbabwe is a divided society, and in this time of great upheaval and suffering it is crucial that peaceful ways be found to reconcile, rebuild and heal the country," the statement said.

"WCC has a long history of accompanying the people of Zimbabwe in their struggle for independence and freedom, and will continue to stand in solidarity with the people and churches in Zimbabwe."

Similarly, a joint mission from the South African Council of Churches and the South African Catholic Bishops Conference visited Zimbabwe and expressed publicly their horror at the devastation, especially in the main urban centres of Harare and Bulawayo. Upon their return to South Africa, the two organizations, working ecumenically, raised a significant amount of material aid, especially blankets, tents and food for the displaced persons. However, in an act of particular vengeance, officials at the border were ordered not to allow the urgently needed aid to enter Zimbabwe without paying import duties, further delaying help for the suffering. By the time the goods were cleared, the cold weather season had almost ended.

8. New Ecumenical Thresholds

"Helping becomes an excuse for exclusion." Sam Kabue

The words just hang there before the participants at a WCC conference on reconciliation and healing: so powerful, such simple words, coming from a man blind since childhood. They serve to introduce one the WCC's more recent additions to its programmes based in Africa. It is a centrepiece for the mission of accompaniment to disabled people in Africa and around the world. It is a plea not for help, not for healing, but for inclusion. These words were part of a paper given by Sam Kabue, coordinator of the Ecumenical Disabilities Advocacy Network (EDAN) established by the 1998 Harare assembly. EDAN was given the mandate to support the work of individuals, churches and non-church organizations concerned with issues affecting disabled people globally.

The network advocates for the inclusion and participation of persons with disabilities in all spiritual, social, economic and structural life of the church and society and to maintain and sustain an active network of people with disabilities. The disabled will focus on improving their situation by providing space for their contributions and gifts to the ecumenical movement. EDAN was adopted as a programme within the Justice, Peace and Creation team of WCC in 1999, based in Nairobi under the auspices of NCCK and AACC, where its activities are very much in solidarity with the work of the social, economic justice and women's programme.

EDAN members believe fundamentally that *all* people, with or without disabilities, are created in the image and likeness of God and are called to an inclusive community in which they are empowered to use their gifts. This is all people who are called to holiness in Christ irrespective of the physical condition of their bodies and the level of psychological participation in the struggles of life. Through the Holy Spirit, the inclusive community is called to repentance, transformation and renewal (Gen. 1:27; II Cor. 5:17).

The churches in Africa need to integrate into their theological education a curriculum for pastors on the issue of disability. Theologians and pastors must be enabled to articulate a holistic approach to the question of disabilities in the life of the church. From its formation, EDAN recognized that if a long-term impact was to be made in influencing the church to provide space for the expression of the disabled in its spiritual, social and development life, it would be necessary to put in place programmes that engage the leadership of the church at various levels.

To accentuate this, shortly after EDAN was set up, a five-day workshop was held at St Paul's United Theological College, in Limuru, Kenya, with participants from the United Theological College of the West Indies, Kingston, Jamaica; Stockholm School of Theology, Stockholm; Escola Superior de Teologia (Lutheran School of Theology) in Brazil and the Asian Theological Seminary in the Philippines. Included were representatives of the EDAN network from the Caribbean, Sweden, Korea, Latin America, Ghana and North America.

Kabue described his own deep personal disappointment after his Presbyterian church refused him ordination to the ministry because of his blindness. Instead, he has devoted his life to working on the issues of the differently-abled for more than 15 years. He said conversations on disabilities tended to be received with a lot of enthusiasm but faded away as soon as the immediate awareness was gone. It was important to maintain this awareness through establishing courses and training in work with the differently-abled within theological schools in Africa and around the world.

A West African EDAN consultation was held in Accra, Ghana in 2002 and a follow-up in September 2003. Focus of the events was on the human rights of persons with disabilities. Despite the fact that most governments in Africa had ratified the worldwide UN disabilities convention, very little awareness had been raised within the churches about their rights. Employment was another issue because companies and governments were not required to cease job discrimination against disabled people, as is the case in many countries. One of the biggest causes of disability are the many millions of landmines left unmarked in rural areas where there have been wars and violence, dating back in some cases to liberation struggle days, despite the 1997 International Landmine Ban (the Ottawa Convention) when 122 countries signed on to a law banning the use of landmines. Countries like Angola, Mozambique, Sudan, Somalia, Democratic Republic of the Congo (DRC), still have millions of uncharted mines scattered throughout their territories.

Kabue also addressed a plenary session of the WCC Conference on World Mission and Evangelism at Athens in May 2005 whose theme was healing and reconciling communities. He strongly condemned religious groups that offer "miraculous healing" and denominations that emphasize a "charity approach" towards the disabled.

"More often than not, persons with disabilities feel alienated, marginalized, embarrassed and, in some cases, offended by the treatment meted out on them by the church." Some church teachings, doctrine and theology, "have made the word 'healing' an anathema in the ears of persons with disabilities," Kabue said, warning against "commercial fixes and religious groups which offer miraculous healing in the setting of superficial acceptance and friendship."

Many churches in Africa, and a growing charismatic movement worldwide, stress faith as an integral part of returning to health, sometimes called "divine healing," organizers of the Athens meeting noted. But Kabue said "the more liberal theology of traditional organized churches ... has its share of keeping people with disabilities outside" – the "charity approach" being the most negative aspect. Few churches have procedures for initiating "the intellectually disabled into sacraments," he said. EDAN is a good example of reconfiguring the ecumenical movement so that programmes can be "owned" by the WCC, AACC and NCCs.

Following are excerpts from his paper, which created considerable debate at Athens, not all of it positive:

> The terms "healing" and "reconciling" are all so common to us especially in the ecumenical fraternity to the extent that it is assumed that they mean the same and evoke the same positive feelings to all of us. This is certainly not the case. To the people of South Africa to whom apartheid is still fresh in their memory, and to those of Sudan who are just emerging out of years of conflict and suffering, the terms will have an understanding of bringing hope and a sense of creating harmony with neighbours that were once enemies. In societies which are still hopelessly torn apart by armed conflicts and dominated by the experience of death and suffering, the terms will have no meaning and their use will be considered as a consistent reminder of the suffering.
>
> As the WCC interim statement "A Church of All and for All" rightly points out: 'No social group is ever the same, and disabled people are no exception to the rule. We come from a variety of cultures, and are thus culturally conditioned in the same manner as every person. We have experienced different kinds and levels of medical care and differing social attitudes. We have come to an acceptance of our disabilities by diverse routes. Some of us have been disabled since birth, while others have been victims of accidents or have had disabilities develop later in life. In the case of disability, it is often assumed that healing is either to eradicate the problem as if it were a contagious virus, or that it promotes virtuous suffering or a means to induce greater faith in God. If your disability is as a result of sickness or accident, the term healing comes with the yearning and hope for recovery for as long as you have not accepted that it is a new condition in your life. To those who have been disabled since

birth and have gone through the necessary processes of adjustment, healing has little to do with their disabilities until others remind them of this understanding. To them, disability and sickness are two very different things and healing applies to sickness and not to disability.

Let me make it clear at this point that there is no doubt in my mind that healing is biblical and applicable in the Christian faith. However, its understanding as it relates to persons with disabilities is made complex by differing teaching, doctrines and theology.

One might want to ask, are the healing stories today a matter of faith, reality or imagination? Most important, in this modern age of information, communications and technology, the assistive devices to enable persons with disabilities to function in the society and to take part in nearly all aspects of society's life, is it a miraculous cure or fixing of impairments in the body the central reason for presenting those who bear these impairments to God? Were this the case, then the soul which is the ultimate subject of the gospel mission, is less important than the physical body. People, irrespective of their bodily condition, need to hear and to be reached with the gospel. They need to partake in getting the gospel to others. Their impairments can neither be a cause for their remission of sin nor excuse for their failure to play their part in the extension of the kingdom.

I have mentioned differing teaching, doctrine and theology. These have at times led to serious and unhelpful paternalistic and patronizing attitudes in the church. The interpretation and belief among some churches that there is relationship between disability, sickness and sin has made them develop an attitude of pity and sympathy to those disabled or sick. To them, the presence of people with disabilities in the church is a sign that the church is unable to combat the devil that is the source of these infirmities. The response to this is endless prayers for those in this condition and when these prayers do not yield the expected result, the victim is blamed for having no faith.

The healing stories in the New Testament and especially those in the gospel had a hidden dimension that modern society should consider as it deals with disability in the modern concept of healing and reconciliation. Jesus made precedents in including the sick and the disabled as a focus of concern in his ministry. He chose to use healing to unite them with the rest of the society. Prior to his time, they were excluded, ignored and considered unclean.

There are approximately 26 different scriptures on people with such infirmities as paralysis, blindness, deafness or physical disabilities in the Gospel. There are, in accordance to the Judeo-Christian culture and practice of the day some distinct characteristics in all of them. They have no names; they are poor, unemployed, beggars or servants; they are patronized, treated with contempt, publicly rebuked and humiliated. It is from this state of affairs that Jesus declares that he came to set the captives free and to give release to the oppressed.

At the beginning of the 21st century, as was the case before the Christian era, sectors of the population who are unable to compete or to perform at the levels that society demands are, in contemporary terms, discarded. Among them, we find a high proportion of people with sensorial, motor and mental disabilities. We will find them living in any of the great cities of the world: men and women of all ages, ethnic backgrounds, colours, cultures and religions who, because they have a disability, live in abject poverty, hunger, dependence, preventable disease and maltreatment by those who are "able".

It is the role of the church in this new century to face the reality of humanity in the image of a disabled Jesus on the cross; the reality of people with disabilities who are rejected and abandoned. It is painful that the churches throughout the world have not addressed more vigorously the sufferings of marginalized, poor, blind, deaf, and physically and mentally limited people. We do not need pity, or mercy, but compassionate understanding and opportunities to develop our vocations, possibilities and abilities.

It is important to be aware that, in some parts of the world and in some churches, there has recently been a return towards over-protection and even disregard of disabled persons. In some places, evangelical groups have manipulated us. Even worse than being ignored, manipulating disabled people could become the church's new sin.

The more liberal theology of the mainline churches too has its share of keeping persons with disabilities outside. The charity approach to disability has been the most negative aspect in their address to disability concern. They are largely responsible for the growth and maintenance of a "helping" profession, which relegates persons with disabilities to a receiving end. Helping becomes an excuse for exclusion and this is characterized by separate schools, rehabilitation centres and other caring institutions. We had difficulties to get any persons with disabilities here [to Athens] because no church wanted to consider them in their delegations since they do not fall into the familiar classifications. The situation is no different in the WCC or its regional and national councils.

Eminent persons programme

Another ecumenical accomplishment on the continent is the Eminent Persons Ecumenical Programme for Africa (EPEPA) which is a joint initiative of the All Africa Conference of Churches, Church World Service and the World Council of Churches. Prominent African institutions and leaders have often called for the establishment of an eminent persons' group as an instrument for conflict resolution. EPEPA is to be instituted as a strategy for the churches to play a critical role in peace-making and peace-building in Africa.

The essence of the EPEPA is crucial in breaking new grounds for cooperation within the ecumenical movement to serve on a sustainable basis as principle architects for intervention where needed in Africa. The three ecumenical institutions have recognized the urgent need to bring the programme to fruition. The AACC would play a critical role in facilitating the process on the continent.

EPEPA is an arrangement whereby distinguished and experienced persons are identified when a situation arises requiring particular skills in diplomacy, mediation, conflict resolution and wide diplomatic experience. The team is then organized, given a clearly understood mandate and prepared for the task of peace-making, after which they are enabled to travel to trouble spots with the objective of attempting a cessation of hostilities through dialogue. One such example was the Commonwealth Eminent Persons Group that went to South Africa in 1986. It had two WCC leaders on it – Canada's Archbishop Ted Scott, former WCC central committee moderator (1975-83) and Dame Nita Barrow, of Barbados, a former WCC president (1983-91). The EPG came close to achieving its mandate until the apartheid government reneged on its commitments, launching attacks on Zambia and Zimbabwe while the eminent persons were in South Africa. They immediately withdrew in protest.

As the EPEPA is envisaged, members would talk and listen to factions in conflict or potential conflict, suggest solutions where possible, offer mediation or seek assistance from the international community.

This ecumenical initiative arises from the felt need of the churches to be able to intervene in the many current multi-dimensional conflicts facing the continent. EPEPA reflects a deep commitment to work together for life, truth, justice and peace. The proposed programme affirms the capacities of the sub-regional fellowships and the NCCs in mediating peace and reconciliation.

The Eminent Persons Ecumenical Programme for Africa was affirmed by the AACC at its assembly held in Yaoundé in 2003. There will be a tripartite coordinating committee to implement the EPEPA, co-chaired by the leaders of CWS, WCC and the AACC. About 12 persons will be chosen on the basis of expertise and experience. CWS would nominate three persons including a fundraiser. AACC and WCC each will nominate four persons. The EPEPA shall be the voice of the church in Africa speaking to such bodies as the African Union (AU), the United Nations, and the European Union, among others.

Safe school zones

There is a fundamental conviction that primary and secondary schools on the continent can be made much more attractive to students if they can learn and study in a secure environment, free from violence; and that schools can be a stabilizing influence on society at large. This is an initiative of Church World Service (CWS) in partnership with the churches in Africa. The problems facing Africa's children are huge and frightening:

• increasing numbers of children are abandoned to the streets because of neglect, violence, poverty or orphaned by parents who have died of AIDS;

• educational systems are gravely affected by the AIDS pandemic in countries like Malawi, Zambia, Zimbabwe and Uganda, where more than 30 percent of teachers are HIV-positive;

- many children are trapped in a downward spiral of war, disease, and deepening poverty;
- African children are generally worse off than they were 14 years ago when the United Nations Convention on the Rights of the Child (CRC) was approved by the heads of state of all countries including those in Africa;
- violations of the basic human rights of the children have become a common and disturbing occurrence in many African countries; and
- children in sub-Saharan Africa are more likely to be sick, less likely to be in school, and far more likely to die in childhood than in any other region of the world.

In September 2002, CWS embarked on an initiative to press governments and the newly formed African Union to approve legislation declaring schools as "safe zones" free from violence, civil conflict and abuse from teachers, parents and adults especially. This was an overall ecumenical effort to explore collective strategies to overcome hunger, poverty and disease, focusing on measurable results within an achievable time frame. The initiative is grounded in a theological understanding of God's covenant relationship with humanity (Heb. 1:1, Luke 3:22, Rom. 4:17) and this understanding is foundational to CWS's vision and call to focus on Africa's children.

The initial consultation took place in Nairobi where church leaders from 31 countries in sub-Saharan Africa concluded that one of the most urgent tasks for the ecumenical community is child welfare. The School Safe Zones (SSZ) offers a conceptual and pragmatic framework for implementing this resolve to make "Africa Fit for Children".

Research also suggests that investing in human capital, especially in early educational development, is one of the most effective ways to battle poverty and social inequality. Education is the key to acquiring individual capacity and building national human capital to lay the foundation for sustainable economic growth and social development.

Climate and water resources

While the entire planet suffers greatly from the impact of climate change, Africa, which comprises just 14 percent of the world's population, and has just one percent of the world's industrial output, suffers in a unique way because of its central location in the Intertropical Convergence Zone. Most of the industrial pollution in the world is caused by the 30 or so OECD (Organization for Economic Cooperation and Development) industrialized countries but the destructive consequences are shouldered by the people of Africa. Owing to the tropical location of the continent, winds carrying pollutants from highly industrialized countries pass over the continent every seasonal cycle.

According to Professor Jesse Mugambi of the University of Nairobi who is a member of the WCC Working Group on Climate Change, these winds have irreversibly destructive consequences for Africa evidenced by prolonged droughts, unpredictable torrential rains causing massive floods which displace millions of people and destroy large amounts of property.

The WCC cooperates with a number of churches and ecumenical partners in Africa to study and raise awareness about global warming caused by climate change which aggravates natural disasters, increases the spread of tropical diseases, causes water scarcity and encourages the increase of plagues of insects such as locusts. The effects of climate change add to the already-existing environmental destruction brought about by resource-extraction in mining, forestry, mono-culture and toxic waste dumping. The loss of ice cover on the peaks of Mount Kenya and Mount Kilimanjaro signals changes in the hydrological cycles of the region.

While some countries in the north, primarily the US, argue that climate change and its attendant devastation is not caused by human action, the scientific community disagrees entirely. The WCC has focused for a number of years on the human causes of climate change in cooperation with church-related agencies, the AACC and other partners, especially as it relates to the loss of water sources in such river basins as the Nile, the Niger and the Zambezi. Massive deforestation adds to the causes of extreme drought which have been particularly evident in recent years in southern and eastern Africa, accompanied ironically by unprecedented floods at the same time in countries like Mozambique and Malawi, both of which are signals of the adverse consequences of global warming. The water agenda is especially high on the list of priorities of church-based development organizations.

Resource extraction from Africa (gold, diamonds, bauxite, uranium, petroleum, copper, titanium, tin, iron, chrome, coltan) does little to benefit the peoples of the countries from which this raw material is taken. And in return, the industrialized countries using these resources for processing their materials create the pollution which Africa must bear. At the same time, Mugambi writes, "the people of Africa have been reduced to destitution through the economic policies of globalization which enrich the North while Africa's indebtedness continues to escalate."

The most recent report of the Intergovernmental Panel on Climate Change (IPCC) confirms that industrialization and burgeoning automobile use is the direct cause of global warming and that the region of the world most adversely affected by global warming is Africa.

In a paper for the WCC working group, Mugambi argues that the emergency action by African governments and the international community are simply "charity" and "relief" and their results are merely temporary. "Will Africa continue to depend on these temporary actions every year while the industrialized nations continue to pollute? Pointing to the Kyoto Protocol and the mandatory reduction by industry and the automobile of carbon dioxide emissions, the WCC insists that these protocols must be adhered to in order to correct the damage done already. Yet the world's only superpower, the US, refuses even to sign on to the protocol which is due to expire in 2112."

Faith communities in Africa, according to Mugambi, must be accompanied to challenge the state by maintaining a "critical distance" so that policies and practices which increase the already massive environmental damage to Africa are not implemented. Often these negative "grants-in-aid" are seriously damaging to the natural environment.

"The African cultural and religious heritage takes very seriously the natural environment. The African community includes everyone and everything: God, spirits, ancestors, the present generation, future generations, plants, animals, insects, inanimate things. God, humanity and nature – all belong to the same ontological reality," writes Mugambi. He says this world-view was undermined by the modern missionary enterprise from North America and Europe which tended to "look down" on this respect for the environment, teaching instead that God has given human beings the responsibility and power to "subdue" and "exploit" God's creation. Ironically, says Mugambi, it is in those areas of tropical Africa where Christianity is most dominant, that the environment is most degraded. "Christians have contributed towards the destruction of their habitat through over-exploitation of natural resources. This is a matter requiring not only repentance, but corrective action."

African Christians have to be reminded in their quest to reconstruct and rebuild communities that they must be responsible stewards of creation. "When God had completed the work of creation, God saw that it was 'very good'. What have we done to God's beautiful creation? It is no longer good at all so we Christians through the ecumenical movement must take responsibility to restore divine beauty. Such restoration will, in the long term, be fruitful because nature will replenish and heal the wounds inflicted by human beings through irresponsible industrialization," Mugambi says.

Statistically, Africa's contribution to industrial pollution is negligible at present but the majority of people must live with poor access to clean water, reliable fuel and electricity, forcing them to destroy forests for heat and light. The WCC Working Group on Climate Change proposes:

- African elites must turn their attention to the plight of the majority, which lives in destitution;
- Africans living in rural areas will have to do more afforestation on the arable and semi-arable lands;
- the wetlands, including river valleys and lakeshores, will have to be protected;
- soil conservation will need to be done systematically to improve the quality of arable land and reduce siltation of rivers and lakes;
- rainwater harvesting technologies will need to be pursued vigorously;
- renewable energy technologies will have to be made more efficient and affordable for rural and peri-urban communities; and
- programmes, now under way with WCC and its partners, for environmental education and rehabilitation, especially at the local level involving faith communities, will need to be increased.

Accountability and transparency

Slowly, over the years, as WCC hosted more and more "round tables" between donors and ecumenical groups, it became clear that a seeming lack of accountability and transparency was hampering the ability of the churches and related institutions to access needed money for their work and projects. From 1997 on it also became apparent that there was a serious need for common accounting and reporting standards among the various ecumenical bodies in order to improve Round Table responsibilities in these areas.

A series of "encounters on accounting and reporting" was held and it became apparent that common practices would greatly facilitate stakeholder requirements. With support from two donors, Bread for the World and ICCO, the Dutch interchurch organization, various financial officers, programme managers, partners, external auditors and others, along with the WCC Africa Office, began to look at common standards and decided there needed to be a handbook that the various churches and agencies could use to clarify reporting.

The result in 2004 was the WCC-published *Accounting and Reporting Standards: Contributions from Ecumenical Bodies* which is already widely used for accounting and reporting but also covers related topics that will help build healthier ecumenical bodies with organizational

Making a Garden of Eden
Rather than dream of going to heaven,
Wake up and make a garden of Eden,
Make wherever you are a heaven
God will bless you as you do!

This theme song of the Utooni Self-Help Community Group some 90 km east of Nairobi, celebrates what was a barren wasteland 30 years ago, having been stripped bare of its trees by carvers who made curios for the tourist industry. The area is semi-arid with no permanent water source and a low average rainfall. In 1978 Joshua Mukusya, a rural development worker with the NCCK, joined with a group of 135 families to form a self-help group to deal with all the challenges they faced at Utooni: water shortages, poor food supply, schooling, lack of security, culture, afforestation, soil conservation and so on. Each had its own committee mainly made up of women.

Every Monday, each member-family sends someone to work together on an agreed upon project. They work on each other's farms and homes in turn each week. In monetary terms the labour is worth millions of dollars. Today the results are stunning. There are 42 km of beautiful terraces which conserve soil and retain moisture on the slopes that have all been rehabilitated into fertile farms. More than 200 sand dams have been built serving as reservoirs for millions of litres of rainwater. More than 8,500 domestic water tanks have been built so that every family has at least one tank, as well as the schools and community buildings.

Utooni's market is at Kola where the community members exchange their harvest. Buyers and sellers come from elsewhere to trade. Commerce is growing at Kola and water consumption continues to rise among the 1,000 persons who live there. Brick-making has become an industry. Trees have been planted and the forest cover is revitalized. Visiting groups come to learn. Kola now has a housing scheme and a post office which serves as their bank.

The community's motto is "Without Vision We Perish". They control their own future, set their own priorities using their own labour and resources. They meet with politicians, NGOs, church leaders but on their own terms. "We rely on no one but God and ourselves."

(Mugambi, 2005)

development, sustainability and plenty of practical advice. The handbook is not mandatory, and is more of a guide. It does not prescribe specific solutions but it does help build up credible institutions.

Ecumenical Enablers

The Ecumenical Focus on Africa (EFA) provides a way in which the WCC and the ecumenical movement can include not only leaders of churches and related organizations or the staff persons and members of the various national councils and sub-regional fellowships, but it is also a way for individuals to make their own direct contributions to journeys of hope in Africa today.

The challenges facing Africa require a wide range of partnerships with a shared commitment to create a better future for Africans, especially children and young people. This is the kind of accompaniment the Harare assembly called for. It is already happening at many church levels but some experiences have been undertaken and extended to include, for example, partnerships between sectors in Africa and abroad – business people, educators, students, health professionals, philanthropists. All of them are goodwill ambassadors active in the future in Africa.

William Temu, the WCC's director of management, has some experience with a group of young African women and men called "Ecumenical Enablers" or, sometimes, "Ecumenical Accompaniers", who are volunteer African enablers of WCC.

"When I first came to WCC as Africa area secretary in 1997, I was an African, but I had no idea how big my continent really is and how big the ecumenical job is. It was far too big for one person. So, I began to think I needed a pool of volunteers with various skills and interests and with a huge commitment to the WCC," Temu explained.

Soon there was a group of men and women, including independent finance and management consultants, health consultants, a practising lawyer as well as people working with ecumenical and other Christian organizations such as FOCCESA, and CORAT Africa (Christian Organization Research and Advisory Trust). The enablers were described by Temu as people willing to take on assignments for WCC, committed to ecumenism and skilled in their areas of expertise. Their numbers varied but usually there were about ten people. From time to time WCC would facilitate meetings in Geneva or in Africa to bring them together. There are also now WCC enablers in the Asia and Pacific regions as well.

They introduced themselves at a meeting in Geneva in 2001 with remarks such as: "I use 50 percent of my time for ecumenical enabling because human dignity is one of my priorities."... "...working for the church is not a job but a calling and it knows no boundaries but the movement to real unity can be painful..." "It is a miracle for me to be with the enablers and to work closer in the ecumenical journey. Having a lot of experience working as a facilitator with women leaders I look ahead with deep faith to serve as an ecumenical enabler." "Normally the first priority of a lawyer is to make money but I am more rewarded working with churches and I look ahead with deep faith to serve as an Ecumenical Enabler." "...enabling means for me to be an 'encourager' for people in need of being listened to..."

EEs, as the enablers call themselves, are an integrated part of the Africa Desk at the Geneva headquarters although they live and work in countries such as Botswana, Nigeria, Kenya, Sierra Leone and elsewhere and now represent a "pilot way" of working to be agents of change following the Harare assembly. Their goals are those of WCC: to promote alternative visions of its mission of hope, peace and reconciliation and to reconcile Christian denominations, doctrines, divisions, and to work towards unity, offering the world a credible vision of communities reconciled.

The concept of ecumenical enabling is still fairly new, says Temu, but it is intended to build local expertise while helping churches overcome financial and organizational crises. An enabler ideally is:

- a WCC representative in their own situation and must be familiar with the WCC's policies and activities, especially the EFA, and liaise with local councils;
- a listener/provocateur able to listen keenly to discussions and provide summaries; but also able to stimulate discussion and raise questions as a way of engaging in WCC issues;
- a guarantor of accountability, making sure things are done "decently", that funds are used properly and the finances can be explained to non-financial people;
- a person who can follow up with the local Christian Council concerns of WCC at affordable costs; while at the same time accompanying and supporting the NCC to decide how best to proceed; and
- able to celebrate diversity in leadership and management.

In the world of ecumenical enabling there are positives and negatives. When the group met in Geneva they listed some of these negatives as: unclear agendas, lack of clarity of the enabler's role, no level playing field among stakeholders, pretence and hypocrisy by some leaders, lack of a will to change, unacceptable accountability, and a culture of wastefulness. On the positive side: integrity and commitment, good management and willingness to learn and change, humility and legitimacy found in faith, mission and call to service.

9. The Gift of African Women

For some, the ecumenical journey of hope began a few days before the 1998 WCC Harare assembly with a brilliant festival to celebrate the culmination of the Ecumenical Decade: Churches in Solidarity with Women (1988-98). A thousand women and 30 men from all over the globe were in Africa to celebrate 10 years of ecumenical solidarity at Harare's Belvedere Teachers College. The aim of the meeting was to celebrate the end of the decade but also to project the image of African women as **strong keepers of the faith** to be seen **in a positive light** and in **solidarity with each other** who were **fulfilling many roles as a part of society** as **makers and keepers of peace in conflict situations.**

African women are essential for reform and progress. They possess a moral standing as the steady foundation on which the church in Africa is built. They are the fundamental energy under God in the regeneration of the ecumenical movement in Africa. Even though not formally part of the hierarchical order in most male-structured churches, it is the African woman who bears the same pain of exclusion that Jesus does in the community of believers. The family, the very social institution that provides life and living in the African community, survives because of womanhood.

Water was the symbol of the Decade festival. Water brought by women from every continent and region, symbolizing their unity in diversity. It is a powerful symbol of life: sometimes salty, fresh, polluted, scarce, over-abundant, controlled, the cause of conflict. Biblically, water has many images: waters of birth, water that cleanses, refreshes and heals. The waters of baptism are a powerful inclusive mark of unity as Christians and a sign of equality for all. And so it came reverently into the worship, a symbol of unity and commitment to the church.

"What an amazing mosaic we make, gathered in this place! I often boast and tell people that I come from the best continent in the world. Some people think otherwise. But today just spoil me and join me in believing that we are in God's presence on a continent that God loves very much... Africa is the birthplace of humanity so we are meeting literally on sacred ground." Dr Musimbi Kanyoro, a Kenyan who is general secretary of the World YWCA, preached at the opening worship on "From Solidarity to Accountability".

"Why had God enabled us to be here in Harare? Can you remember that Jesus asked for accountability from those who had come to see his predecessor John the Baptist, in the wilderness?

What did you go out to look at? A reed shaken by the wind? What then did you go out to see? (Luke 7: 24-25) Our presence here calls for accountability."

She asked the women what they went to Africa to see and told them to be accountable for what they saw:

Poverty, disease, disaster: "We are on a continent that is not poor but has a lot of poverty. The poverty goes to the extremes of misery and in fact generates many other problems. Our lives as African women are often marked by endless struggles due to economic constraints from unjust practices. We are also a continent that is ill, especially from AIDS. Many of the dead and dying are members of our families."

War and the aftermath of wars: "We are here from many countries – from Angola where landmines are rude evidence of the futility of war. We are from Rwanda, Congo, Burundi, and we bear the marks of genocide in the Great Lakes. We are from Liberia, Sierra Leone and Mozambique and we carry the emblem of child soldiers.

Violence: We women know about rape in homes, on the streets in broad daylight, more often by men we trust. We wonder why the rape of African women does not make headlines. We wonder why solidarity from other women has not come for us!"

Kanyoro asked what was new about these things the visiting women had seen.

"Nothing. Jesus, when he was on earth saw the problems facing the people with his own eyes – the poverty, inequality, religious and economic oppression, joblessness, depression, illness and the outcasts. He was filled with compassion.

"We too know all these things but we are not a dying continent because we refuse to give up on God and on ourselves. And on our church. Every day is a jubilee day for Africa because the jubilee is for the downtrodden, it is about the love of God who proclaims mercy to the condemned."

Women are fully part of the Journey of Hope and wish to be, Kanyoro emphasized. She said women can no longer just call for solidarity because "we need to be part of the refining and redesigning and reconfiguring process we hoped for during this Decade. Accountability entails that we are aware the process of change can be painful."

Her challenge to the church, which she said has too many male leaders and too much patriarchy, was that "we will not accept our gifts being minimized, but rather we will lift up all the gifts of the people of God. We will not accept that power can only be shared with a few, but rather we will act with knowledge that sharing with all only increases power. We will not accept responsibility for the anger of men, but rather we will understand it and push for a continuous dialogue between men and women. We will not accept that what we bring to the churches is unworthy of the churches' time and energy, but rather the death and resurrection of Jesus Christ has made time for all of us. We are worthy participants at the table and we are called to act like we belong, because we do indeed belong."

Looking to the future beyond 1998 where, in a few days the eighth assembly of the WCC would approve the Ecumenical Focus on Africa's (EFA) journey of hope, Kanyoro focused on the accompaniment of the churches with men and women in the new vision of Africa. "We thank God together for not giving up on us during this Decade. We are strong together. We are Children of God. Our playing small does not serve the world. ... We are meant to shine, as children do. We were born to manifest the glory of God that is within us and within everyone. And as we let it shine, we unconsciously give other people permission to do the same. As we are liberated from our fear, our presence automatically liberates others. This is accountability."

As Mercy Oduyoye writes: "the African family may be used as a symbol of what Christians mean by ecumenism, a household whose ruling morality and ethics are of Christ, whose religion is the religion of Jesus of Nazareth, and whose faith is anchored in the Christ of God. The ecclesia becomes a kin-group, a community of Christ believers, called together by and around the Christ event. The family is a community within which the members feel at home. To be separated is to experience alienation and exile, and therefore one surrenders individualism in order to promote full individuality. And if the African family is the most credible motif of ecumenism, then surely the African woman is the perfect symbol of the struggle for unity because she carries the burden of life in the household of God. She mediates life by not only being the path to new life but also the one who provides nourishment for the household economy."

The "Voices of the Decade" who were the women's presenters to the WCC's Harare assembly, were unanimous in praising the progress. Voices affirmed the deep call for human and social rights of women. Voices deplored violence in all its many forms against women and children. Voices also declared that the struggle is an on-going process that eventually would make the new millennium truly new, especially for women in Africa. The assembly accepted that it was being called to move from solidarity to "accountability". And other Voices cautioned the WCC about any delays in removing obstacles to the full inclusion of women in every aspect of life, both in church and society. These Voices, whose words were adopted by the assembly which stated that there is no turning back in "the journey of faith". The theme of accompanying African brothers and sisters in their "journey of hope" that emerged from the African plenary became intertwined at Harare with the "journey of faith" from the Decade so that the two would walk hand-in-hand in the Ecumenical Focus on Africa. "The WCC," said the assembly plenary session on the Decade, "has heard clearly the challenge to account for its commitment to the aims of the Decade in all its workings and policies. We also hear the call to strengthen the churches' solidarity with women."

Lessons from African women theologians

A critical part of the Journey of Hope is the place African women leaders and theologians have played in increasingly important ways to accompany the changes towards a new Africa.

For many years the strong and collaborative leadership of Mercy Amba Oduyoye of Ghana has provided the ecumenical movement with a voice in the struggles with colonialism and patriarchy in Africa and on behalf of the women of Africa. She developed a role as the "mother" of African women's theology. As a senior staff person at WCC (deputy general secretary 1987-94) and as one of the most prolific thinkers and writers in African and international theological circles, Oduyoye helped in the launching and creation of the Circle of Concerned African Women Theologians in 1989. The Circle, as it is commonly referred to, is an interfaith association that aims at producing theological literature by encouraging and mentoring women to research, write and publish in the wide scope of religion and culture. One of these women theologians, now on the WCC staff, Dr Nyambura Njoroge, of Kenya calls Oduyoye "auntie" and in 2004 outlined for the American Society of Missiology some of the key areas of women's concern in Africa. The following excerpts from her paper indicate how the role of women in the journey of hope is critical to a new ecumenical Africa. Njoroge is involved at WCC with the empowerment of women in theological education and ministry.

The Circle

The Circle is organized according to three European languages, English, French and Portuguese, which obviously tells much about the colonial past and reality.

The WCC and the ecumenical movement have played a significant role in providing opportunities and resources for African Christian women to discover one another and to grow in many diverse ways. A consultation in 1978 at Cartigny, Switzerland laid the groundwork for the creation of the Circle. Eight African women were among 53 women from all regions who gathered for the first time and among them was Mercy Amba Oduyoye, then a Ghanaian university lecturer teaching at the University of Ibadan in Nigeria in the religious department. She was the most seasoned of the eight Africans. At times the women met according to continents. Following is part of what African participants said:

> Is our theological education culturally relevant? Many of the women in the group felt that the emphasis in their education was on the academic rather than the practical. And that the practical skills they will need to minister to the people in their communities are neglected in their education. Affirming that the true Christian is involved in the world, the women felt that theological education relevant to their culture would enable them to work within the community from a basis of sound biblical and theological principles: not that they neglect the academic and biblical part of their training but that they be shown how to use it in their daily lives and work.
>
> Recognizing the tension that often exists between the church and the culture, the women agreed that this tension should not be ignored but explored throughout their theological education. Looking specifically at theological education for women, the group felt that many theological institutions are still unresponsive to the needs of women. Realizing that male students, as well as female, need a broader understanding if they are to minister to both women and men, we should work for a larger number of women on theological faculties as well as attempting to influence how male professors think and teach. Finally, we must encourage other women to study theology and seriously consider ordained ministry as a vocation.

African participants resolved to look for the other women in Africa studying theology and bring as many as possible together in a consultation of women in theology, to find out just what women theologians are doing in Africa, to question the meaning of ministry and women's part in it, to look critically at theological education in Africa, to encourage women to become more active in the emerging theologies and to discover how the church can be more responsive to the issues and needs of women.

Mercy Amba Oduyoye left Cartigny clothed with a passion for justice and great courage. She did not allow any difficulties to deter her and in 1980 came the first conference of African Women Theologians in Ibadan, Nigeria. She spent the rest of the 1980s reaching out, recruiting and sharing her vision and commitment. In 1987, she moved to the WCC and the following year convened the first planning committee for the inauguration of the Circle which took place in Accra, Ghana, September 1989 with 69 women present.

In addition to reaching out, recruiting and mentoring other women to share in her dream and vision, Oduyoye brought with her great open-mindedness and a deep Christian commitment that is tolerant of other religions. She writes: "The women of the Circle are practitioners of African Traditional Religion, Christianity, Islam and Judaism and maybe others too. We do not ask for religious affiliations in the Circle, only that one should consciously live by a belief in God". The Circle is both an ecumenical and multi-faith movement, even though the membership is largely Christian. Hardly anyone gets to know Oduyoye's denominational affiliation because what matters to her is reflecting, exploring and analyzing the impact of faith, religion and culture in the life of African women in their religious communities and society to create sound theological literature. Tirelessly, she provided empowering leadership and helped to nurture a collaborative model of working together that is captured by Musimbi Kanyoro:

> It was agreed that the Circle should not become an organization with a structure and headquarters. While it was obvious that the Circle would need some funds for its work, it was resolved that it must be driven by commitment of African women to write and publish and not by external factors such as money. The Circle was to be a space for women to mentor each other by doing communal theology. Thus the Circle was to remain an open-ended forum, always hospitable to new people. Hierarchical structures of leadership were not essential. The important fact was for African women to nurture and support one another as writers. The Circle women would engage in debate and dialogue with all other theologians, women and men, in Africa and beyond.

Despite being multi-faith the Circle has a strong and sound biblical and theological basis that is embodied in the choice of the gospel story of Jairus' girl-child presumed dead who was called to get up or arise – *Talitha cum!* – by Jesus. It is also important for women in the Circle that this story is intertwined with the story of the bleeding woman who touched Jesus for healing (Mark 5:21-43; Luke 8:40-56). For the launching of the Circle, Teresa Okure, a Nigerian religious sister and New Testament theological educator and scholar, wrote the Bible study on these two women and connected them to African women.

> The daughter of Jairus and the woman with the flow of blood: two women who met Jesus at a critical point in their lives, when all hope of cure and restoration

was gone, one at the age of 12, the other after 12 years of illness, one through the intervention of the father, the other by the sheer will to live. Women who were as good as dead, physically and socially, but who were personally touched by Jesus and empowered thereby to arise and live; women who, by living, proclaimed God's marvels and God's reign. These two women have much to teach us. Let us lend supportive hands to one another and help one another to arise. For Africa will not arise unless its womenfolk, the mothers and bearers of life, arise. What an awesome thought! What a heavy responsibility on our part! May God give us the will to arise and the desire genuinely to help one another and the whole continent to arise.

When Oduyoye retired from the WCC, she decided to deepen the vision of "the will to arise" by building the Talitha Cumi Centre, the home for the Institute of African Women in Religion and Culture at Trinity Theological Seminary in Accra. The centre hosts seminars on gender and theology on a variety of issues for people in Ghana and once every two years, it hosts an international seminar for Circle members and their partners. Through the leadership of this great daughter of Africa, who is always spreading the mission and vision of the Circle, African women theologians have a solid legacy.

Collaborative model: the strength of the Circle

The Circle was born during the WCC's Ecumenical Decade which helped to create critical awareness of women's theological concerns in the churches and theological institutions. It also increased forums where African women theologians, pastors and leaders of church women's organizations could develop their theological knowledge and voices.

By the end of 20th century it had become clear that the global HIV and AIDS pandemic had affected more Africans than in any other continent and that women and children were most vulnerable. In 2001, a small group of women theological educators at Yale Divinity School extended an invitation to Circle members to attend a conference on "Gender, Faith and Responses to HIV/AIDS in Africa" held in February, 2002. This collaboration led to the invitation of four women from Yale to the third Pan-African Circle Conference held in Addis Ababa, in August 2002. The theme was "Sex, Stigma and HIV/AIDS: African Women Challenging Religion, Culture and Social Practices".

The success of the Circle was born and nurtured by women who believe in reaching out, recruiting, mentoring and opening doors for others to come in and share their dreams, vision, skills and potentials in the creation of theological literature that takes seriously women's experiences, perspectives and God-given gifts. Aware of our vulnerability and powerlessness we chose to focus on "Transforming Power: Women in the household of God" during the second Pan-African Conference of the Circle held in Nairobi in 1996.

Naming the missing link in God's mission

In the formation of the Circle a few African Christian women named the missing link in God's mission as the lack of affirmation of women's full humanity and denial of women's full participation in God's mission in the church and society. Even today there are people who cannot comprehend that women are equally endowed with theological minds and leadership qualities, especially if they happen to be black.

It is not that women do not theologize and articulate their faith and struggle to comprehend the divine in their lives but it is that their voices are not heard, heeded or taken seriously. Unfortunately, the Bible has been misinterpreted and misused to deny women (and people of African descent) our God-given identity and power and likeness with the divine despite the biblical affirmation that human beings, female and male, are created equal in God's image. Mercy Amba Oduyoye brilliantly named this missing link, reminding us that "a bird does not fly with one wing" at her inaugural speech launching the Circle.

In a recent article "Gender and Theology in Africa today" on the Circle website, Oduyoye has elaborated the crux of the matter and gives a glimpse of the issues and concerns that have preoccupied the Circle members as they struggle to create a "two-winged theology" in Africa. This article illustrates the power dynamics between women and among men and "among nations", because, as people who have been subjected to slavery and colonization by foreign powers, critical analysis of racism, apartheid and imperialism are essential in women's writings. Oduyoye helps the reader to see some of the age-old gender stereotypes in theology, religion and culture and how they impact on African women. The article also profiles the Circle's commitment to a collaborative model of doing theology in what has been called "communal theology". Church theology, leadership and our understanding of God's mission in Africa have been largely articulated by foreigners and African men and the Circle wants to bring this long legacy to an end. This explains that the most recent activity by the Circle is the project on "Engendering Theological Education in Africa" to transform the theological curriculum in Africa by mainstreaming gender. Oduyoye writes, "Recognizing and becoming sensitive to gender in theology leads to a theology that is liberative, one that does not remain theoretical but demands ethical choices that will empower the transformation of relationships that have been damaged by sexism and misogynist attitudes."

Biblical and cultural Bible studies

From the beginning the Circle acknowledged that religion and culture are the basis of theologizing and as Christian women, the Bible has a central place in this discourse. Hence contextual Bible studies have been critical. However, in addition to biblical hermeneutics, the Circle has identified cultural hermeneutics as a necessary step for in-depth understanding.

All questions regarding the welfare and status of women in Africa are explained within the framework of culture. Women cannot inherit land or own property because it is not culturally "right". Women may not take leadership because it is culturally the domain of men... However, it is not enough simply to analyze culture without reference to the people who maintain the culture and on whom the culture impacts. Here is where the need arises for a gender-sensitive cultural hermeneutics because it doubles in addressing issues of culture while being critical of that culture from a gender perspective. The church is a part and parcel of the analysis. It is in the church that the dilemma of how Africans should live as Christians and cultural people thrives. Since the Bible forms the base and informs African Christians on what they can validate or not validate in their culture, we must start from the framework of reading the Bible with cultural eyes. The culture of the reader in Africa has more influence on the way the biblical text is understood and used in communities than the historical culture of the text.

Imperialism and globalization

Women are also living and working in a highly globalized and changing world, which demonstrates Africa's interdependence with the rest of the world and its impact on our lives as women and as Africans. Musa Dube has focused on this area in her creative ways of retelling and contextualizing the gospel and by articulating the post-colonial theories. In her writings, Dube always attempts to put Africa within the context of imperialism and globalization processes. Dube's analysis, in a context where others argue that globalization has redeemed Africans from the African village to the joys of the global village, shows how the need for decolonizing our minds, theology, church and literature is key to our success in creating life-giving theologies.

With this comes the urgent need for the Circle to contend with the social injustices and death-dealing challenges that have condemned millions of Africans to a life of extreme poverty and a culture of silence, violence and senseless death, including social and ecclesiastical death. Reflecting on the Lord's Prayer in the context of globalization, Dube asserts:

As a black African woman of Botswana – who is a survivor of colonialism and the subsequent neo-colonialism of globalization – I live in the deep shadow of death. To live with the intensification of poverty in African countries, to live with wars and coups, to live with corruption and exploitation, to watch helplessly as beloved friends, neighbours, and relatives slowly shrivel as HIV/AIDS gnaws at them, is to live where death and life have become identical twins... This context of death-dealing challenges me to reflect on what it means to profess Christian faith and to pray the Lord's Prayer in the global economic era. I am confronted with a crisis that necessitates a re-examination of the Lord's Prayer. What, in other words, is God's vision for God's creation? What are the roles of Christian men and women, individually and corporately, in bringing God's kingdom on earth? Is there any vision that is pledged to God and to each other when Christians recite the Lord's Prayer? If so, is this a vision we can implement? And, how? These questions shall be the subject of my reading of the Lord's Prayer.

Social injustices and gender-based violence

Since the "African woman" is not a monolithic entity, the Circle has attempted to unpack the plight of African women in different contexts and their contributions in the church and society. It has tried to demonstrate to churchwomen (including women from African Instituted Churches) their capacity to resist social injustices and gender-biased harmful rituals and to become agents of transformation and bearers of hope. From the beginning gender-based violence and injustices as sources of misery, suffering and death have taken centre stage. Silence surrounding the area of human sexuality and violence against children and women has been a major concern from the beginning. Breaking the conspiracy of silence and stopping gender-based violence have become even more urgent in the global HIV and AIDS pandemic era.

No doubt speaking out on issues of human sexuality, HIV and AIDS status, gender-biased rituals and gender-based violence, and especially rape and incest require a lot of courage, spiritual stamina, creative and constructive solidarity. Circle women and others have written on widowhood, wife inheritance, childlessness, single parenting, female genital mutilation, etc., but perhaps the greatest courage has been shown by Thandeki Umlilo, a religious sister from South Africa who, in *Little Girl, Arise!* tells her experience of incest and sexual abuse by her father, brothers, uncle and other men from the time she was four. At age 50, Umlilo writes:

> For too many years have I lived in the valley of dead bones. Incest and abuse violated the essence of me and held me bound in deadly shame, guilt and self-rejection – a human being that housed a withdrawn, timid and vulnerable child. Today, however, I experience myself as alive, able to take risks, eager

to live life to the fullest, knowing the joy of freedom, deeply appreciating the woman that I am, the person whose very source is the giver of all life.

This transformation is the hope I hold out to all people who have been abused or victimized in any way. My story in its very frankness is to tell all victims of abuse that we are not sure of our experience. Within us is the power to transcend any trauma and to rise victoriously in the glory and splendour of New Life. The second purpose is to make as many people as possible, especially the perpetrators, aware of the devastating effect of abuse. My hope is that this awareness-raising will enable perpetrators to treat themselves and all persons with respect and dignity that is rightfully theirs.

Umlilo chose to tell her story that speaks for many African women who have suffered the same incest, sexual abuse and rape but who, unlike her, are not so fortunate to go through the process of counselling, spiritual guidance and healing. Among friends, African women continuously share personal encounters with gender-based violence, including incest and rape, if not their own, those of their daughters, sisters, nieces, cousins, aunties, mothers and friends. Some of these women suffer social death because of deep psychological trauma while others commit suicide. Social death has become such a reality among people living with HIV and AIDS because of stigma, discrimination and silence surrounding the pandemic. The survivors of rape and incest are also deeply traumatized and usually suffer from shame and guilt throughout their lives.

Unfortunately, sufferers and survivors of rape have increased (including girl-children) because of the many war-torn and conflict-infested countries in Africa where rape is used as a weapon of war (as elsewhere) and the lack of privacy in refugee camps. African women are also subjected to sex slavery among warring rebel groups and soldiers as well as the trafficking of sex workers outside the continent.

Much is at stake in the battle against gender-based violence in Africa. It has contributed to the rapid rate of HIV infection among women and girl-children. Nevertheless, it is no secret that unhealed wounds of incest, rape and sexual abuse affect the sexual life of the survivors and it has been the cause of dysfunctional marriage relationships. Certainly, this is an area that demands in-depth research and creative pastoral theology, care and counselling that addresses their pain and suffering. This is why the Tamar Campaign has become important for many women in southern Africa and the reason some Circle members would like to see it spreading across the continent.

Theology of lamentation

Not surprisingly our death-dealing context and senseless suffering have forced some in the Circle to turn to a theology of lamentation as has been the case in most of my writings. It is not enough to argue like John Mbiti, a pioneering African theologian, that "one would hope that theology arises out of spontaneous joy in being a Christian, responding to life and ideas as one redeemed". I can attest to the fact that when I am deeply depressed, disillusioned and angry and lack words because of the deafening silence of the church on social injustices and evil, such as the ones named above, the only language I understand is lamentation and that is when I have written most of my articles. Similar views about lamentation have been expressed by others. Circle member Denise Ackermann, a South African, writes:

> Stigma is nourished by silence. Internalized trauma, fear or rejection, cultural restraints and wrong understandings of sin and punishment, all rob people of the ability to speak out and to name their reality. I suggest that our scriptures have given us a language that can deal with suffering. In the ancient language of lament we have a way of naming the unnameable and of crying out to God in situations that are unbearable. What is lament? It is a form of mourning but it is more purposeful. It signals that relationships have gone terribly wrong and it reminds God that God must act as partner in the covenant. It is both individual and communal. It is a primal cry that comes out of the human soul and beats against the heart of God. It calls God to account for our human suffering. Lament is risky and dangerous speech; it is restless; it pushes the boundaries of our relationships, particularly with God; it refuses to settle for things the way they are.

African Christians need to recognize and acknowledge the deep valleys of death that Tamar (the raped daughter of King David), Musa Dube, Thandeki Umlilo and many others have so eloquently named as a missing link in African theology and mission. We must hold ourselves accountable, our churches, governments, religious and political leaders and even God by using every possible language including art to name our suffering and culture of violence and death as we seek for ways of addressing the misery, loss and grief they bring in our lives.

Empowering women in theological education

We in the Circle must hammer away at the fact that we cannot be effective, empowering and responsible leaders without the right skills, tools and resources. In addition to writing theological literature, a lot of work needs to be done in uplifting and empowering our sisters, especially in the lusophone (Portuguese-speaking) countries where we have hardly any women with advanced theological training and who find it difficult to contribute theological literature.

Lack of scholarship grants remains the largest hindrance in empowering women through theological education. On the other hand, theological institutions must be willing to change to meet the practical needs of women, their experiences and perspectives that shape their theologies, teaching and research methodologies and ways of doing ministry. However, our greatest hope and encouragement is to see the slowly but steadily growing body of theological literature being listed in required readings in theological institutions and the new project on mainstreaming gender in theology. Recall the words of Oduyoye:

> The power of definition of what is theology has to be exercised by a community of women and men in theology. The academic world remains uncertain as to how to assess the alternative epistemologies and methodologies that women claim mainstreaming gender in theology demands. But like it or not, the concern for gender has opened up a new academic field, and this has to be acknowledged and appropriated to make the academy responsible and responsive to the world out there. The presumed right of church and bishops to determine what is to be believed stands in the way of mainstreaming gender in theology as long as leadership in the ecclesia remains male.

Bearers of hope and life

In our small and delicate ways the Circle has demonstrated great potential in recruiting, mentoring and nurturing a generation of bearers of hope and life against many odds. Our courage to speak out, to tell the truth and write about our joys and sorrows in the family, church (and other religious communities) and society have become a threat to some who would rather we remain silent "in our place".

But we have chosen to touch the cloak of Jesus and to hear his voice calling us to arise! We have chosen to participate fully in God's mission and to name the missing links in African theology, mission and life, for the Lord says, "See, I have inscribed you on the palms of my hands; your walls are continually before me." (Isaiah 49:16) This is the true identity and power with the divine that we yearn for as we seek to be moral agents and bearers of hope, empowerment, liberation, justice, peace, healing and fullness of life. Women are determined to learn from others and to make a difference.

The Tamar campaign

The Tamar narrative comes from a neglected and marginalized biblical text which is found in few lectionaries. It is based on the rape narrative of Tamar, the daughter of King David, by her half-brother Amnon (2 Samuel 13:1-22), the subsequent attempts by Tamar to make the crime public and how David, Absalom, Amnon and other males conspire to cover up the rape and incest.

The use of the Old Testament text is the brainchild of the Ujamaa Centre for Community Development and Research (formerly the Institute of the Study of the Bible and Worker Ministry Project ISB&WM) at the School of Religion and Theology in the University of KwaZulu-Natal, Pietermaritzburg, South Africa. It began in 1996 with a workshop on violence against women using the words from second Samuel to help poor, working-class and marginalized African Christian women talk about violence and how the laws of the state and church grant men all the privileges to prosecute, divorce and excommunicate.

The first workshop, as described by Bible scholar Gerald West and Phumzile Zondi-Mabizela, coordinator of the Worker Ministry, asked the women four questions:

1. What is the text about?
2. Who are the male characters and what is the role of each of them in the rape of Tamar?
3. What is Tamar's response throughout the story?
4. Where is God in this story?

The participants, working in the safe space of a workshop, quickly identify with the story which they say typically is about: domestic violence, the "cunningness" of men, guilt, power, silencing of women and loss of dignity. Identifying the men they say the actions of Jonadab, David and the servant in the Samuel narrative made the rape possible even though Amnon was the rapist. So, the men are accomplices. Absalom, they said, played a weak and ambiguous role, offering Tamar, his sister, a home but telling her to keep quiet about the rape.

When they discussed question three, the African women noted that Tamar was a strong and articulate woman who had argued and pleaded with her brother, Amnon and she had refused to keep silent.

Generally the women participants in the workshop felt that even though God was not mentioned directly in the text, that God had been with Tamar and that God would judge David, Amnon and Jonadab. Some said, through the story, God showed the weakness and slyness of men.

Since that first event in 1996, many workshops have been held using this contextual Bible study process where people can speak out for themselves. In 1998 Zondi-Mabizela became coordinator of the Women and Gender programme at ISB&WM and since then Tamar's story has been used in dozens of Bible studies to create space for women (and some men) to break the silence about abuse in its many and varied contexts.

One of the sites in which this Bible study was first used was at the Uniting Reformed Church in Hammarsdale, a semi-rural community near Pietermaritzburg, in 1999. The two-day workshop with young people and the lay leaders of the church was facilitated by Zondi-Mabizela using the story of Tamar. Violence against women and children was one of the key concerns among church members. There were a large number of young people present, particularly young women.

Local participants were divided into small groups on the basis of age and gender, including a group for older men (among them, the church's pastor), a group for older women, a group for young men, and two groups for young women.

The groups were asked: "What will you now do in response to this [Tamar] Bible study?" They replied that they wanted to deal specifically with their own modern-day context in response to the story from Samuel. They did not want to explain it all away as ancient history. The seriousness which the young women, in particular, took this story into their own daily reality and the challenging questions about what ISB&WM staff intended to do about it, resulted in plans to launch the Tamar Campaign, committed to initiating a regional (and perhaps national) campaign in which to commemorate Tamar and her story. From that first Hammarsdale event, the Tamar story and its ramifications have become continental and wider.

The Tamar Campaign was launched in 2000, with the aim of encouraging the churches to speak out against all forms of violence against women and children, especially physical, sexual and psychological violence by men. There is a related goal of supporting and accompanying survivors of violence. Many churches wanted to bury the issue of gender violence as something that belonged in the private sphere as opposed to being openly discussed by congregations and communities.

In response to this hidden agenda it was decided to launch 16 days of activism in which there would be no violence against women, from November 25 to December 10, 2000. Ministers were asked to preach on gender violence, its causes and consequences, on the Sundays during the 16 days. The first campaign changed many lives. Tamar's protest has given many women voice. Young men have been infuriated by the actions of the many men in the Samuel text who were accomplices in the rape of Tamar. This has encouraged them to promote a different culture of respect and protection of their loved ones. Church leaders have used the text as a tool to encourage a spirit of openness. The Tamar Campaign was soon international.

In August 2003 the narrative reached the Circle chapter in Nairobi which organized a 10-day women's seminar with 100 in attendance. These were women theological educators, students and women in ministry (pastors and leaders of churchwomen's organizations) from several churches. Each day started with contextual Bible study and one morning the women read the Tamar narrative. At the end of the session, women were encouraged to share their stories and knowledge about rape and incest in their ministry and theological studies. To the surprise of the coordinators, 30 percent of the women spoke from personal experience of their own rape, including incest and child sexual molestation.

Following a 2002 Conference on Theological Education and Ecumenical Formation with the theme "Journey of Hope in Africa", programme staff of WCC were approached to help fulfil the commitment made in the plan of action on "contextualization of theological education" in the context of increased child sexual molestation, incest and rape in Africa and the part these crimes play in the spread of HIV/AIDS. A workshop using the Tamar story was set for 2005 in Nairobi.

Its objectives were to:

- raise critical awareness of the wide range of increased violence against children and women and in particular the heinous crime of sexual violence on female bodies of all ages and its extreme forms in war-torn situations in Africa; and

- introduce the methodology and strategy used in the Tamar Campaign to break the conspiracy of silence and end sexual violence through contextual Bible studies that bring together socially engaged biblical scholars, theologians and pastors with "ordinary" readers of the Bible (literate or not), who share their resources in order to find empowering and liberating ways of living.

The workshop was the collaborative work of FECCLAHA, St Paul's Theological College, Limuru and WCC and in partnership with the Ujamaa Centre. Forty-five participants (25 women and 20 men) and facilitators from 20 sub-Saharan countries attended, among them lay theologians, administrators of theological institutions, pastors and social scientists. Participants were drawn from a wide range of WCC member churches as well as Pentecostal churches and represented anglophone, francophone and lusophone countries.

The workshop had three major components:

- contextual Bible studies on 2 Samuel 13:1-22; 2 Samuel 11:1-27 and Mark 5:21-6:1 and sessions on different kinds of violence against children and women; and case studies on rape, incest and child sexual molestation;

- launching of the Tamar Campaign in Africa by planting 30 trees on the grounds of St Paul's, Limuru; and

- worshiping in local churches in Limuru and Nairobi with the opportunity to preach or speak about the campaign.

Participants appreciated the opportunity to engage in such a difficult topic that has been shrouded in denial, deep-rooted secrecy, conspiracy of silence and ignorance despite the fact that experts acknowledge that sexual violence happens more often in Christian homes, manses, rectories, churches and church-related institutions than anywhere else.

There was overwhelming consensus that for contextual Bible studies to be effective on any topic, proper training of facilitators must take place and resources on the methodology be produced to accompany the training. A good example on how the methodology can be misunderstood and misused was experienced at the campaign launch dinner where an invited guest preacher used the wrong biblical narrative on Tamar (Genesis 38:12-30). Moreover he used inappropriate imageries and stories on women in his sermon.

Fortunately for the workshop, Gerald West, one of the facilitators and initiators of the Tamar Campaign, had produced a resource manual: *Doing Contextual Bible Study* to provide a sample of nine Bible studies shaped extensively by communities of the poor and marginalized in South Africa that come from real life contexts. Additional books and articles were made available to each participant to introduce them to the basic principles of contextual Bible study and the wide range of violence against children and women.

In addition to the symbol of trees signifying the beginning of a new journey for all those who will benefit from the Tamar Campaign, the WCC workshop also used the symbols of light (candle) and life (water) as a way of suggesting a variety of symbols that people can use to launch the campaign in their local context.

During the Bible study on King David and Bathsheba (wife of Uriah), participants were able to name this narrative as a rape case instead of the traditional interpretation of adultery. Both this narrative and that of Tamar and Amnon, demonstrated that a number of people are usually involved in the rape of one woman and how the crime also leads to further violence – creating a conspiracy of secrecy and silence and a chain of violence.

At the tree planting launch, a sample of eight cases of rape reported in Kenyan newspapers in January and February 2005 were read aloud while two women held the newspaper pages with the stories and pictures. This was a powerful moment of the reality in Kenya (in a peacetime context) to the extent that some participants were overcome with emotion and were unable to plant the trees because they were having to relive their own stories.

At the dinner, in a quiz by the Nairobi Women's Hospital (a private hospital that has a centre that provides services to sexually violated women, children and men – about five percent of all cases are male – free of charge if they report within 72 hours) on sexual violence, it was enlightening, as well as shocking, to learn that 45 percent of cases that are reported at the hospital are of girls under the age of 15.

Prior to the workshop the planning committee hosted by St Paul's College did a lot of promotional work on the launch of the Campaign among churches, NGOs and UN agencies that focus on gender-based violence as a way of creating partnerships and alliances beyond church institutions. The workshop provided an occasion for ecumenical learning and educational skills. However, the greatest challenge is to raise funds to support training of facilitators and to encourage theological educators and theologians to develop relevant curricula and liturgies for churches and teaching institutions to keep the vision alive.

The Tamar narrative is giving survivors of rape, incest and people living with HIV and AIDS the courage to break the conspiracy of silence and secrecy surrounding their lives.

According to West and Zondi-Mabizela, the Tamar Campaign goes beyond sexual violence. "In the area of economic justice, we can provide resources, including Bible studies, which contribute to building basic economic literacy. We often use these opportunities to introduce the campaign. Because the campaign addresses issues which are a growing problem in our communities, it is usually received well. People are always shocked and disappointed to find that there are texts that are hardly ever read in our churches. When we ask groups to write down their plans of action after workshops, one of their goals is to challenge their leaders to read the texts which we use for the campaign."

In the midst of great misery, suffering and senseless death, people are finding words and actions of encouragement that remind them that death does not have the last word. Upon hearing the cry of Tamar, women and men are expected to act to end violence, restore dignity, health and to nurture peace in our lives.

Appendix One
African Ecumenical Covenants

OUR COVENANT WITH GOD

We, the people and churches in Africa, give thanks for the manifold blessings bequeathed upon us by God.

We acknowledge that African leaders have committed crimes against their own kith and kin in the past and at present times.

We repent now of our sins against each other and beseech you O God to heal our land and deliver us from all evil.

Our hearts are yearning to be freed from despair so that we may endure in faith, because of God's promise to restore our dignity and fulfill all our dreams.

May God grant us the wisdom and knowledge to harness the growing public goodwill towards a new vision of life for our people in Africa and for the rest of the world. Let us renew our faith in the God of love in whom our future is safe and our grief is turned into great joy.

We, African people on the continent and in the diaspora, having been reminded afresh of our difficult past, but, inspired by the stories of resistance with courage and sacrifice of our fore parents, and empowered by the signs of hope such as increasing acceptance of democratic governance, the end of the apartheid regime in South Africa, and the Truth and Reconciliation Commission of South Africa, hereby renew our commitment to reconstruct and rebuild our communities and work tirelessly for a future of Africa full of life in abundance. We commit ourselves to:

- continue the unfinished task of transforming our social, political and economic systems and institutions for an inclusive and just society; seek and pursue peace and reconciliation for our people and communities;
- establish appropriate ethical values in work, governance and management, and good stewardship;
- do everything in our means to overcome the scourge of HIV/AIDS; and
- affirm the right of African children to hope for a bright future, which we shall help to work out with all our strength and all our ability.

We therefore renew our covenant with God in fulfilling these promises and invite men and women of goodwill, and especially this assembly, to accompany us in this journey of hope.

December 1998, Harare.

COVENANT DOCUMENT ON HIV/AIDS

Preamble

The Lord God is the creator of heaven and earth; the creator of all life forms in the earth community. He created all life and everything good. In this HIV/AIDS era, he sees the misery of his people, who are infected and affected by this disease; he has heard their cry on the account of this epidemic. He knows their sufferings and he has come down to deliver them from HIV/AIDS. So he calls to send us to the infected and affected, to bring his people, his creation, out of the HIV/AIDS epidemic. Now therefore this assembly recognizes God's call to us and hence makes this covenant with God today:

1. Life and HIV/AIDS Prevention

We shall remember, proclaim and act on the fact that the Lord our God, created all people and all life and created life very good (Gen. 1-2). We shall, therefore, seriously and effectively undertake HIV/AIDS prevention for all people – Christians and non-Christians, married, single, young and old, women and men, poor and rich, black, white, yellow, all people everywhere – for this disease destroys life and its goodness, thus violating God's creation and will.

2. Love and HIV/AIDS Care

We shall remember, proclaim and act on the fact that love is from God and everyone who loves is born of God and knows God. Those who say, 'I love God', and hate their sisters and brothers are liars, for unless you love your sisters and brothers whom you see, you cannot love God whom you have never seen (I John 4:7-21). We shall, therefore, do all that is necessary and within our power to encourage both men and women to love, care, support and heal all those who are infected and affected by HIV/AIDS in our communities, countries and continent.

3. Treatment and HIV/AIDS Drugs

We shall remember, proclaim and act on the fact that the earth and everything in it belongs to the Lord and that he has given it over to all human beings for custodianship (Ps. 24:1; Gen. 1:29). We shall therefore, openly and persistently undertake prophetic and advocacy roles for all the infected who are denied access to affordable HIV/AIDS drugs until anti-retrovirals are available to all who need them.

4. Compassion, HIV/AIDS Stigma and Discrimination

We shall remember, proclaim and act on the fact that the Lord our God, is a compassionate God, who calls upon us to be compassionate, to suffer with those who suffer, to enter their places and hearts of pain and to seek lasting change of their suffering (Luke 6:36; Matt. 25:31-46). We shall therefore, have zero tolerance for HIV/AIDS stigma and discrimination and do all that is necessary to eliminate the isolation, rejection, fear and oppression of the infected and affected in our communities. We shall declare HIV/AIDS stigma and discrimination an unacceptable sin before God and all believers and in all our communities.

5. Poverty and HIV/AIDS

We shall remember, proclaim and act on the fact that the Lord our God, who created all the resources of the earth, blessed both women men and gave them the resources of the earth for their sustenance (Gen. 1:28-29). We shall, therefore, work to empower all the poor and denounce all the cultural, national and international structures, laws and policies that have condemned billions to poverty, thus denying them their God-given rights and, in the HIV/AIDS era, exposing them to infection and denying them quality care and treatment.

6. Gender Inequalities and HIV/AIDS

We shall remember, proclaim and act on the fact that the Lord our God created humankind in his image. In his image, he created them male and female, he blessed them both and gave both of them leadership and resources in the earth; he made them one in Christ (Gen. 1:27-29; Gal 3:28-29). We shall, therefore, denounce gender inequalities that lead boys and men to risky behaviour, domination and violence; that deny girls and women leadership, decision-making powers and property ownership thus exposing them to violence, witchcraft accusation, widow dispossession and survival sex – fueling HIV/AIDS infection and lack of quality care and treatment.

7. Children and HIV/AIDS

We shall remember, proclaim and act on the fact that the Lord our God welcomes children. He has given his kingdom to them and he is the father of all orphans (Mark 9:33-37; 10:13-16; Ps. 68:5; Ps. 146:9). We shall, therefore, work to empower and protect all children and denounce all the national and international structures, cultures, policies, laws and practices that expose children to sexual abuse and exploitation, HIV/AIDS stigma and discrimination, dispossession and poverty, thus exposing them to HIV/AIDS infection and lack of quality care.

8. Church, People Living with AIDS and HIV/AIDS

We shall remember, proclaim and act on the fact that we are one body of Christ and if one member suffers, we all suffer together with it; that the Lord our God identifies with the suffering and marginalized and heals the sick (1 Cor. 14: 26; Matt. 25:31-46). We shall, therefore, become a community of compassion and healing, a safe place for all PLWAs (people living with HIV/AIDS) to live openly and productively with their status.

9. Human Sexuality and HIV/AIDS

We shall remember, proclaim and act on the fact that the Lord our God created human sexuality and created it good (Gen. 2:18-25). We shall, therefore, test for infection, denounce sexual violence, abstain before marriage, be faithful in marriage and practice protected sex to avoid HIV/AIDS infection and plunder on life, for all life is sacred and prevention should be seriously pursued to protect life.

10. Justice and HIV/AIDS

We shall remember, proclaim and act on the fact that the Lord our God sees, hears, knows the suffering of people and comes down to liberate them (Ex. 3:1-12; Luke 4:16-22). We shall, therefore, declare the Jubilee and we shall proclaim liberty throughout the land and to all its inhabitants (Lev. 25:10), for unless and until justice is served to all people in the world, until justice rolls down like waters and righteousness like an ever-flowing stream, HIV/AIDS cannot be uprooted.

Compiled by EHAIA and adopted
at the AACC 8th General Assembly
Yaoundé, Cameroon, 22-27 November, 2003

THE KIGALI COVENANT

Love your neighbour as yourself.

Mark 12:31

This Covenant with God and with each other is based on the second commandment given to humanity.

We, Christians, from the churches in Africa and beyond, thank God for making it possible for us to gather at the workshop on Lasting Peace in Africa in Kigali, Rwanda, from 14th to 19th April, 2004.

We came to Kigali, to stand in solidarity with the people of Rwanda who suffered terribly the horror of genocide that claimed the lives of more than one million innocent people in 1994. We listened to the testimonies of the survivors of the genocide, and visited genocide remembrance sites where we saw with our own eyes evidence of people's inhumanity to people. We accept guilt for inaction during the genocide in Rwanda before God and offer our apology, as some Rwandese churches did, to the people of Rwanda.

We saw the remnants of the genocide in the form of bones, skulls and dilapidated clothing and personal belongings of babies, children, youth and adults. They were frighteningly displayed as a reminder of the dark hundred days the Rwandan genocide lasted, at the NTARAMA MEMORIAL (formerly a Roman Catholic Chapel) as well as the KIGALI MEMORIAL CENTRE. We also heard stories of women of the genocide who were raped and who are today living with HIV/AIDS and bruised bodies; child-headed households and totally handicapped persons. These, the ecumenical family must undertake to assist in any way possible. As we pondered on the genocide stories, we were convinced that the perpetrators of the genocide killed their humanness, cut their relationship with God, before they could take away the humanness of others. The depth of the horror challenged us to deeply reflect on ways and strategies with which we can build ever-lasting peace in Rwanda in particular and the rest of Africa in general. The abuse, anger, tension, humiliation, trauma, pain and tears inherent in any genocide experience like those of Rwanda remind us of the events leading up to the crucifixion of our Lord Jesus Christ. (Matt. 27)

The false accusations and torture of the innocent are truly degrading, to say the least, and an affront to the Gospel of Christ. Hence, like Peter, the Apostle, the best human response would have been to encourage the victims to draw their swords in revenge; and yet Jesus ordered Peter, His disciple, to put away his sword. Christ, the Master warns that those who kill by the sword would die by the sword. (Matt. 26:48-52)

This is an experience that teaches us to struggle for peace at all costs. This is why as Christians we teach and preach confession and repentance before the message of peace, reconciliation and love to all and sundry. We thank God for the victory of Easter – for bringing us back to life, for bringing Rwanda back to life. The significance of Easter being that Christ rose from death in a victorious way. We are therefore grateful to God, the sustainer and giver of life for the hope and courage found within and among Rwandans who embarked with determination on the process of reconstruction of this beautiful country and reconciliation of its sons and daughters. Many countries on our continent have the potential of repeating the Rwandan experience and now that we have time to prevent a similar occurrence, we commit ourselves that never again should such a degree of violence and crime against humanity be allowed to occur in any of our countries. Consequently, we, in the workshop dwelt on identifying issues such as manipulation of ethnic identities, dominant tribal attitudes that have the potential to destabilize the continent of Africa and do hereby covenant with God and each other to:

- Share widely our experience and invite all persons of good will to work for peace in Africa and the world at large.
- Work and promote good governance practices that protect the integrity and dignity of creation.
- Stand up and speak against behaviour, pronouncements and practices that have the tendency to set one group of people against another.
- Challenge the youth and the leadership of churches and governments to feed the minds and souls of their people with love, peace and rec-

onciliatory messages so that painful experiences in human memory are not exploited.

- Pledge to ensure that never again should Africa experience genocide.
- Pledge with the World Council of Churches, All Africa Conference of Churches, the sub-regional fellowships, National Christian Councils and all other confessional and religious bodies to help build the capacity of our churches in advocacy and be proactive in the prevention of conflicts.
- Regularly call on organizations such as the African Union and the regional economic blocs to ensure that rapid response mechanisms are in place to prevent wars and acts of genocide.

We were touched and overwhelmed by reports on the efforts of the Rwandan government, churches and humanitarian agencies for the solidarity and acts of healing given to the victims of the genocide, even though more resources are needed to complete the task of restoration. We therefore call for a strong advocacy effort and support of the healing process currently taking place in Rwanda. While we plead for support for the efforts of the Rwandan government, the churches are encouraged to witness to its prophetic ministry by standing for truth, justice and reconciliation. As we renew our covenant with God and each other, we assure all genocide victims across the globe that you are in our hearts as we seek to fulfill these promises. We invite men and women of good will to accompany us in this journey aimed at the restoration of the integrity of humanity in our troubled world.

Kigali, Rwanda, April 18, 2004

Appendix Two
Statements on Africa from WCC Central and Executive Committees

AFRICA: CHALLENGES
FOR THE ECUMENICAL MOVEMENT

Central Committee, Geneva, 26 August – 2 September, 1999

1. Introduction

Africa has changed so radically, and so often, in these last few hundred years. The Africans have been used and abused; the evil of apartheid grew and prospered; the rich mineral resources of the continent became fair game for others and the standard of living of Africans declined. But the heartbeat of Africa is still strong and steady as witnessed at the Africa Plenary of the eighth assembly, in Harare, Zimbabwe. There is indeed a renaissance in Africa and there is indeed a new vision being born in African theology and spirituality.[1]

Eric Hobsbawm, the most outstanding British historian now living, describes the twentieth century in terms of extremes. In his celebrated book, *The Age of Extremes* he argues that, from the point of view of history the twentieth century was a short one spanning 1914-1991.[2] He advances very convincing reasons. But for Africa the twentieth century was quite a long and tortuous one. It started in 1884 with the partitioning of the continent at the Berlin Conference, and ended in 1994 with the inauguration of Nelson Mandela as the first truly democratically elected president of a new South Africa. The two reference points signify the twin legacy of the experience of Africa in her relationship with Europe – that of exploitation and domination on the one hand, and resistance and struggles on the other. The defeat of apartheid was the end point fulfilment of the vision articulated by the Pan-Africanist movement – the vision of political independence for the whole of Africa, from Egypt to South Africa, and from Eritrea to Congo.

Paradoxically, while the era of colonial domination was being buried in Pretoria, a new question sprang from the earth in Rwanda – the question of viable and inclusive governance systems for Africa and the economic and cultural benefits derived therefrom. The most gruesome and meticulously planned slaughter of human beings took place in Rwanda precisely as Mandela was being installed president of post-apartheid South Africa. In fact some of the journalists who covered Mandela's inauguration were redirected to Rwanda to cover the genocide. So in South Africa and in Rwanda, "Africa was witnessing, at once, the most hopeful and the most distressing events imaginable."

2. The Partitioning of the Continent, the makings of the first dream for a better Africa, and the Nation-State Problematic

In the introduction to his voluminous and most comprehensive book, *The Scramble for Africa*, Thomas Pakenham opens with these words: "The scramble for Africa bewildered everyone, from the humblest African peasant to the master statesmen of the age, Lord Salisbury and Prince Bismarck." Exactly 115 years ago decisions were arrived at in Berlin that were to determine the future and destiny of Africa and her people.

In the Berlin Conference of 1884-1885 Africans were not consulted much less represented. Present at the conference were all European nations except Switzerland. USA did not attend. David Livingstone, the "missionary-explorer" was most insightful when he coined the "3 Cs"; commerce, Christianity and civilization, as the strategy for opening up Africa to Europeans. To the "3 Cs" Africans would, of course, add a fourth, "conquest". Livingstone argued that trade, not the gun, would liberate Africa. But even a casual evaluation would show that trade, like the gun, was harmful to Africa. Either way you look at it the African was the loser. For the participants at the Berlin Conference, Africa was recognized merely as a great reservoir of imperial treasure. The natural resources featured prominently on the agenda but not the people of Africa. The people did not matter even when they were defining "the conditions under which future territorial annexations in Africa might be recognized."

If the Berlin Conference initiated the colonial project, the liberation project has its genesis in the first Pan-African Congress in Paris, 1919. The Congress called for freedom, democracy, justice, economic betterment and human dignity for the African people. This message from Paris was sharpened further at the Fifth Pan-African Congress in Manchester in 1945 at which the delegates from Africa and the diaspora stated, "**We are determined to be free and we shall be free. We will fight in every way we can for freedom, democracy and social betterment.**" That vision was to guide the African struggles for liberation. It was finally fulfilled with the end of institutional apartheid in South Africa in 1994.

Whether we look at the Africa of 1884 or the one of 1999, economics is a powerful factor in determining the relationships between the outside world and Africa. Cecil Rhodes did not mince words when he confessed that:

> "... my cherished idea is a solution for the social problem, i.e. in order to save the 40,000,000 inhabitants of the United Kingdom from a bloody civil war, we colonial statesmen must acquire new lands to settle the surplus population, and to provide new markets for the goods produced in the factories and mines. *An empire*, as I have always said, *is a bread and butter question*."[3] (emphasis added)

This clearly demonstrates that Africa was colonized more for her economic significance to Europe than for anything else. Everything else was either secondary or was a means and strategy to that end. Today the bewildered African peasant and even the European statesman must be totally lost as to where or even what Africa is.

In the struggle against colonialism, nationalism became both a means and an end in itself. Little, and in some cases, no efforts were made to link the aspirations of the people and practical realities of what would constitute a new nation to be born out of the struggle. As Frantz Fanon clearly puts it,

> "National consciousness, instead of being the all-embracing crystallization of the innermost hopes of the whole people, instead of being the immediate and most obvious result of the mobilization of the people, will be in any case only an empty shell, a crude and fragile travesty of what it might have been. The faults that we find in it are quite sufficient explanation of the facility with which, when dealing with young and independent nations, the nation is passed over for the race, and the tribe is preferred to the state."[4]

With independence the reins of power were passed to the leaders who had been ushered in by the masses, acting more on spontaneity than a rational understanding of what such independence entails. On their part the elite middle class, who were the only ones well placed to assume political leadership seized the opportunity to grab. To them independence simply meant hoisting a flag, composing a new national anthem and taking over the positions of the out-going colonial personnel. Independence therefore was reduced to "flag-independence". The economy was not in the scheme of things as far as this leadership was concerned. Taking over, and not transformation of the economy, was the basic objective.

So one of the things that went wrong with the first African dream was that the national economy at independence was not set on a new footing. The second one was the adoption of the nation-state as a model for the new independent "nations" of Africa.

Soon after attainment of political independence the African leader was to discover that he could not deliver goods to the people. He had no economic base of his own. The economic system the leader inherited could only be maintained (not developed) by the colonial master he was supposed to have kicked out. That indeed was a rude reality, and what was even more shocking to the African leader was to learn that his own survival as a leader, and the survival of his government, depended on subsidies from the former colonial power. The pride of nationalism melted away and the new African leader simply settled down to amass wealth for himself and family, and could not care less whether the national economy was plundered to the ground. In fact he became the greatest looter of the economy even as his lifestyle was characterized by conspicuous consumption totally oblivious to the abject poverty of the masses. Since the masses were now an enemy he needed a bigger army and bigger police force to control them. Disproportionate budget allocations vis-à-vis social welfare, like health and education, were directed towards security.

Too unpopular to face free elections, the African heads of states discovered new tactics and strategies for staying in power, such as one-party rule. In most cases elections were postponed *sine die*, or the president simply decreed all other political parties except his own to be illegal. Military coups d'état or assassinations became the only alternative methods of change in ruling. That is why Africa has hardly any former presidents but many late heads of state.

The role of the intelligentsia began to be ambiguous. Many succumbed to the patronage of the political leadership. They served to rationalize the status quo and were rewarded accordingly. The majority of journalists fell into this category; they dared not write anything critical of the government, and least of all the president, who by this time had acquired the venerated title of the "Father of the Nation". Nor did they dare advocate for the poor and the oppressed. Artists even composed songs full of lavish praise of the man (without exception all presidents were, and still are, men) describing him *sine qua non* as far as the existence of the nation and its people were concerned. Those intellectuals are distinguished by their intellectual dishonesty.

A small number of intelligentsia, though, dared to be honest to themselves and kept faith with the people. They spoke out. They risked imprisonment and even death. They criticized the political leadership either, in the first instance, satirically as in the enormous body of literature in the African Writer Series, or lately, directly. Those were the first candidates of African exiles, who today are numerous in Europe, North America and elsewhere.

With the number of "enemies" increasing by the day, protection of his regime became the highest preoccupation of the African head of state. He was least concerned about the state of the national economy or that of the citizens, most of whom he suspected of disliking him all the while.

The flawed nation-state model

The second problem, and arguably the main root cause of the woes of Africa, is the nation-statism which was adopted at independence. The most frequently cited reasons for the failure of governance and stability in Africa are corruption, ethnicism and nepotism, and external exploitation. Hardly mentioned, especially in the mass media, are the flaws and failures of the nation-state model itself. But there is now a discourse emerging that seriously questions the legitimacy of the nation-state for Africa.

Already by the 1980s it was clear that the nation-state model was not functioning well in Africa. It was a flawed model and political independence did not redress the situation, because, according to Basil Davidson, "the first generation of African leaders failed to re-establish vital inner links with the poor and dispossessed of this [continent];" or, "it was the failure of post-colonial communities to find and insist upon means of living together by strategies less primitive and destructive than rural kinship networks, whether the ethnic clientism or its camouflage in no less clientist multi-party systems."[5]

If you have someone on your back, against your will, the most natural thing to do is to get him off your back. That is the priority. Thereafter when you have rid yourself of the oppressive weight on your back, you then pause to decide what to do with the attained freedom. It seems that is what happened with Africa. At the time of colonialism the most pressing issue was to attain political freedom. Even those who foresaw some of the dangers inherent in the impending post colonial nation-state and even warned against them, finally accepted independence within the colonial framework. Nkrumah, for instance, while accepting the British government's offer to lead the then colonial Gold Coast to independent Ghana, said to the Ghanaian people that "there is a great risk in accepting office under this new constitution which still makes us half-slaves and half-free." Very few understood, much less heeded Nkrumah's warning.

The majority of leaders were preoccupied with the promises of independence and that resonated with the aspirations of the people. Nationalism therefore had much less to do with national cause, and more to do with the demands of a social nature and content. The Malagasy nationalist, Jacques Rabemananjara, remarked in 1958 that, "one thing's certain in today's political vocabulary, the word nationalism means, generally, the unanimous movement of coloured peoples against western domination. What does it matter if the word doesn't really describe the phenomenon to which we like to apply it?"[6] It is because of such pragmatism that the struggles for political independence have been seen in terms of social struggle through which aspirations like getting back the land, better education and better health services for all would be fulfilled.

It is important to note that some African leaders, though, had alternative views to the nation-state model but they stood no chance of promoting their ideas. In 1946 Africans representing twelve French colonies held a congress in Bamako with the intention of forming "a political movement dedicated to the realization of two large independent federations instead of twelve nation-states".[7] Their counterparts in the British colonies also had discussions about forming federations either before or shortly after independence. But the British and French were so intent on transferring power to post-colonial nation-states that they could not tolerate anything to do with potential federations. Their concern with the emerging nation-states in Africa was not so much whether they served African interests but that they should be in line with British or French national interests. As Davidson comments,

> "[A]fter 1950 the British in power persisted with a remarkable complacency in shepherding the British colonies, not into a society of interrelated states such as the pioneering nationalists desired for their continent, but into accumulation of newly invented and entirely separate nation-states, a very different thing."

For their part the French strategy was to elevate their colonies in membership in *la plus grande France*. The only nationalism they recognized was the French nationalism.

Once those objectives were set, what the British and the French needed to do was to spot and promote the "right" candidates for leadership in the impending nation-states.

The benefits concomitant with the promised high offices whetted the appetite of the candidates and they became very enthusiastic protagonists of nation-statism and national building. They were indeed the *interlocuteurs valables* after the necessary tutoring and went on to negotiate independence within the rubric of nation-states.

Several critical points were overlooked in the decision by the colonial powers to offer, and for the African nationalists to accept, the nation-state model:

1) The acceptance of the nation-state model for independent Africa meant the acceptance of the moral and political practices of colonial rule in its institutions. The colonial partition legacy had far-reaching implications not only for governance but in social, cultural and psychological aspects of peoples' lives.

2) Nation-statism is to be understood in its ethos and ideology whose practices were incompatible with the interests and aspirations of the people of Africa.

3) No opportunities were offered to discuss credentials and potentials of the nation-state, nor to explore possible alternatives. The model was simply imposed on the Africans who, needless to emphasize, were the weaker party in the negotiations for independence.

4) In many cases the national consciousness, a prerequisite to establishment of the nation-state in Europe (and one that took many decades to develop), existed only in the hope of a few educated elite in Africa. From the point of view of colonial powers the interests and aspirations of the ordinary folk did not count. Their views are summed up in the words of a British observer in 1920, concerning the peasants in Moldavia and Walachia; he said that in respect to politics peasants are "a dead and helpless mass." That means as far as the British and French were concerned, the peasants had no right to be considered in the equation and negotiations for independence of their countries. And subsequently the African leader did not involve the peasants in the governance of the state.

From the point of view of the interests of the African people the legitimacy of the nation-state is further questioned vis-à-vis its (the state's) role in the Cold War era. The African countries became battlefields of super power rivalry. Either of the super powers helped the state to acquire the capacity to control and suppress the people. So, both during the colonial period as well as the post colonial period, the concept and the practice of the state was to be an instrument of control.

The state was not about good governance but control. That led to the privatization of the state, which all the while became a formidable force, not to serve the interests of the people, but in effect and in fact, as a threat to their interests.

Politics in Africa, therefore, has been shaped by that understanding of the nation-state in Africa. It is primarily about access to state power, and the goal of political struggle is to capture the all-powerful state power. In that case, state power in Africa is overvalued, and the struggle over it, is brutal, intense and ruthless.

The big question is how do you turn around, or better still transform the nation-state in Africa to serve the interests of the people. Such is the daunting task ahead for the African people at the dawn of the new century and third millennium. No wonder then that Basil Davidson describes the nation-state in Africa as "the black man's burden". It is to be remembered that the "civilizing of the African savages was once described as the white man's burden."

3. The quest for a new vision

The Pan-Africanist vision of political independence by all means possible was a strong reaction to the European colonial project perfected at the 1884-5 Berlin Conference. For a century, that vision would inspire and guide the liberation struggles in Africa until 1994 when formal apartheid came to an end. With the end of apartheid the Pan-Africanist vision was vindicated. But that did not mean the end of exploitation and domination of Africa by external powers, nor the end of self-authenticated suffering and oppression by despotic African leaders. The challenge now is for Africans to dream new dreams and see new visions. There is need for overarching, long term visions to inform and guide the new struggles against new problems and challenges.

It will be too pretentious for this background note to attempt at formulating such visions. What it attempts to do is to identify possible signs of hope that might lead to articulation of new visions for building a better Africa.

Reconstruction

From Christian theological reflection liberation, as a theme, is derived from Exodus in the Old Testament. The liberation of the Israelites from the bondage in Egypt has inspired many oppressed peoples around the world, and served as a basis for many Christians to legitimize their involvement in the struggle against oppression. That was the case for African struggles against colonialism and apartheid, Latin Americans and Asians against dictatorships of despotic leaders, and African

Americans against racism. Through such struggles liberation came to mean more than political freedom. It became a paradigm for struggle for justice, peace and the recovery of human dignity. Those values could not be attained through the developmentalist paradigm either.

In the 1990s Christian theology has pointed to the imperatives of shifting the "paradigms from the post-Exodus to Post-Exile imagery, with reconstruction as the resultant theological axiom."[8] Mugambi continues to contend that, "the twenty-first century should be a century of reconstruction in Africa." The call for reconstruction is not limited to the theological realm. In secular circles as well there are initiatives for social reconstruction. Even governments have formulated and operated programmes and projects of reconstruction, most notable among them being the South African government's RDP (Reconstruction and Development Programme).

The contemporary Africa may be compared to Europe in the fifteenth and sixteenth centuries when a process of reconstruction followed long periods of cultural stagnation and Islamic onslaught. That reawakening in Europe was envisaged as **renaissance** to signify the rebirth of the society. The need for rebirth of the African society cannot be over-emphasized.

A lot of reflection and work on reconstruction in Africa have been done in the last five years. Several books have been written on theology of reconstruction and on social reconstruction.

In the run up to the eighth general assembly, the World Council of Churches (WCC) carried out a programme under the title of **Towards Reconstruction in Africa**. The objectives of the programme were to listen to the voices of the churches and peoples and learn from their experience of life with God in their country, region and the African situation in general; to promote a culture of life and peace with justice on which should be based the quest for just, participatory and sustainable societies; to enhance the fulfilment of human dignity in Africa and the affirmation of the African identity; to discern the Church's mission in peace-making, conflict prevention and management, and reconciliation at community and national levels, taking into account respective African values; to promote national, regional and pan-African cooperation in the search for peace, sustainable and viable communities; and to enhance the contribution of the churches to the building of democracy; facilitating a coordinated analytical focus on situations of severe human and people's rights violation.

In collaboration with NCCs, AACC and some northern ecumenical partners, the WCC has been able to promote models for active solidarity with Africa, especially with the faith communities and nations at large, in order to identify ways of developing and/or stimulating new forms of solidarity between churches and peoples of each region with the ecumenical family and the international community at large; and encourage the movement of ideas and people in support of the efforts of Africans towards life with dignity and for the creation of sustainable communities.

For continued work under this imperative to be effective we must discover the solid foundations upon which reconstruction is to be effected. We must discover the wholenesses that would guarantee sustainable reconstruction. Wholeness, because there is prevailing alienation and fragmentation experienced by the people in virtually all realms of life – social, cultural, political, economic and even ecclesial.

The renewed efforts and interests in the study of the nature and tenets of the "African Religion" by the African scholars signifies the "thirst" and search for life in all its wholeness. In this vein dialogue between African Religion and Christianity will certainly gather greater currency in the twenty-first century. It is also likely that a dialogue between "palaver" and "ethics of discourse" will be inevitable because of the growing interest in ethical dimensions of African communities. The need for such dialogue is not just for the benefit of Africans but it will be mutual. The deeper scholars understand primal traditions the more they realize the potential contribution of African Religion to understanding and meaning of life of humans and the whole creation. In his reflections of these themes, Bediako of Ghana is convinced that "it is in Africa that the opportunity for a serious theological encounter and cross-fertilization between Christian and primal traditions [African Religion], which was lost in Europe, can be regained; and Africa may well be the place for redeeming wrongs done not to her alone in the name of mission."[9] Miller affirms Bendiako's conviction when he suggests that, "whatever the nature of Africa's future, it is now clear that its religious heritage in the form of African Religion and Christianity as received via the missionary encounter will be in the service of the continent's reconstruction."[10]

Reconstruction of Africa must be informed by a **communitarian ethic**. Community consciousness in Africa is a precious virtue that must be guarded carefully. For Africans life is community centred. "The African thought and action are deeply determined by the community"[11] without which the life of the individual could be greatly deficient. The individual gives to the community and in return receives manifold from the community. Hence there is mutuality between the individual human person and the community. Their interaction generates interdependency which is based on the fact that all members of the community have the task of mutually increasing the life force for the benefit of all. "Everybody's behaviour and ethical action have consequences for the whole community: the good contributes to the increase of life, while the evil destroys or at least reduces life."[12]

The communitarian ethic therefore has a lot to offer in both social and ethical reconstruction in Africa. It could in fact provide a solid basis for economic and political reconstruction as well.

With such rich religious heritage the African has a lot to offer in the dialogue and cross-fertilization between Africa and the rest of humanity. It also means that "Africa's future will not be secured by wholesale adoption of western economic, technical and social models though it is clear that it has been enormously influenced by them. Africa is not an island to itself. But the case is made that the people of this continent must be open to the world from a clear, well articulated perspective, based on Africa's religious and cultural values as well as an inclusive African process, accounting for the needs of all."[13]

As above, the process leading to political independence did not allow for serious search for viable and inclusive governance systems at the time of political independence. There are questions in Africa such as "when is a nation state?" or "what is the role of a nation state?" So reconstruction of legitimacy is central, as a basis for reconciliation and rebuilding. There is great urgency to rebuild institutions, modalities and processes which ensure a broad consensus among the main actors in the society on the exercise of power, institutions of the state and on the acquisition and utilization of resources. The church is just about the only visible institution, apart from the state, all other institutions in the civil society having been systematically disabled during the Cold War era. Hence it is clear that in Africa there is a crisis of institutions and any serious efforts at reconstruction must include reconstruction of institutions of civil society.

Illegitimacy of "liberation" struggles

In Africa the second half of the twentieth century was characterized by liberation struggles. Such struggles were legitimate because they were the means through which Africans were to achieve self-determination and recover the dignity which had been sacrificed on the altar of colonialism. With the end of apartheid the noble project of decolonization was achieved. Except for Southern Sudan and the former Spanish Sahara the legitimacy of other so-called struggles for liberation must be questioned. In this respect the causes and objectives of civil wars in Africa are to be critically analyzed and evaluated by anyone wanting to take a position one way or the other. One thing, though, is clear; the civil wars that are hangovers from the Cold War have no legitimacy whatsoever. Angola is a case in point. UNITA can hardly claim to be fighting for the total liberation of Angola anymore.

The war in Angola is a hangover from the Cold War era which has since degenerated into banditry and cannot in any way, shape or form be termed a liberation process. Worse still is the case of Sierra Leone. That war is sheer madness. The so-called rebels are responsible for the most diabolical atrocities ever. The killings and amputations of many innocent men, women, children and old people especially disqualify the rebel movement in Sierra Leone from any claim or pretences to redeeming the society. Its leaders have no business being part of a government of national unity. Instead they should be at The Hague facing trial for crimes against humanity.

Of late there have emerged new levels and ways of intervention in Africa. A good case in point is the Great Lakes Region (GLR) where we can observe very dangerous developments. Something must be done before these new forms/ways of intervention are institutionalized through private armies. The failure to arrest the process could lead to total disintegration of states like the Democratic Republic of Congo (DRC). Already there is talk of mercenaries in DRC whose main interests are to benefit from the natural riches of the country. As in the case of the rhino's horn, the natural resources are the curse of Africa.

As a result of such interventions and the widespread abuse of power by leaders, the African people are being penalized for refusing to be oppressed and for not allowing their resources to be plundered. This calls the ecumenical movement to find new ways of expressing solidarity and building relationships. How are we to understand our advocacy work vis-à-vis these developments in Africa in the twenty-first century?

Legitimacy of other forms of social intervention

While the need for peace and reconciliation in many parts of Africa cannot be disputed, there is nevertheless the need to be critical of some of the actors and methodologies in this area. Following the genocide in Rwanda and conflicts in [the] GLR (Great Lakes Region) there has been a proliferation of peace makers most of whom are not accountable to anybody. Conflict resolution has become simply fashionable if also very profitable. Similarly in the wake of democratization process, democracy specialists have descended on Africa. There is also a residue of development specialists whose motives are questionable.

Given this scenario it is obvious that conflicts are inevitable. What does peace-making mean here? Peace initiatives based on African traditional/cultural values must be encouraged. In this vein the work of *Nairobi Peace Initiatives* is welcome and should be supported.

Life with dignity in just and sustainable communities
   Caring for life as an overarching focus is very relevant for Africa. Given the enormous senseless and unnecessary loss of lives in Africa today, whether as a result of debt or other causes, we must revisit the whole question of the sanctity of life. The nature of conflicts and the form of violence prevalent in Africa today are very strange to the people of Africa. Traditionally the warriors, or any others doing the fighting, were totally forbidden to kill women and children. That is why we cannot understand what kind of breed are the rebels of Sierra Leone who dare kill and maim children and old people.

Legacy of domination and the struggle for self-determination for human dignity
   There are indications that suggest that in the early decades of the twenty-first century there will be a preoccupation with the search for what it takes to right the wrongs of the previous century, and millennium. In this respect several characteristics are relevant: repentance, forgiveness, reparations, reconciliation and healing.
   This is critical for Africa. Violation of dignity of the African people must be addressed and redressed. This should be the case for Africans both on the continent and in the diaspora. In both situations the African people continue to live with wounded and compromised dignity.
   It is at the same time a problem of impunity. Reparations do not have only to assume material dimensions. Violation of dignity is not only a justice question, it is a deeply theological one. That makes it imperative for the ecumenical movement to accompany the African people in their attempt to deal with the legacy of domination and all its derivatives.
   In this respect racism in the twenty-first century should be considered in a new light. It took the brutal murder of Stephan Lawrence for Britain to accept there was institutionalized racism in the London Metropolitan Police Force. What lessons do we learn from that development for the ecumenical work on racism in the years ahead?

Identities and Security
   De-construction and Reconstruction should be understood as initiatives for regionalization and are indicative of the perceived flaws of the nation state model. In concrete terms the regionalization has found expressions in the formation of Southern African Development Community (SADC), Economic Community for Eastern and Southern

Africa (COMESA), East African Cooperation (EACOOP) and Economic Community for Western African States (ECOWAS). What does this say to the issue of territorial integrity? Africans have generally agreed to keep the boundaries set by the colonial powers. But the regionalization initiatives suggest there is a strong desire to transcend geographical boundaries to achieve certain social, cultural and economic interests.

There is a very interesting process that gives ecumenical parallel to the economic regionalization. This has led to formation of Fellowship of Councils of Churches in Eastern and Southern Africa (FOCCESA), Fellowship of Christian Councils in Western Africa (FCCIWA) and Fellowship of Councils and Churches in the Great Lakes and Horn of Africa (FECLAHA). Alongside with AACC these fellowships are key ecumenical partners. At its launching in March 1999, FECLAHA committed itself to strive to encourage the citizens of that region to live as a people without boundaries. In so doing they are saying the boundaries created by the partitioning of Africa were for purposes of exploiting and dominating Africans. To that end those regionalization initiatives are exercises in de-construction of what was undertaken by the Berlin Conference. But they could also be seen as building blocks for reconstruction based on legitimate interests of the African people.

Conclusion

The excitements of the new millennium have to be tempered with the new responsibilities we will have as an ecumenical movement. The present millennium has been a complicated tapestry of history with some wonderful achievements. But there have also been some intensely sad and tragic times. The millennium ends with new forms of colonialism replacing the conquests of the last few hundred years. There is so much wrong that we have to set right in this new millennium. There are memories to be healed and broken relationships to be reconciled. God grant that we might see this magic January 1, 2000 as a challenge rather than merely a celebration[14] and that it may be the millennium of righting the wrongs, redeeming the history and discovering harmony with Creation.

NOTES

[1] Kobia, S.: paper presented to Faith and Order Commission, June 1999, Toronto, p. 5.
[2] Hobsbawm, E.: *The Age of Extremes*, 1994. Vintage Books, New York, p. 3.
[3] Hobson: *Imperialism: A Study.*
[4] Fanon, F.: *The Wretched of the Earth*, p. 148.

[5] Davidson, B.: *The Black Man's Burden*, 1993. E.A. Educational Publishers Ltd., Nairobi, p. 291.

[6] Ibid. p. 164.

[7] Ibid. p. 172.

[8] Mugambi, J.N.K.: *From Liberation to Reconstruction*, 1995. E.A. Educational Publishers Ltd., Nairobi, p. 5.

[9] Miller, Harold: "Perspectives on the Closure of an African Century", unpublished paper presented to a Mennonite retreat, Limuru, Kenya, Dec. 1998, p. 12.

[10] Ibid.

[11] Bujo, Benezer: *The Ethical Dimensions of Community*, 1998. Paulines Publications Africa, Nairobi, p. 182.

[12] Ibid.

[13] Miller, op. cit. p. 13.

[14] Kobia, op. cit.

STATEMENT ON PEACE IN ANGOLA

Sent to the WCC Central Committee from the Executive Committee of the Council of Christian Churches in Angola, August 1999

The leaders of the member churches of the Council of Christian Churches in Angola, at the 41st meeting of its Executive Committee, 5-6 August 1999, at the Formation and Culture Center in Luanda were aware and fearful of the daily worsening political, social, economic and cultural situation. There is thus need for action to be taken to avoid a humanitarian catastrophe greater than previous ones.

We acknowledge that Angola has been the victim of a long series of wars which have not succeeded in bringing peace. On the contrary, the country has been progressively destroyed with increasing numbers of people dying, displaced persons, refugees, disabled people and street children, together with a culture of violence which is reaching uncontrollable levels.

We, the leaders of churches gathered in this Executive Committee, acknowledge the urgent need to call the nation to reason so that it can find a rational way to solve the conflict.

In this context we, the leaders of the churches of this council, acknowledge that Angola and the life of Angolans are a gift from God which no one has the right to destroy.

Encounter between men and women of goodwill is a defence against any form of violence and we thus continue to believe that only agreement between all Angolans can save Angola from permanent conflict.

For us to be patriotic in our context must mean taking wise decisions which will save the life of all Angolans, create an environment favourable to the achievement of their hopes as a people created by God in God's image and make possible social, economic, religious and cultural development.

So that this can be our destiny:

1. We acknowledge that we are men and women of unclean lips and that we dwell in the midst of a people of unclean lips and we thus commit ourselves to:
2. Confess our weaknesses and develop attitudes which are worthy of the creator's (God's) will for us;
3. Continue to work for unity and cooperation between the churches and the vital forces in the nation which are concerned to develop a peaceful, democratic and prosperous country;
4. Encourage in this context our communities, the Angolan people in general and political and religious leaders to place at the top of their agenda the cessation of violence and the peaceful resolution of our conflicts;
5. Appeal to all Angolans and to the international community to recognize the grave humanitarian situation the country is experiencing and to join forces with us so that sufficient resources can be mobilized and honestly used for the most vulnerable communities.

Finally, as we move to the end of the century, we must celebrate the Jubilee, this is the time of grace that is offered to us so that peoples enslaved in all ways may be freed and able to hear the message that says, "God will speak peace to his people, to his saints, to those who turn to him in their hearts. Surely his salvation is at hand for those that fear him. Mercy and truth will meet, justice and peace will embrace, the Lord will give what is good to our land." (Psalm 85:8-13)

AFFIRMATION OF ECUMENICAL EFFORTS FOR PEACE AND JUSTICE

Letter to the Rev. Gaspar Domingos, Council of Christian Churches in Angola (SICA), 3 September 1999

Dear Rev. Domingos,

The Central Committee of the World Council of Churches, meeting in Geneva, 26 August – 3 September 1999, received with appreciation the statement of the Executive Committee of the SICA on peace in Angola. We appreciate your courage and the actions that you have taken that are an eloquent witness for peace and justice in your country.

We know well the enormous task that lies ahead of you. The need for Angolans to come together and to reason together has never been so urgent. This is critical to be able to reverse the present situation of mass assassinations. As your statement affirms so clearly, the life of every Angolan is a gift of God and no one has a right to destroy it. As we affirm the sanctity of life we also support the initiative mentioned in the appeal to Angolans to take wise decisions, decisions that could save Angolan lives.

We thank you for your presence and that of Rev. Caetano in the meeting of the Central Committee. That presence was of great benefit. The discussions and decisions taken with respect to the Decade to Overcome Violence are of particular interest and importance for Angolans and for the situation of your country. Your repudiation of all forms of violence in the resolution of conflict corresponds to the policies of the WCC and to the spirit of the Decade, whose objective is to overcome violence.

In the light of the above, I wish to express that the WCC is ready to accompany the Council of Christian Churches in Angola in the pursuit of peace, justice and reconciliation. We hope to receive soon news of the implementation of your plans of action.

In anticipation of receiving your plans, we express the wish that your ministry of peace and reconciliation be fulfilled for your people and your country. May the grace of our Lord Jesus Christ be with you as you pursue this important ministry.

Rev. Dr Konrad Raiser
General Secretary

MINUTE ON PEACE AND RECONCILIATION
BETWEEN ETHIOPIA AND ERITREA

Adopted by the Central Committee,
Geneva, 26 August – 3 September 1999

The World Council of Churches and many of its member churches and related agencies around the world have been deeply concerned about the conflict between Ethiopia and Eritrea, which has been raging with ever greater intensity since May 1998. We have grieved at the terrible, mounting toll of human life this war is again inflicting on peoples who have suffered so terribly and for so long from war, repression and abject poverty. Immediately after the outbreak of hostilities, the General Secretary wrote to the leaders of the two countries, imploring them to stop the fighting and to resolve the border issue, which was the immediate source of contention, by peaceful means.

Earlier this year an ecumenical delegation led by the WCC, including a representative of the All Africa Conference of Churches (AACC) and the Fellowship of Councils and Churches in the Great Lakes and Horn of Africa (FECCLAHA), visited both Ethiopia and Eritrea, to express the concerns of the churches around the world and to offer whatever assistance the WCC and the wider ecumenical movement may be able to render. The delegations met with government leaders, and especially with Orthodox, Protestant, Roman Catholic and Muslim leaders, who on both sides have formed religious committees to promote a peaceful solution.

These two religious committees will be meeting for a third time soon at the invitation of Norwegian Church Aid. Fervently hoping that the conversations they resume now may lead to agreement on joint steps to be taken for peace, the Central Committee of the World Council of Churches, meeting in Geneva, 26 August – 3 September 1999, conveys to the religious leaders on both sides our encouragement and the assurance of our prayers.

We know from our own experience how difficult is the road to peace, but we know that God Almighty expects all those who believe in Him to travel that road. We know how demanding is the way to justice, but God is a God of Justice. We know how long is the way to reconciliation, but God wills that we live together as sisters and brothers who love and care for one another. Be assured that we stand ready to accompany and support you when you are ready and able to travel together for the sake of God and all God's people. May God inspire your deliberations, unite your spirits, and equip you to bring a word of hope, a word of peace to the leaders of your countries and to all those who look to you for spiritual guidance.

MINUTE ON NIGERIA

Adopted by the Central Committee,
Geneva, 26 August – 3 September 1999

Bishop Michael K. Stephen of the Methodist Church of Nigeria has informed the Central Committee about the actions taken by the churches in Nigeria in response to the Memorandum and Recommendations on Nigeria adopted by the Central Committee in 1997. Among those recommendations was an appeal to the churches to keep the human rights situation in that country under close review and to inform the WCC of their actions, and to encourage the churches of Nigeria in their witness for human rights, justice and peace in Nigeria. The political situation in Nigeria has changed significantly since then, and the leadership of the Christian Association of Nigeria has taken a strong stand for justice, identifying itself with the suffering people of the country.

The Central Committee of the World Council of Churches, meeting in Geneva, 26 August – 3 September 1999,
- welcomes this report from the churches of Nigeria;
- commends them for their witness and their response to its earlier request; and
- requests the Officers to write to the Christian Association of Nigeria, conveying the gratitude of the Central Committee for the churches' efforts, encouraging them to continue to be a prophetic voice in the nation, and offering them support as they pursue reconciliation in Nigeria.

STATEMENT ON THE SITUATION IN THE SUDAN

Adopted by the Central Committee,
Potsdam, Germany, 28 January – 6 February 2001

Background. The conflict in Sudan has been on the ecumenical agenda for over three decades. The roots of the conflict lie in its history of slavery and colonialism and date back to 1956 when the country gained independence from Great Britain. The situation today, however, has become increasingly more complex than when the almost thirty-year long conflict began. The main causes of the conflict are to be found in:

* The divide-and-rule policy of the colonial rulers, manifested in the "Closed District Act" of 1935 that barred freedom of movement between the Northern and Southern provinces of Sudan;
* Unequal development policies between the North and the South that gave rise to present disparities;
* Religious rivalry, enforcement of cultural hegemony, tribalism and racism;
* Failure of the Government of Sudan to implement the spirit of the 1972 Addis Ababa Peace Accord that gave rise to the present environment of total lack of faith and trust amongst the Southerners against the Government in the North;
* The reluctance on the part of the Government of Sudan to abide by the Declaration of Principles (DOP) agreed to between the parties in the framework of mediation by IGAD (the East African Intergovernmental Agency for Development); and
* The refusal by the Government of Sudan to accept separation of religion and state in the Constitution.

From 1971 the WCC, in cooperation with the AACC, engaged actively in a mediation effort with the South Sudan Liberation Movement and the Government of Sudan that led to the 1972 Addis Ababa peace agreement. Though this agreement brought a cessation of hostilities and a substantial reform of government of a united Sudan, it eventually collapsed, giving rise to a new civil war.

In view of the new intensification of the fighting, the WCC Central Committee adopted a Minute on the Sudan in August 1992, expressing concern about the situations in South, East and West Sudan that had displaced thousands of civilians, especially including children. It called on the United Nations to promote a cease-fire in Southern Sudan and a disengagement of troops, together with resumption of the stalemated Abuja negotiations. The Central Committee reaffirmed the need for the WCC to remain in contact with the parties to the conflict in efforts to promote a just and lasting peace.

Again in September 1997 the Central Committee adopted a Statement on Sudan, where it welcomed the common position taken by the church leaders in North and South Sudan in their paper: "Here We Stand United in Action for Peace." That paper called for a stop to the war and dialogue for peace among the armed factions in the South and between them and the Government of Sudan. The Central Committee urged all parties, their supporters abroad and those seeking to assist in the achievement of a negotiated peace to support the resumption of the IGAD Peace process, to cooperate with it, and to place their various initiatives within the framework of the IGAD principles.

The Sudanese churches have been unceasing in their own efforts to promote peace at all levels. The New Sudan Council of Churches has undertaken a significant, innovative new effort in this direction through a series of People-to-People Peace Conferences in Southern Sudan. These have resolved a series of ethnic and communal conflicts and brought hope and stability to some of the areas most affected by the hostilities. The Khartoum-based Sudan Council of Churches has also developed an active programme in advocacy and grassroots peacemaking, especially among women and youth.

At the regional level, the IGAD Peace Process – that started with much promise and hope with the acceptance of the Declaration of Principles by the parties to the conflict – now shows signs of stagnation despite zealous efforts of the IGAD Secretariat as well as of Northern States members of the IGAD Partners Forum to keep the negotiations on track. These have not been sufficient to remove the primary obstacle in the way of negotiations, namely the reluctance on the part of the Government of Sudan to accept the principles of separation of religion and state and to implement fully the IGAD Declaration of Principles. As a result, impatience with the slow progress of negotiations has led to insistent new calls by the people of the South, and of their churches, for self-determination and independence from the North.

The current situation. In the late 1990s the Government's oil exploration efforts in Southern Sudan, in cooperation with Western and Asian petroleum companies, succeeded in producing some 150,000 barrels a day in the Upper Nile. Oil production has contributed to an escalation of the conflict and hardened the determination of the Government of Sudan to pursue a military solution to the conflict. The churches in Sudan, together with ecumenical partners abroad, have called for a just sharing of oil resources and have demanded that the oil revenue be spent on improving the situation of the people and not on promotion of the war effort through purchase with oil revenues of more sophisticated arms.

In its war effort the Government of Sudan has used air power ever since the war began in Southern Sudan. In recent times, however, aerial bombardment has targeted civilians and taken an increasingly heavy toll through high altitude bombing. Densely populated civilian areas like Kotobi and Lui have been bombed repeatedly, resulting in loss of life and destruction of property. One of these bombings that occurred in the hometown of Bishop Paride shortly after he addressed the Eighth WCC Assembly in Harare was vigorously protested immediately by the WCC Officers to the Government of Sudan through its embassy in Zimbabwe.

The continuing bombing has further increased the suffering of the people already caught in the midst of this seemingly endless conflict. Bombing missions have not spared NGOs involved in humanitarian relief operations, a number of whose aircraft have been destroyed. These air strikes eventually drew international attention. They were suspended for a period in the middle of last year after UN General Secretary Kofi Annan intervened, but were resumed with a vengeance later. On 29 December 2000 the Sudan air force bombed the Episcopal Church Cathedral in Lui, Equatoria Province, completely destroying it. The raids continue unabated taking a continuing heavy toll of casualties.

The Central Committee of the World Council of Churches meeting in Potsdam from 29 January to 6 February 2001, profoundly conscious of the unbearable suffering of the Sudanese peoples, especially those in the South, as a result of more than thirty years of civil war:

> *calls* on the Government of Sudan to cease immediately the bombing of civilian targets of Southern Sudan, Nuba Mountains, Southern Blue Nile and other marginalized areas, and to abide by international law;
>
> *calls* for the establishment of a no-fly zone in these areas, except for protected access of aircraft transporting humanitarian supplies;
>
> *urges* the Government of Sudan, the SPLA and other warring parties to abide by the Geneva Convention and to allow independent observers to monitor the situation;
>
> *reminds* the Government of Sudan of its responsibility to guarantee the safety and security of all its citizens both in the North and in the South;

notes with concern that the oil revenue earned by the Government of Sudan is diverted to its war effort and contributes to the escalation of fighting in Southern Sudan rather than being utilized to meet the urgent needs of the people affected by the hostilities;

requests member churches to undertake lobbying and advocacy efforts with governments and oil companies based in their countries for the cessation of further petroleum exploration and development in Southern Sudan until such time as a peace agreement is reached between the parties;

reiterates its conviction that any lasting peace in Sudan must be negotiated with the support of partner states in the region through the IGAD peace process and the Declaration of Principles enunciated thereunder;

reassures the churches of the Sudan of the continuing support and prayers of the World Council of Churches in their peace efforts;

appeals to WCC Member Churches to intensify their efforts to encourage and support the joint peace initiative of the Sudan Council of Churches and the New Sudan Council of Churches; and

urges churches and church-related agencies to continue to provide necessary humanitarian support to the Sudan for the needs of refugees and displaced persons, those in desperate situations of poverty, and the victims of war, including especially those disabled as a result of wounds inflicted through war, mines and bombing.

MINUTE ON THE PEACE PROCESS IN SUDAN

Adopted by the Central Committee,
Geneva, 26 August – 3 September 2002

At its last meeting (Potsdam, February 2001) the WCC Central Committee adopted an extensive statement on the situation in Sudan. That statement drew attention to the urgency of efforts to resolve the conflict and called on the member churches, ecumenical partners and related agencies to engage in a series of advocacy actions to this end.

Through the Sudan Ecumenical Forum, the WCC and other ecumenical partners have intensified their monitoring of developments, and provided new support to the churches of Sudan and their advocacy for peace and reconciliation.

In late June 2002, the General Secretary visited the North and South Sudan at the invitation of the Sudanese churches. There he renewed the WCC's pledge to continue to accompany the churches in their struggle for a just and lasting peace in Sudan.

Simultaneously with this visit the Government and the Sudan Peoples Liberation Army/ Movement (SPLA/M) met in Machakos, Kenya under the auspices of the Inter-Governmental Agency for Development (IGAD) for further negotiations on a peaceful resolution of the conflict. On 20th July 2002 they signed an agreement known as the "Machakos Protocol". The Sudanese churches, though still concerned with the increased incidents of violence in Upper Nile, have expressed unequivocal support for this commitment of the parties to enter into negotiations for a peaceful and comprehensive resolution of the conflict, based on the IGAD Declaration of Principles (DOP). They welcomed the Machakos Protocol as a valuable framework for the ongoing peace negotiations, and especially the specific agreement of the Parties to incorporate provisions for the Right to Self-Determination for the people of South Sudan and on State and Religion in a Final Agreement.

The Central Committee welcomes the Machakos Protocol and reiterates its support for the IGAD Peace Process, and expresses appreciation for the persistent efforts of the Sudanese churches to pursue peace against heavy odds. At the same time, it is concerned about the reported escalation of fighting around Tam in Western Upper Nile and Yuai in Eastern Upper Nile, in serious breach of the provisions of the earlier Nuba Mountains Ceasefire Agreement brokered by the USA and Switzerland, resulting in further serious loss of life and displacement of civilian population.

In this new context, and in light of the Decade to Overcome Violence, the Central Committee urges member churches to:

- remain constant in prayer for the churches and people of Sudan;
- support and encourage the churches of Sudan in their continued witness and work for justice, peace and reconciliation;
- monitor and exchange information on developments related to the Machakos Protocol; and
- assist the Sudanese churches to gain access to future negotiations within the framework of the IGAD Peace Process.

STATEMENT ON ZIMBABWE

Adopted by the Executive Committee,
Geneva, 11-14 September 2001

The Executive Committee of the World Council of Churches, meeting in Geneva, 11-14 September 2001, expresses its deep appreciation to the Zimbabwe Council of Churches and to the church leaders for the Pastoral Letter to the Nation made public in Harare in late August of this year.

The member churches of the WCC have become increasingly concerned about the deteriorating economic and social situation in Zimbabwe and the rising tide of violence there. Part of this violence has been instigated by the encouragement given by the government of Zimbabwe to the War Veterans to occupy white-owned commercial farms. These invasions have claimed many lives of both white and black citizens. Compounding this violence were widespread acts of political intimidation in the months before the 2000 parliamentary elections. These have continued almost unabated. Early this year, the War Veterans began to attack and occupy private businesses. Pressures applied by international financial institutions for structural adjustments of Zimbabwe's economy have exacerbated the impact on the people of the nation by further undermining the social welfare system and public health services at a time when the HIV/AIDS pandemic had already stretched it to the limits.

Zimbabwe's African neighbours and others around the world have been deeply troubled by all these developments in this nation that they had regarded to be a model of how racial tolerance, economic development and political democracy can contribute to a successful transition from colonial rule.

The WCC has a deep and long-standing attachment to the people of this land and to their churches. This began during the period of colonial rule, continued through the struggle for independence, has been sustained in the years since, and was renewed with the holding of the Eighth WCC Assembly in Harare in December 1998.

The ZCC pastoral letter reflects our concerns and has been issued at a critical time. Its urgent call for an open national dialogue on the crucial issues facing the country was warmly welcomed by the people of Zimbabwe. It makes clear and constructive recommendations on ways to lead the society as a whole away from the brink of self-destruction. These are addressed to the government, all political parties, the private sector and civil society as a whole. We sincerely hope that no particular addressee, especially the government and the ruling party, will view it as an attack on them or their institutions; but rather that all will welcome the church leaders' offer to facilitate the national dialogue and cooperate with them in pursuit of non-violent approaches to conflict transformation.

It is noteworthy that the church leaders have chosen to assume responsibility for their own national situation, and have made little reference to those outside Zimbabwe's borders whose impact is continually felt in this land. It is crucial, however, that the international community also take the churches' words to heart. Threats of further economic sanctions or to suspend all foreign aid until after the 2002 presidential elections could well impair the national dialogue and push Zimbabwe over the edge.

We therefore commend the approach taken by the recent Commonwealth meeting in Abuja, Nigeria. It recognizes the fact that "Land is at the core of the crisis in Zimbabwe and cannot be separated from other issues of concern... such as the rule of law, respect for human rights, democracy and the economy. A programme of land reform is, therefore, crucial to the resolution of the problem."

Zimbabweans are capable of restoring responsible governance, the rule of law and the democratic process in their country, and can put in place a responsible process of land reform that will do justice to all involved. They cannot, however, do this alone. International financial institutions and especially those governments that made financial commitments to facilitate a fair process of peaceful land redistribution during the Lancaster House independence negotiations, must fully assume their obligations as well. In Abuja, the United Kingdom renewed its commitment. We hope that the U.S.A. will follow suit. Without these nations' assistance and the understanding and help of the international community, the nation will remain in jeopardy.

We continue to pray fervently that the people of Zimbabwe, their government, political parties and civil society as a whole will heed the call of the churches now, before it is too late. May God continue to bless and guide Zimbabwe in this critical hour of need.

MINUTE ON ZIMBABWE

Adopted by Central Committee,
Geneva, 26 August – 2 September 2003

The present socio-economic and political crisis in Zimbabwe is a serious challenge to the churches in the country and a matter of concern to the wider ecumenical family. The challenges faced by the people and churches in Zimbabwe are multifaceted and complex. The 'fast track' land resettlement programme implemented by the government of Zimbabwe over the last two years has led to serious human rights violations. The process of resettlement is carried out in a manner that has circumvented legal procedures and created an air of uncertainty amongst the people particularly the new settlers. The disruption caused to the commercial agricultural sector by 'fast track' resettlement has endangered food security. The government's handling of the situation through recourse to violence and introduction of contentious legislative measures has compounded the crisis, isolating the country and bringing it to the brink of ruin.

We share the pain and suffering of the people of Zimbabwe as a result of escalating violence and repression of fundamental human rights by the state and groups encouraged and supported by the government. The violence, intimidation, unlawful arrest and torture perpetrated by the police, ruling party militia and other state agents must come to an end. We particularly deplore actions of the government to introduce new laws and amend existing laws with intention to clamp down on political opponents, human rights defenders, representatives of trade unions, students, teachers, lawyers, and jurists. We express solidarity with the churches of Zimbabwe as they witness to the challenge of the present crisis, and affirm the Executive Committee Statement from September 2001.

We urge member churches of WCC to condemn acts of violence. We encourage the Zimbabwe Council of Churches as they strive to increase their efforts to seek a peaceful resolution of the conflict between the government and the opposition in the country in order that they may together address the basic grievances of the people.

We call on the General Secretary, the Africa Peace Monitoring Group and the Commission of Churches on International Affairs of the World Council of Churches to:

• continue their support of the churches to seek a peaceful resolution of the conflict, restore the rule of law and put an end to arbitrary arrests, torture and killings;

- support and encourage the efforts of the Zimbabwe churches to work towards constitutional reforms that reflect the aspirations of the people on the principles of good governance, rule of law and democratic norms;
- support and encourage the initiatives of Zimbabwe churches to redress the inequities of land distribution;
- provide a platform to the churches of Zimbabwe for a comprehensive, inclusive and coordinated ecumenical accompaniment to facilitate sharing and exchange of information and analysis, and to undertake advocacy for peaceful resolution of the conflict.

STATEMENT ON LIBERIA

Adopted by the Central Committee,
Geneva, 26 August – 2 September 2003

1. Liberia has been in the throes of civil strife and wars since the 1980s. A peace agreement signed between the Liberian army and the rebels resulted in the election of Charles Taylor as President of Liberia in 1997. In 1999, Taylor was accused of destabilizing neighbouring countries, especially Sierra Leone, from which he profited massively by supporting rebels operating in the diamond mining areas. In May 2001, the UN Security Council imposed an arms embargo on Liberia because of Taylor's activities to destabilize the region by promoting conflicts and trading weapons for diamonds with the rebels in Sierra Leone.

2. Meanwhile, rebels belonging to Liberians United for Reconciliation and Democracy (LURD) who were fighting Taylor's army, initially operating from bases in Guinea, made progress and gained more and more territory in the North and West. Also, another rebel group, the Movement for Democracy in Liberia (MODEL), gained control of strategic areas in the South and East, thus cutting off Taylor from his other main source of revenue – timber. Around March 2003, fighting intensified and the rebels opened a number of fronts and between them were able to control two thirds of the country before reaching the outskirts of the capital, Monrovia.

3. As a result of the escalation in fighting a large number of people, including internally displaced persons and refugees from neighbouring countries, were again uprooted and forced to move in search of safety and security. Soldiers from Taylor's army who were not paid wages for several months indulged in widespread looting and plunder. The complete breakdown of law and order and disruption of humanitarian services further added to the suffering of the already beleaguered population.

4. On the 4th of June a high level Liberian Peace Conference was convened in Accra, Ghana, under the auspices of the United Nations – International Contact Group on Liberia (ICGL). While the talks were in progress the UN Special Court in Sierra Leone for war crimes indicted Taylor for crimes against humanity and issued warrants for his arrest. After considerable difficulties and painstaking negotiations the parties finally agreed to a cease-fire on the 17th of June, 2003. Despite the cease-fire agreement fighting continued as Taylor prolonged his departure from Monrovia and the rebels tried to make last minute gains.

5. On the 1st of August, the UN Security Council adopted Resolution 1497 (2003). The Resolution authorized the establishment of a multinational force to support the implementation of the 17th of June cease-fire agreement including establishment of conditions for the initial stages of disarmament, demobilization and reintegration activities to help establish and maintain security in the interim period, until the installation of a successor authority. On the 18th of August, ECOWAS and the United Nations brokered a power sharing agreement between the current government, the rebels, political parties and civil society, for a transitional government that will take charge in October 2003 and prepare the country for democratic elections before the end of 2005.

6. The leadership of the Liberian Council of Churches remained present in Accra and in consultation with the representatives of the parties to the conflict through the duration of the peace talks and kept churches world-wide informed of developments. The AACC and churches in Africa and the US called on the African leaders and the United Nations to work towards a comprehensive resolution of the conflict. The World Council of Churches sent letters of support to the churches in Liberia and to the UN Secretary General calling on him to support the Accra Peace Initiative and encourage the parties to agree on the presence of a credible peace keeping force.

7. The Central Committee meeting in Geneva, Switzerland 26th August – 2nd September 2003 therefore:

a) *Expresses* its appreciation and support for the role of ECOWAS, ECOMIL, AU, the inter-religious council, the churches and leaders of the Liberian Council of Churches for their efforts to promote peace and accompany the parties to the conflict in their negotiations at Accra, Ghana, to arrive at an agreement to cease hostilities and to form a transitional government;

b) *Condemns* the spate of violence unleashed by the military forces of the government of Liberia under the leadership of Charles Taylor and the LURD and MODEL rebel groups that resulted in horrific conditions and untold human sufferings which left the majority of the people on the streets for days with little or no access to clean water, sanitation and food;

c) *Welcomes* the UN Security Council Resolution 1497 (2003) and expects that an all inclusive political framework agreed between the parties on the 18th of August, for a transitional government, can be implemented and a conducive climate created for free and fair elections in Liberia before the end of 2005;

d) *Urges* member churches to uphold and support the peace and advocacy work of the Liberian Council of Churches and its members in prayer and thanksgiving for their continued witness to the gospel of Jesus Christ, the Prince of Peace;

e) *Calls* on churches and church-related agencies around the world particularly those in the United States, because of its historical links with Liberia, to provide much needed humanitarian assistance to the people and to accompany the churches as they seek to promote a just and durable peace, and restore harmonious community life where all people can contribute to the establishment of a society with justice and dignity for all.

MINUTE ON SUDAN

Adopted on 19th February 2004

In January/February 2001, the Central Committee of the World Council of Churches adopted a major statement on the situation of the conflict in Sudan in which it inter-alia appealed to member churches of the Council to intensify their efforts to encourage and support the joint peace initiative of the Sudan Council of Churches and the New Sudan Council of Churches. It also reiterated its conviction that lasting peace in Sudan must be negotiated with support of partner states in the region through the IGAD Peace Process and the Declaration of Principles enunciated thereunder.

The Executive Committee meeting in Geneva February 2004 welcomed the progress made by the Peace Process in Sudan and appreciated the work done by the Sudan Ecumenical Forum in support thereof. It however, noted with concern that some intricate issues like sharing of political power, integration of armed forces of government of Sudan and Sudan People's Liberation Movement, and application of Sharia law, given the provisions of the Machakos Protocol, still need to be addressed. Also, the status of the so-called "marginalised areas" – the Nuba Mountains, Southern Blue Nile, and Abyei need to be resolved soon to prevent the situation from becoming an obstacle in search of just and lasting peace. The recent reports of international agencies not being able to deliver much needed aid and assistance to people of Darfur are greatly disturbing. The situation in this area is troubling and explosive. There is a risk that if the fighting continue between the Government of Sudan and the two rebel groups, the whole peace process may be jeopardised.

The Executive Committee acknowledges the excellent contribution of IGAD, under the leadership of the Kenyan mediator, Lt. Gen. Lazaro K. Sumbeiywo, and the 'troika' countries of the United States, the United Kingdom and Norway in their efforts to bring an end to Sudan's twenty years civil war. The Committee is encouraged by the success of the IGAD Peace Process as a regional initiative of groundbreaking magnitude. It is a sign of hope for Africa that given the political will and determination, the people of the region can resolve their disputes and conflicts.

The Executive Committee

reiterates the WCC's expression of solidarity and continuing prayers for the people and churches in Sudan as they intensify efforts towards a comprehensive and just peace for all the people of Sudan.

encourages the churches in Sudan to continue to pursue their efforts for 'south-south' and 'south-north' dialogue to enhance the process of healing and reconciliation in the country as a whole.

urges the Government of Sudan and the Sudan People's Liberation Movement to bring the Peace Process as soon as possible to a final conclusion, in order for the reconstruction of the country to begin.

calls upon the WCC to continue to monitor developments through the Sudan Ecumenical Forum particularly, in respect of the on-going conflict in the western region of Darfur that has resulted in an alarming deterioration in the humanitarian and human rights situation and threatens to unravel the gains made in the peace process; and in respect of disarmament, demobilisation and the threat of small arms and light weapons that pose a major challenge to a sustainable peace in Sudan.

calls to the attention of member churches and related agencies of the need to prepare for large scale reconstruction and rehabilitation tasks and the humanitarian needs in the post-conflict period and urges them to respond generously through the Action of Churches Together.

STATEMENT ON SUDAN

Executive Committee, August 2004

1. Sudan has been plagued by war for all but a short period since its independence in 1956, primarily due to unequal distribution of wealth and power sharing, between north and south, centre and periphery. It is the largest country of the continent and shares boundaries with nine African states. Unless the Government of Sudan finds the way to peaceful co-existence between all Sudanese people and also with its neighbours, lasting and just peace will be difficult.

2. The first civil war lasted for 17 years before a peace deal was brokered with the facilitation of the World Council of Churches (WCC) and the All Africa Conference of Churches (AACC) in 1972. In 1983, civil war erupted again between the government of Sudan and the Sudan people's Liberation Army/Movement (SPLA/M) as a result of failure to implement the 1972 agreement. Estimates are that 2.5-3 million people have died as a result of the war and over 4 million have fled their homes, many to neighbouring countries. Religious intolerance has made the conflict deeper.

3. The conflict between the North and the South finally has the potential to end, due to the peace framework developed by the Inter-Governmental Authority on Development (IGAD). The signing of

the Machakos Protocol in July 2002 marked a turning point towards a just and lasting peace between the government and SPLA/M. This protocol brought a cessation of hostilities and recognition of the right of self-determination for Southern Sudan. It was followed by five other protocols signed in 2003 and 2004. The agreements in the last three protocols addressed the most contentious and difficult issues. After six years of an interim period there will be a referendum in the South when the people will have the right to vote on unified Sudan or for separation. The success of the peace process is largely due to the pressure placed on both parties by the IGAD countries under the leadership of Kenya and the "friends of IGAD" – Norway, Italy, the United Kingdom and the United States of America.

4. A Comprehensive Peace Agreement is expected to be signed shortly. This agreement will have two basic components: a comprehensive cease-fire and modalities for its implementation. Negotiation for the Comprehensive Peace Agreement has already begun and both sides have expressed optimism that a final agreement will soon be concluded.

5. There has been an active participation in Sudan from the WCC and member churches for more than 20 years. The Sudan Ecumenical Forum (SEF), to facilitate the role of the churches in peace making, appointed Rev. Dr Sam Kobia Special Ecumenical Envoy for Sudan in 2002. Churches and related agencies in Denmark, Germany, the Netherlands, Norway, Sweden, the UK and the US actively accompany the Sudanese churches throughout this difficult period.

6. While the ecumenical movement was monitoring the hopeful developments in the negotiation between the Government and the SPLA/M, reports started to come about the serious atrocities in Darfur. The UN officials have referred to the conditions in Darfur as the worst humanitarian crisis in the world today. The conflict between the rebels (the Sudan Liberation Army and the Justice and Equality Movement) and the pro-government militia, known as the Janjaweed, has resulted in a campaign of terror, led by the latter, against the predominantly African civilian population. Almost a quarter of the population of about 6 million people have fled their homes. It is estimated that around 30,000 people have died over the last 17 months and fears have been expressed that many more may die over the next months unless a political solution is found.

7. The World Council of Churches, the All Africa Conference of Churches, the Sudan Ecumenical Forum and the churches of Sudan have made several statements and other interventions condemning

the atrocities in Darfur and have urged the Government of Sudan to bring them to an end.

8.   The Executive Committee of the World Council of Churches meeting in Seoul from 24-27 August 2004, conscious of the agony and affliction of the people of Sudan and especially the women and children in the South and in Darfur:

8.1 *On Southern Sudan*

- *welcomes* the peace protocols signed between the Government of Sudan and the Sudan People's Liberation Army/Movement on 26 May 2004, and encourages the parties to sign a final comprehensive peace agreement as soon as possible and ensure its full implementation;

- *acknowledges* the efforts and the sacrifices made by the people of Sudan in their struggle for peace and appreciates the support given by IGAD and the Governments of Kenya, the US, Norway, the UK, Italy and Switzerland and urges the international community to ensure the signing of the comprehensive peace agreement and to monitor its implementation;

8.2 *On Darfur*

- *expresses* its deep concern and dismay at the ongoing humanitarian disaster and the gross human rights violations;

- *urges* the Government of Sudan to fulfil its obligations to protect its civilian population and to disarm the pro-Government militia – the Janjaweed – and calls on the parties to the conflict to respect the cease-fire and work for peace and reconciliation;

- *calls* on the African Union and the United Nations to insist on the full deployment of independent Human Rights and cease-fire monitoring teams, investigate war crimes and provide for the presence of adequate international peace-keeping force.

- *appeals* to the neighbouring countries and the SPLA/M to assist in establishing alternative routes for the delivery of humanitarian assistance to Darfur.

8.3 *On the role of the churches*

- *encourages* the Sudan Council of Churches, the New Sudan Council of Churches and the Sudanese churches to fulfil their specific ministry of forgiveness and reconciliation at all levels of society;

- *expresses* its appreciation to the Sudan Ecumenical Forum for the intensive and effective advocacy and efforts undertaken during the last ten years and urges it to continue with its international advocacy work;

- *appreciates* and encourages the Action by Churches Together (ACT) International to continue its humanitarian support and urges all humanitarian actors to provide generous support for all those in need in the affected areas in Sudan;
- *urges* the ecumenical fellowship to enhance the capacity of the Sudanese churches and its councils to enable them to respond effectively to the emerging challenges;
- *calls* on the WCC, the AACC and the SEF to join the efforts to advocate for generous and substantial international support for the task of rehabilitation, reconstruction, repatriation, healing and reconciliation work of the churches.

MINUTE ON SOMALIA

Executive Committee, August 2004

1. Somalia has been without an effective, recognised government for the last 13 years. According to UN statistics, as a result of the civil war about 1 million people have died and hundreds of thousands of Somalis have fled to the neighbouring countries, other parts of Africa as well as to Europe and North America.

2. The Inter-Governmental Agency for Development (IGAD) Facilitation Committee under the leadership of Ambassador Betheul Kiplagat, the Moderator of the CCIA, has made substantial contribution to seek a lasting solution to the national crisis of Somalia. The current peace initiative is more inclusive than the previous one, with participation of all key stakeholders, the warlords and traditional leaders. Somali businessmen who have a major influence both at political and economic levels are also involved. These efforts have been directed towards securing nomination for 275 members of parliament from the Clans and Sub-Clans. Recently, the IGAD Ministerial Facilitation Committee inaugurated the new Somalia Parliament. After this, as a next step, there will be elections of Speaker, Deputy Speaker and nominations of Prime Minister and Ministers.

The Executive Committee of the World Council of Churches meeting in Seoul from 24-27 August 2004, aware of the major crisis of Somalia:

supports the effort of the IGAD Ministerial Facilitation Committee as it seeks lasting peace for Somalia;

requests the WCC to share information with the member churches about the current developments on Somalia for the purpose of awareness building, advocacy and assistance for rehabilitation, resettlement and reconciliation;

encourages the WCC to work in collaboration with other civil society groups active in Somalia;

appreciates and encourages the efforts of Ambassador Betheul Kiplagat and the Ministerial Facilitating Committee and assures them of its support;

calls on the member churches to keep people of Somalia in their prayers.

MINUTE ON ZIMBABWE

Executive Committee, August 2004

1. There is long standing ecumenical co-operation and relationship between the World Council of Churches and churches in Zimbabwe, which dates back to the country's struggle for independence. The ecumenical body and its partners supported the liberation movement through the widely acclaimed Programme to Combat Racism (PCR). The Central and Executive Committees have issued several statements, also pastoral visits have been undertaken at different times. The WCC has also supported and coordinated election monitoring.

2. Since independence, the unequal distribution of land remained unresolved. While almost all Zimbabweans agree that a fair redistribution of land is critical, the process has been a matter of deep division. There is also general agreement among the churches in Zimbabwe on the rationale for land distribution. The disagreement however continues to be on how the plan has to be executed. The adoption by the government of the fast track procedure on the land question has polarised and divided the country.

3. Following the loss of the constitutional referendum in February 2000, parliamentary elections were held in 2001. ZANU PF won by a narrow majority over the newly formed Movement for Democratic

Change (MDC). The elections were widely criticised by international observers as not being free and fair. In 2002, presidential elections were held and Mugabe sought a sixth term. Morgan Tsvangirai, the leader of MDC, challenged him, in particular. The elections were marred by violence and vote rigging widely condemned as unfair and not free by international observers, including a team of church observers coordinated by the ZCC, the AACC and the WCC. Mugabe won the election but his victory was not accepted by MDC and the political stalemate has been punctuated by growing instability, chaos and violence. Parliamentary elections are scheduled for 2005 and presidential elections for 2006.

4. The country has witnessed a collapse of its economy with massive shortages of all basic foodstuffs, including maize, the staple food for most people and other essential items such as electricity and petrol. The collapse of the currency and outright shortages of money have left the few who are employed with cash that is hardly of any value. Zimbabwe's once strong health sector too, has collapsed and the country ranks as one of the highest in the world for HIV/AIDS with some 34 per cent of the population positive and an average of 2,800 deaths-a-week from AIDS-related illness. There has been a massive out-migration of Zimbabweans both to Southern Africa and overseas.

5. Human rights abuses are widespread and corruption has become rampant at all levels of society. There is a break down of law and order, and the role of law enforcement agencies is selective. Furthermore, attacks on civilians by extra-judicial squads of politicised youth and so-called war veterans are a daily occurrence. One of the most difficult problems facing the country as it approaches elections – 2005 and 2006 – are draconian laws against freedom of expression. There is no independent media and people therefore have to rely on information provided by state-owned newspapers, radio and television.

6. As the Executive Committee meets in Seoul, the Zimbabwe Council of Churches is organising a retreat with the Heads of Member Denominations on the theme "COMMON VISION TOWARDS A ZIMBABWE WE WANT" from 23-26 August, in Carribea Bay, Kariba. The church leaders are expected to discuss the current national crisis and come out with a message and an ecumenical plan of action.

The Executive Committee of the World Council of Churches meeting in Seoul from August 24-27, 2004, aware of the national crisis of Zimbabwe:

> *calls* on the ecumenical fellowship to pray for peace and reconciliation in Zimbabwe;

encourages the WCC through the CCIA to support the initiatives of the churches in addressing the national crisis, including the urgent humanitarian needs;

requests the General Secretary of the WCC to send an ecumenical team to the churches in Zimbabwe as a sign of encouragement and solidarity;

supports the initiative of the church leaders in Zimbabwe to convene a retreat on the theme "A Common Vision Towards a Zimbabwe We Want";

calls on the WCC through the CCIA to support the churches' mediation role between ZANU PF and MDC;

urges the Zimbabwean churches to work towards constitutional reforms that reflect the aspirations of the people on the principles of good governance, rule of law and democratic norms;

reiterates its support for the initiative of the churches to address issues of land distribution, economic, social and political reforms;

acknowledges the need for the international ecumenical family to assist the Zimbabwean churches in their pastoral efforts for reconciliation and trauma healing in Zimbabwe;

calls on the WCC to urge the Zimbabwean Government to end the political violence and intimidation of civilians and repeal all repressive legislation and unjust laws, such as the Public Order Security Act (POSA), the Access to Information and Protection of Privacy Act (AIPPA), and the Broadcast Service Act and also to request the government to provide a free political space, including the complete overhaul of electoral laws and institutions, to enable all elections to be held under free and fair conditions.

Acknowledgements

This brief, but hopefully comprehensive, account of a living narrative of hope for the ecumenical movement in Africa is a product of real struggle for the renewal of vision and alternatives for a future work of faith in the continent. For this I thank Rev. Dr Samuel Kobia, general secretary of the WCC, for the inspiring conversations about possibilities for Africa and the durable truth that the churches represent for the continent.

This is a work in progress and without the commitment of Dr Kobia and others like Melaku Kifle of the Commission of the Churches on International Affairs (CCIA), who were instrumental in facilitating access to vital information and providing the logistical support, this effort would have been impossible. I also want to thank the book's editor, Hugh McCullum, himself the author of several books on Africa and the ecumenical movement, for several focused readings and improvements of the original texts that finally produced a more refined manuscript. Much of the primary sources used in this work were found at the AACC archives. Thanks to Bishop Mvume Dandala, the general secretary, for allowing me to have the access to these facilities.

I am especially indebted to the following ecumenical scholars, Rev. John Gatu, Musimbi Kanyoro, Mercy Oduyoye, Philomena Mwaura, Musa Dube, Sebastian Bakare and many others whose words of wisdom whisper in our thoughts unknowingly.

Nicholas Otieno,
Nairobi, Kenya

Abbreviations and acronyms

AACC   All Africa Conference of Churches
ACK   Anglican Church of Kenya
ACM   African Common Market
ACT   Action by Churches Together International
AICs   African Instituted (Independent) Churches
AIDS   acquired immune deficiency syndrome
APMG   Africa Peace Monitoring Group
ATIEA   Association of Theological Institutions in East Africa
AU   African Union

BEACON   Building Eastern African Community Networks
BWIs   Bretton Woods Institutions

CCIA   Commission of the Churches on International Affairs
CMS   Church Mission Society
COMESA   Common Market for East and Southern Africa
CESCR   Committee on Economic, Social and Cultural Rights
CUV   Common Understanding and Vision
CWS   Church World Service

DOV   Decade to Overcome Violence
DRC   Democratic Republic of the Congo

EATWOT   Ecumenical Association of Third World Theologians
ECA   Economic Commission for Africa
ECOWAS   Economic Community of West African States
EDAN   Ecumenical Disabilities Network
EDICESA   Ecumenical Documentation and Information Centre
          for East and Southern Africa
EFA   Ecumenical Focus on Africa
EHAIA   Ecumenical HIV/AIDS Initiative in Africa
EPEP   Eminent Persons Ecumenical Programme

FOCCESA   Fellowship of Christian Councils in East and Southern
          Africa

FOCCICA	Fellowship of Christian Councils in Central Africa
FOCCLAHA	Fellowship of Christian Councils in the Great Lakes and Horn of Africa
FOCCIWA	Fellowship of Christian Councils in West Africa
G8	Group of Eight Industrial Nations
GLEF	Great Lakes Ecumenical Forum
HIV	human immunodeficiency virus, the infection that causes AIDS
IDPs	internally displaced persons
IGAD	Intergovernmental Authority on Development
IMC	International Missionary Council
IMF	International Monetary Fund
JCA	Joint Church Aid
LWF	Lutheran World Federation
MCK	Methodist Church of Kenya
MDG	Millennium Development Goals
NCCK	National Council of Churches of Kenya
NCCCUSA	National Council of Churches of Christ in the USA
NEPAD	New Partnership for Africa's Development
NGO	non-governmental organization
NSCC	New Sudan Council of Churches
OAIC	Organization of African Instituted (Independent) Churches
OAU	Organization of African Unity (now AU)
PCR	Programme to Combat Racism
PCEA	Presbyterian Church of East Africa
PROCMURA	Programme for Christian Muslim Relations in Africa
REOs	regional ecumenical organizations
SADC	Southern African Development Community
SAPs	structural adjustment programmes
SCC	Sudan Council of Churches

SEF	Sudan Ecumenical Forum
SPLM	Sudan People's Liberation Movement
SREA	sub-regional ecumenical assembly
SRFs	sub-regional fellowships
TRC	Truth and Reconciliation Commission
WARC	World Alliance of Reformed Churches
WCC	World Council of Churches
WCCE	World Council of Christian Education

Bibliography

Abundant Life in Jesus Christ: 6th Assembly, All Africa Conference of Churches, Harare, Zimbabwe, 25-29 October, 1992, Nairobi, All Africa Conference of Churches, 1992.

Bakare, Sebastian, *Jubilee in an African Context: The Drumbeat of Life*, WCC, 1997.

Barrett , David B. and Padwick, T. John, *Rise Up And Walk*, Nairobi, Oxford University Press, 1989.

Barrett, David B., Kurian, George T., and Johnson, Todd M., eds. *World Christian Encyclopedia: A Comparative Study of Churches and Religions in the Modern World*, Oxford, New York, Toronto, Oxford Univ. Press, 2001, 2 vols.

Baur, John, *2000 Years of Christianity in Africa: An African history 1962-1992*, Nairobi, Pauline Publications, 1994.

Bent, Ans J. van der, *Voices of Unity: Essays in Honour of Willem Adolph Visser 't Hooft on the Occasion of his 80th Birthday*, WCC, 1981.

Brian, Ion and Heller, Dagmar, *Ecumenical Pilgrims: Profiles of Pioneers in Christian Reconciliation*, WCC, 1995.

Briggs, John, Oduyoye, Mercy Amba, Tsetsis, Georges, eds., *A History of the Ecumenical Movement: Volume 3, 1968-2000*, WCC, 2004.

Chipenda, Jose B., Karamaga, André, Mugambi, Jesse N.K., and Omari, C.K., *The Church in Africa: Towards a Theology of Reconstruction*, Nairobi, All Africa Conference of Churches, 1990.

Cheru, Fantu, *African Renaissance Roadmarks to the Challenge of Globalization*, London, ZED Books, 2002.

Devereaux, Stephen and Maxwell, Simon, *Food Security in sub-Saharan Africa*, London, ITDG Publishing, 2001.

Drumbeats From Kampala: First General Assembly, All Africa Con-ference of Churches, Kampala, Uganda, 20-30 April, 1963, SPCK, London, 1963.

Dube, Musa, *HIV/AIDS and the Curriculum, Methods of Integrating HIV/AIDS in Theological Programmes*, WCC, 2003.

Dube, Musa, ed., *Africa Praying: A Handbook on HIV/Aids-Sensitive Sermon Guidelines and Liturgy*, WCC, 2004.

Duchrow, Ulrich and. Hinkelammert, Franz J., *Property for People, Not for Profit: Alternatives to Global Tyranny of Capital*, London, ZED Books, 2004.

Ellis, Stephen, ed., *Africa Now: People, Policies, Institutions*, Ports-mouth, NH, Heinemann, 1996.

Fabella, Virginia and Oduyoye, Mercy Amba, eds, *With Passion and Compassion, Third World Women Doing Theology*, Maryknoll, NY, Orbis, 1998

Fahrenholz, Geiko Muller, *The Art of Forgiveness: Theological Reflections on Healing and Reconciliation*, WCC, 1997.

For a New Africa with Hope and Dignity, WCC, 2004.

French, Howard W., A *Continent for the Taking: The Tragedy and Hope of Africa*, Knopf, New York, 2004.

George, Susan, *Another World is Possible, IF...*, London, Verso Books, 2004

Gifford, Paul, *African Christianity: Its Public Role*, London, Hurst, 1997.

Halperin, Jean and Ucko, Hans, eds, *Worlds of Memory and Wisdom: Encounters of Jews and African Christians*, WCC, 2005.

Hick, John, *Disputed Questions in Theology and the Philosophy of Religion*, Yale University Press, New Haven, Conn., 1993.

Jacques, Geneviève, *Beyond Impunity: An Ecumenical Approach to Truth, Justice and Reconciliation*, WCC, 2004.

Kato, Byang H., *Theological Pitfalls in Africa*, Evangel Publishing House, Nairobi, 1975.

Kessler, Diane, ed., *Together on the Way: Official Report of the Eighth Assembly of the World Council of Churches*, WCC, 1999.

Kinnamon, Michael and Cope, Brian E., eds, *The Ecumenical Movement, an Anthology of Key Texts and Voices*, WCC, 1997.

Kobia, Samuel, *The Courage to Hope: The Roots of a New Vision and the Calling of the Church in Africa*, WCC, 2003.

Kobia, Samuel, *The Quest for Democracy in Africa*, NCCK, Nairobi, 1993.

Le Carré, John, *The Constant Gardener*, Stodder & Houghton, London, 2002

Logan, Willis H. ed., *The Kairos Covenant: Standing with South African Christians*, New York, Friendship Press, 1988.

Mages, Lauren, *African Religion: The Moral Values of Abundant Life*, Maryknoll, NY, Orbis, 1997.

Mananzan, Mary John et al, eds, *Women Resisting Violence: Spirituality for Life*, Maryknoll, NY, Orbis, 1996.

Martin, Guy, *Africa in World Politics: A Pan-African Perspective*, Trenton, N.J., 2002.

M'Biti, John S., *African Religions and Philosophy*, Nairobi, East African Educational Press, 1969.

M'Biti, John S., *Bible and Theology In African Christianity*, Oxford, Oxford Univ. Press, 1986.

McCullum, Hugh, *The Angels Have Left Us: The Rwanda Tragedy and the Churches*, (Risk Book Series), WCC, 1995, repr. with afterword 2004.

Mugambi, Jesse, N.K., ed, *Development in Africa: The Democracy and Role of the Churches*, Nairobi, All Africa Conference of Churches, 1997.

Mugambi, Jesse N.K. and Magesa, Laurenti, eds, *The Church in African Christianity: Innovative Essays in Ecclesiology*, Nairobi, Initiatives, Publ., 1990.

Mudimbe, V. Y. *The Idea of Africa*, Bloomington, IN., Indiana University Press, 1994.

Musimbi, R.A. Kanyoro, *Introductions in feminist theology introducing feminist cultural hermeneutics, an African perspective*, Shyfield Academic Press, New York, 2002.

Mwaura, Philomena M, and Chirairi, Lilian D., eds, *Theology in the Context of Globalization: African Women's Response*, Nairobi, EATWOT Women's Commission, 2005.

Nairobi to Vancouver 1975-1983, Report of the Central Committee to the Sixth Assembly of the World Council of Churches, WCC, 1983.

Nyerere, Mwalimu Julius K., *Ujamaa Essays On Socialism*, Dar es Salaam, Oxford University Press, 1968.

Oduyoye, Mercy Amba, *Who Will Roll the Stone Away? The Ecumenical Decade of the Churches in Solidarity with Women*, WCC, 1990.

Oduyoye, Mercy Amba, *Hearing and Knowing: Theological Reflections on Christianity in Africa*, Maryknoll, NY, Orbis, 1986.

Onwubiko, Oliver O., *Building Unity Together in the Mission of the Church: A Theology of Ecumenism*, Nsukka, Nigeria, Fulladu Publishing, 1999.

Pobee, John Samuel, ed., *Africa Moving Towards the Eighth Assembly, Harare, 1998*, WCC, 1998.

Shenk, David W., *Justice, Reconciliation and Peace in Africa*, Nairobi, Uzima Press, 1997.

Special Focus on Africa - The Journey Of Hope, WCC, 2002.

Sugirtharajah, R.S., ed., *Voices From the Margin: Interpreting the Bible in the Third World*, Maryknoll, NY, Orbis 1991.

Sundkler, Bengt and Steed, Christopher, *A History of the Church in Africa*, Cambridge University Press, 2000.

Thairumn, Kkihombu, *The African and the AIDS Holocaust: a Historical and Medical Perspective*, Nairobi, Phoenix Publishers, 2003.

Tutu, Desmond, *God Has A Dream*, London, Rider, 2004

Uka, Emele Mba, *Missionaries Go Home? A Sociological Interpretation of an African Response to Christian Missions: A Study of Sociology of Knowledge*, Bern, Peter Land, 1989.

Utuk, Effiong Sam, *Visions of Authenticity: The Assemblies of the All Africa Conference of Churches, 1963-92*, Nairobi, All Africa Conference of Churches, 1995.

Villiers, Marq de, *Into Africa: A Journey Through the Ancient Empires*, Key Porter Books, Toronto, 1997.

WCC Focus on Africa, the Journey of Hope, WCC, 2002.

You Shall Be My Witnesses: Official Report, General Assembly, All Africa Conference of Churches, Lomé, 18-25 August, 1987, Nairobi, All Africa Conference of Churches, 1988.

Young, Josiah U., *African Theology: A Critical Analysis and Annotated Bibliography*, Westport CT, Greenwood, 1993.

Young, Josiah U., *A Pan-African Theology; Providence and the Legacies of the Ancestors*, Trenton, NJ, African World Press, 1992.

Young, Josiah U., *Black and African Theologies: Siblings or Distinct Cousins*, Maryknoll, NY, Orbis 1982.

IMPRIMERIE
LUSSAUD
OFFSET & NUMERIQUE

L'impression et le façonnage
de cet ouvrage
ont été effectués
à l'Imprimerie LUSSAUD
85200 Fontenay-le-Comte